W9-AUC-713

OIL SPILL JACK

A Memoir

JOHN J. GALLAGHER

with

Tristan Davies

Oil Spill Jack, Copyright© 2015 by Gallagher Marine Systems
All Contents© 2015 by John J. Gallagher

Published by Gallagher Marine Systems
305 Harper Drive
Moorestown, NJ 08057
www.gallaghermarine.com

ISBN: 978-0-9862094-6-8 (Hardcover edition)
ISBN: 978-0-9862094-7-5 (Paperback edition)

All rights reserved. No part of this book may be used,
reproduced, distributed or transmitted in any form or by any
means, or stored in a database or retrieval system, without prior
written consent of the author and publisher.

Some names have been changed to protect the identity and
privacy of the person involved.

DEDICATION

I dedicate this book to Anne Ellis Gallagher, my wife and mother of my wonderful children, Sean, Michael, and Annie.

To
Brian Fay

Regards
John J Gallagher

CONTENTS

OIL SPILL

JACK

FOREWORD

I am honored to author this introduction to the biography of Jack Gallagher, or "Jack" as he is simply known to all in the oil spill response industry. I was first introduced to Jack through my brother-in-law, Bob Driscoll, in December 1989. Bob had often told stories about the exploits of his best friend, Jack Gallagher, for many years before our first meeting. I was summoned by Bob for the purpose of meeting Jack and to discuss the possibility of forming a company around Jack's reputation and expertise. Bob had always thought that Jack and I were very much alike and somehow sensed, or believed, that we would work well together. Jack had a copy of a Senate or House Bill working its way through Congress and that Bill, if it were to become law, Jack believed would create an industry around the work he had dedicated the better part of his then professional life to. A little over six months later, that Bill became a law known as the "Oil Pollution Act of 1990," the foundation for Gallagher Marine Systems (GMS) and the oil spill response industry as we know it today.

The hopes of forming a company around Jack were short-lived for Bob Driscoll as he was tragically fighting a battle with cancer that he would lose in September 1990. However, my formal introduction to Jack at that initial meeting was the beginning of a friendship and career working with one of the finest and most amazing men I could ever hope to know. It is hard to believe that more than 25 years have passed, but I guess the adage is true that "time flies when you are having fun."

When the advent of the super tanker collided with the growing environmental movement, oil spills and oil spill response became an international concern. Many hands contributed to the growth and development of the marine oil spill response industry, but one man as much as any other and, to my mind, contributed the most. All who know Jack are familiar with his many colorful stories of dodging missiles, responding to marine casualties, inventing oil spill related technology, or key events which shaped his life. These adventurous stories serve as the basis for this book of Jack's life and serve to chronicle the history of marine oil spill response from its infancy to present times.

Jack Gallagher began his journey as a restless patent attorney and engineer in the late Sixties when he met a client who dabbled in the nascent field of cleaning oil spills. Jack's baptism in the business came with the accidental spill of a large amount of fuel oil into the Potomac in the fall of 1970. Three factors intersected for Jack on that job: The spill received tremendous coverage, as the monuments down the Potomac were being oiled; Jack re-discovered his innate organizational and problem-solving skills; and he was reunited with the water, a love of his since his high school experience in the Naval Reserve. From that response in late 1970, events moved very quickly. Jack was unconsciously drawn into the Industry in part by the uncertainty and endless challenges presented in preparing for and in responding to an oil spill. He worked tirelessly, soon abandoning his legal practice to focus entirely on spill response. The casualties became larger and more complicated, and at every turn Jack was solving new problems as they arose and creating better ways to do what was needed.

Jack may not have been the father of the oil spill contingency planning, but surely he was one of the earliest practitioners, and amongst the best. Jack was also well ahead of his time in seeing the potential benefits of electronic contingency plans and perhaps deserves credit for developing the first computerized oil spill contingency plan in the 1970's. In a departure from simple pro-forma documents with boilerplate instructions, Jack's contingency plans were site-specific, meticulously surveyed, with pertinent local detail, conscientious of credible scenarios and contingencies, with clearly defined chain-of-command, and well-defined individual roles and responsibilities. Jack's plans were effective and useable for those who had to implement the plan. One of his first clients was the Strategic Petroleum Reserve (SPR) along the Gulf Coast. Jack was retained initially not to prepare a contingency plan, but rather to develop a spill-response training program for its operators. He had no sooner completed the first training session when misfortune struck. A major blowout occurred at one of the Strategic Reserve sites, West Hackberry, Louisiana. As fate would have it, this was the exact location and scenario that Jack had chosen as an example for his training exercises. What was meant to be three days in Louisiana turned into two years of periodic first-response to spills and then ultimately, the writing of response plans for each of the five SPR sites.

Although Jack enjoyed being "at the end of the dock and covered in oil," he knew there was more to be done than simply responding to disasters. The opportunity for growth presented itself in a vice presidency with Lamorte Burns, a correspondent of P&I Clubs headquartered in New York City. Here Jack learned the insurance side of the business, an education that would become invaluable. He also gained access to the burgeoning world of the personal computer, which was to change literally almost every aspect of response. It was the beginning of what Jack would call his Automated Response System, which became an important piece of the company that at this point Jack had yet to found.

The spills kept getting bigger and bigger, more complex and varied. Then, in the spring of 1989, the mother of all tanker spills occurred: the *Exxon Valdez*. As a consequence of his continuing relationships with the P&I Clubs, Jack was among the first people responding to that historic spill on behalf of Britannia, the P&I insurer for the *Exxon Valdez*. The roster of respondents reads today like a Who's Who of the early spill response industry. Not only did Jack participate in important ways, he studied the response itself.

Before the Deepwater Horizon spill, the real mother of all oil spills occurred during the first Gulf War in 1991. Following an appearance as an "oil spill expert" on the MacNeil-Lehrer Report, Jack was contacted by Saudi Aramco and subsequently retained by them to oversee the protection of the kingdom's desalinization plants which were threatened by the massive spill. That's a good story in and of itself, and led to the birth of Gallagher Marine Systems.

At the same time Jack was establishing Gallagher Marine Systems, Jack also agreed to accept the Directorship of the newly formed Center for Marine Environmental Protection and Safety (CMEPS) at the Massachusetts Maritime Academy (MMA) in Buzzards Bay. I had the chance to witness Jack develop a curriculum and programs to teach spill response management, rather than direct it. The program at MMA exceeded our expectations, as it was the only program of its kind and we had people coming from all corners of the earth. We quickly established a good and large reputation. We trained shipping executives, terminal managers, harbormasters, and crews along with other parties from around the world, interested in the way we believed spill responses should be managed. One of Jack's innovative programs was the course known as the "OPA 90 Qualified Individual" that was developed in cooperation with the American Bureau of Shipping; and which quickly became the industry standard. OPA 90 had created the Qualified Individual (QI) as the person responsible for implementing a vessel of facilities response plan, but it did little to spell out the true range of real-world responsibilities of a QI and potential extent of his/her role in a response. Today, the QI is one of the fundamental aspects of modern spill preparedness and response in the United States and is a position that Jack Gallagher deserves credit for shaping.

Jack's narration ends with the *Selendang Ayu* casualty of 2004, which was arguably one of the furthest flung and most technically demanding spills ever handled by anyone. While this monumental job ends Jack's story, it marked a beginning of sorts for Gallagher Marine Systems. The next few years saw a large shake out in the oil spill business, and while GMS continues to perform oil spill responses, we are no longer primarily an oil spill response concern. Gallagher Marine Services today is a marine services company that provides myriad technical services for its shipowner/operator clients, from crew training to inspection readiness. There is not a day of the year when one of GMS' employees is not on a ship somewhere in the world. GMS drafts and maintains the response plans for its client fleet of over four thousand vessels, and of course, we respond to disasters when they occur, fulfilling the role of the Qualified Individual that Jack Gallagher pioneered.

Readiness and response are in a different world than they were when Jack, aboard a friend's yacht, oversaw the cleanup of oil that was accidentally discharged during the testing of a new burner at Georgetown University's power plant on the Potomac in 1970. The spills are fewer, the responses quicker, and the means of cleanup much more sophisticated. It took a long time to reach this point, however, and Jack Gallagher was there the entire way. I invite you to enjoy Jack's narrative, both as an important explanation of how an industry came to be, but also, and perhaps more so, as the terrific sort of story that Jack is universally known for telling.

PRELUDE

It was the early spring of 1989. I stood on the deck of a disabled oil tanker, photographing the strong points and chafing gear on the towlines in preparation of an impending tow to Southern California. In the water around the ship, I could make out a ring of black Sea Sentry boom—a boom that I had designed and that Goodyear manufactured for the Navy Supervisor of Salvage. As I continued on a report for the British Protection and Indemnity Club that had the insurance cover on the ship, a crewmember approached me. "Mr. Gallagher," he asked, pointing to my camera. "Don't you want to have your picture taken on board the *Exxon Valdez*?"

It was only a few days after what was at the time the largest ship casualty and response to ever take place in United States waters. We had thousands of people working on it, from the Port of Valdez all the way down through the Aleutians and over to Kodiak Island. The environmental impact was profound, and the response of the media was as well. Even more important, perhaps, was the political and economic impact resulting from that spill. The *Exxon Valdez* disaster would lead to Congress passing the Oil Pollution Act of 1990, universally known today as OPA 90. The law would irrevocably change the way casualties were going to be handled, as well as create multiple entities for their remediation and prevention. Not least of those, from my perspective, would be the formation of Gallagher Marine Systems. As I look today at that photograph of myself on the fo'c'sle of the *Exxon Valdez*, I think of how many things have changed since then, but I also remember how far I had traveled to come to that point.

PART I

BROOKLAND, USA

Chapter 1

The Philadelphia Lawyer

I was born in the spring of 1929 in Washington, D.C., at the Columbia Hospital for Women, a couple of blocks away from the White House. As a young boy, I was bothered that I had been born in a hospital "for women." My mother, Lorraine, known as Becky to her fellow nurses, followed her older sister to Washington from Alabama near the end of World War I. She trained as a pediatric nurse at Children's Hospital in Washington, an occupation she maintained throughout the Great Depression and World War II. My father, James Gallagher, whose parents had emigrated from Ireland to Massachusetts in the 1890s, also came down to Washington during World War I. He was too young for the draft when World War I broke out, so he obtained a job with the War Department. In those days, the War Department was housed across from the White House, in a Civil War-era building now known as the Eisenhower Executive Office Building. It was in that neighborhood that my father met my mother for the first time; Children's Hospital in Washington was about a block away.

I was the first of four. My siblings were William, James, and Joan, born in that order. Early on, we lived in various rental homes, starting with apartments and expanding to houses as children were added to the family. We had lived in Northwest Washington for a period, a few blocks from Soldiers' Home; my father would take us for walks through the grounds there. Next, we moved out to Silver Spring in the Maryland suburbs. There, aged four, I met one of my first pals, Johnny Klippstein, the five-year-old son of a neighbor. Johnny and I played a lot in a great spread of woods that stood behind our houses at that time. One day we found a cannonball, which was like a boy's best adventure to us. Later I concluded from where we found it that must have been fired late in the Civil War, when Lieutenant General Jubal Early passed through those woods en route to the Battle of Fort Stevens. The remains of the fort and works, which mark the only battle that Abraham Lincoln witnessed in person, still stand intact at Georgia Avenue and Military Road in Washington. Johnny, who kept the cannonball, went on to become a Major League Baseball pitcher with a distinguished career, winning a World Series with the Los Angeles Dodgers in 1959.

Jack with his brother Billy

My parents finally bought a home in Brookland, the Washington, D.C., neighborhood where I would live until adulthood. I began kindergarten and acquired a reputation for mischief. I remember that the kid who sat in front of me kept jumping up out of his seat during class. One day I brought a fork to school and put it on his seat the next time he jumped up—he sat down on it with a howl. I was punished for that! In retrospect, I was punished a lot. I was continually doodling in the margins of my work, usually airplanes or ships. One time, I was drawing airplanes when I felt a tap on my shoulder. It was the boy behind me warning me of an approaching nun, who jerked him out of his seat, gave him a whack, and then started on me. She instructed me to bring a book of airplanes to school the next day. I brought a book in, as directed, and the nun looked through it until she found the biggest plane she could locate, a PBY Coronado. She told me that I was to make five hundred drawings of that Coronado and bring them to her. I started doing this, but after a bit, I got some classmates to help me, Tom Sawyer-style. Together we did the five hundred drawings. To this day, I can still draw that plane from memory.

When I finished grammar school at St. Anthony's, I was the boy who had the distinction of having been hit by every nun in the place. There were other boys who had been hit in every class they had taken, but I had gained the notoriety of being the one every nun in the school had taken a swat at. I especially remember one, Sister Rosario, calling my mother in for a conference. She told my mother that I was a good boy generally, but when I got talking, I sounded like a Philadelphia lawyer. From my early schooling at St. Anthony's third level to seventh, I was trained by Catholic nuns.

Most of the other boys in my class were going to public school. Wanting to be with them, I entered Taft Junior High School in the seventh grade. This was 1942, and we were well into World War II by then. One of the kids I reconnected with at Taft was Wally Mitchell. When I had first met Wally, in elementary school, he had started a fistfight. I don't know why, but I reminded him of our previous acquaintance and we went on to become best friends for the rest of our lives. Wally's mother, Mrs. Mitchell, was our high school math teacher. Wally and I used to sit across from each other in class and he would sometimes, without my influence, get the giggles. Once he got them, he couldn't stop. His mother looked down and made us move to different places in the room.

Jack and Billy, 1937

Wally and I both became air-raid messengers as the war began to heat up. We were issued helmets, armbands, and gasmasks and were assigned to the same air-raid warden. When the sirens went off, our duty was to go to our warden's house and wait to carry information to other wardens in the event that the phone systems went out. As part of our training, we had to take first aid and other courses. It was instructive, and made us feel like we were part of the war. At Taft, the kids were taught to follow teachers into the hallway in the event of an air-raid alarm. We once had an air-raid signal during school time—a German long-range scout plane had been spotted over the East Coast. As the alarm sounded, Wally and I flew out the door to get our gear and go to our assigned warden's house. Our teacher, who had no idea what we were doing or why we were doing it, started shouting after us. "You boys come back here! You are not supposed to be leaving!" We kept on going.

Wally Mitchell and Jack join the gang

Wally and I eventually joined a regular gang of neighborhood kids who hung out in the alley behind my house. We did minor things that got us in trouble with the police from time to time.

The gang was the type that contained a bunch of different guys, mostly Irish, some of whom were our ages, and some of whom were older, 14 or 15. We'd fight one another, unless guys from outside the neighborhood came around. There was another gang that hung out by the mailbox in front of Hocking's Drugstore on 12th and Quincy Streets on the way up to the Franciscan Monastery on 14th Street. The Gopher twins ran that group (their name was actually Hayden, but they went by Gopher). When Wally and I joined the Naval Reserve, we had to wear our uniforms for the Thursday training meetings. Uniformed personnel at that time could get into the movies at a reduced price, so Wally and I would put on our sailor suits and go up to the Newton Theater, which was up 12th Street from Dr. Hocking's drugstore. However, when we went, we always picked a route that gave a wide berth to the Gophers; they would have run us out of town if they saw us in those suits.

L to R Jack Gallagher, "Bunny Bullets," Raeder Twin 1, Eddie O'Donnel, Bill Walsh, Raeder Twin 2, Joe O'Leary

In the tenth grade, Wally and I moved from Taft Junior High up to McKinley Technology High School. At that time, McKinley Tech was different from all other D.C. schools. It was a technical school founded in the 1920s with three student levels: scholastic, middle, and lower (i.e. mechanical studies). Wally and I entered in the top group. We also joined the Civil Air Patrol, which was then part of the Army Air Corps. One of our jobs was to assist private pilots whose planes were used to help with scout missions on the home front. This part wasn't always so rewarding. One day, Wally and I went out to Congressional Airport, which is now the Congressional Shopping Center on Wisconsin Avenue. We told one of the Civil Patrol pilots that we would wash his plane if we could get a ride with him. We worked all morning to clean his plane, but when he returned, he had a couple of girls with him. He took them up instead of us. We were disillusioned, but didn't quit the Civil Air Patrol. One summer, we were invited to a special camp for the cadets at Dover Army Air Base in Delaware. I remember my father driving me out to Congressional Airport. Air Patrol pilots were to fly us (in formation, no less) over to Dover. As we took off, I could see my father standing by his car on the side of Wisconsin Avenue. I later learned from my sister that after he returned home, he didn't say a word to anyone until I called and told him I was safely at Dover.

Dover Army Air Base was the final training place for P-47 fighter pilots before they went overseas. We cadets were put into barracks on the base and lived the life of the military. We had officer-club privileges and went to selected classes with the pilots to observe their training. One day, we got to fly in a B-26 Marauder, which was built by the Glen L. Martin Aircraft Company near Baltimore. The B-26 was towing targets for the P-47 fighters offshore over the Atlantic. In between rounds of P-47s shooting at the targets we were towing, we each had an opportunity to sit in the co-pilot's seat and manipulate the plane's controls.

L to R Jimmy, Jack, Billy & their Dad James

Later, I joined the Naval Reserve because Wally had joined. The first time I applied, I was turned down because they determined I had bad color perception based on my physical. It was one of the lowest points of my life, to be told that I was 4-F. Within a year, though, the rules were changed and I tried again. This time I was accepted; it had been decided that people with bad color perception could see better through camouflage.

I started going to weekly training classes at the Navy Yard in Washington, D.C. My first summer cruise was on the heavy cruiser USS *Rochester*. We sailed to Bermuda and had liberty there. We were wearing our white summer uniforms and the first thing we did was to go to a hamburger shop. When I bit into a hamburger, ketchup ran down the front of my uniform. Fortuitously, I could fix my neckerchief so that it covered most of the stain. Next, we came on a big hullabaloo at the Arthur Murray Dance Studio. Someone on the ship had been spreading the word that the Arthur Murray place was actually a brothel. Sailors from the ships had been lining up outside the studio, clamoring to get in, and our shore patrol had to break things up.

Wally and I went out to Elbow Beach and met some girls from cruise ships who had called there. Generally speaking, the hotels did not allow sailors into their restaurants or bars, but we found that we could get into the hotel gardens, get picked up by female passengers from the ships, and be invited into the hotel facilities. We managed to do that and soon learned the reason for the prohibition: at the end of the night, some drunken sailor, who had also sneaked in, was taking off his clothes on top of the bar. The girl I had met in the garden that night was from Wilmington, Delaware. She turned out to be a DuPont from that family in Wilmington. We went around for the few days of her stay and had our picture taken together on the beach. It was a platonic thing but it was my first time getting to date such a girl as a sailor on a Navy cruise.

When we got older, Wally and I were two of the few members of the old gang who went to college: Wally to a teacher's college, and I to the University of Maryland. There was a boy up the street, Mickey Vernon, who was in college at the same time. He and I had similar interests, and we began to hang out together. One time, Mickey and I were walking down 12th Street from that same Newton Theater that Wally and I used to go to in our sailor suits when we came to an alley that presented a shortcut. I suggested we turn down the alley, which came out behind my house. But Mickey, who hadn't been in our gang, demurred, saying, "You don't want to go down that alley. There's a gang of guys who hang out in there who'll beat us up." I had to tell Mickey that I was one of those guys and that we would be okay taking that route.

Chapter 2

A Memorable Cruise

In 1948, as I was about to graduate from high school, a truck hit my mother as she was boarding a streetcar on her way to an evening shift at Children's Hospital. The accident gave her a bad fracture that ended up keeping her up in bed for almost a year. As soon as I graduated, I got a night job at the airport cleaning airplanes. In retrospect, it sounds like a bad job, but to me it was a dream come true to be working around airplanes, regardless of what I was doing. I used to work all night so I could come home and stay with my mother to help her in the day, when everybody else was at work or in school. I didn't go to college in the fall so that I could be with her. Though my mother recovered and was not seriously handicapped, it was a long process.

Around this same time, I met Anne Ellis. It was at an 18-30 Club run by one of the downtown Catholic churches. 18-30 Clubs were organizations that catered to that age group, and I went to this one as a lark with a friend of mine, Don Burns. Anne was there with one of her classmates from Holy Cross Academy, Ione Hoffman, even though Anne was still under 18 and was actually contraband. Don and Ione started dating and they thought Anne and I were a good match. I suppose Anne wanted to see more of me, but as I was working most nights at the airport, my going-to-parties schedule was rather limited. Finally, though, I was able to get to a few parties with them, and Anne and I started dating. She lived in a wealthy section in Kenwood, just outside of Bethesda, Maryland, where her father was a well-respected physician. I'd ride the crosstown bus from Brookland out to the District line in Bethesda and then walk a couple of miles out to Kenwood to see her. Her family had three or four cars, so Anne would drive us on dates. Occasionally, I was able to get my father's car, but not very often.

McKinley Technology High School graduation picture

That summer, I had my second Naval Reserve cruise, this time to Jamaica. We set sail on the light cruiser *Portsmouth* from Newport, Rhode Island. It was hurricane season, and a big one was coming up from the south along the Florida coast. The ship put out to sea toward Bermuda to avoid the path of the upcoming storm, but the hurricane decided to do the same thing. We sailed directly through the eye of it. Instead of being scared, I thought that it was a great adventure. I was striking as a fire-control man in the crew that aimed the guns. My assigned workstation was above the bridge, high up on the forward mast. As we entered the hurricane's path, I could look down and see the bow of the ship go underwater, come up, and throw a wave back over the number-one turret and then the number-two turret. The seawater would then rise up to the bridge level and spray it. Although we were rolling close to 45 degrees, I was having a good time.

Wally was on that cruise, too, and he was enjoying it as well. However, a lot of the regular ship company did not show up for duty. Wally and I certainly became seasick at times, but the regular sailors wouldn't admit to it. They said they all had cat fever. On the mess deck, the tables had been stowed, so we had to eat from our trays of food sitting on the deck. There were very few people down there for about three or four days. We had two destroyers accompanying us on either side, but we couldn't see much of them except for their masts because of the hurricane. The sea became so rough that the aircraft carrier stationed behind us lost some planes off its deck during the storms.

I slept two decks below the main deck in a compartment in stacked bunks. One morning during the hurricane, I awoke to the sound of a trashcan rolling around in our sleeping compartment. The deck had water sloshing around it. I found that I was the only person left in the compartment; the others had abandoned it for fear of flooding. No one had awakened me. For a brief moment, I feared that the entire ship had been abandoned. I later learned that the crew, while trying to save a lifeboat that had broken loose up on deck above our compartment, had left a hatch open, allowing water to come through the ladder.

L to R Sitting: Wally Mitchell, Jack, Jack's brother Jimmy; Standing: Mel Tormé at a night club after Naval Reserve training, 1948

When we eventually got to the Caribbean, it was so hot we couldn't sleep in the compartments. Instead, I'd take a blanket up to sleep on the decks. One night I noticed there was a guy sitting on a chair on the fantail. I asked him what his duty was, and he said that he was the stern watch. He said it was pretty easy, that the bridge called around to all watches to report their condition every 15 minutes. He asked if I wanted to try, so I took over the phone and the chair and waited for a call from the bridge. When the call came, I responded as I was told to. I was pretty proud of myself, and looked around for the watch guy. I found him asleep on the deck on my blanket, where I had intended to bunk. I was beginning to learn how the lower ranks of the Navy were being trained.

I took my next and last cruise as a Navy reservist the following summer, learning even more about how the Navy was run. The cruise was to Portugal on the destroyer escort USS *Robert F. Keller*, from the Washington Navy Yard. Rather than the usual two weeks, this cruise was scheduled for a month; cruises couldn't make Portugal and back in a fortnight, so the Navy set it up by starting the voyage for two weeks at the end of one fiscal year and continuing on for the first two weeks of the following one. My youngest brother, Jimmy, who had also joined the Reserve, came on this cruise with me. Because our last names were the same, we were assigned to a lot of the same kitchen duties together. I was still a fire-control man, but we reservists also had work responsibilities, one of which was KP. I remember sitting with Jimmy on the deck of the ship just outside the galley peeling potatoes while the monuments of Washington passed by on the Potomac. When we got to Lisbon a week later, we were in the same spot on the deck, still peeling potatoes. We were seeing Lisbon, but doing it while peeling potatoes.

When we were kids and got out of line, our mother had a saying: "Just wait until the sergeant gets ahold of you. He'll straighten you out!" One day on the *Keller*, a Naval Chief came up to me. Knowing I was Jimmy's brother, he asked in exasperation, "Gallagher, how in the hell did your mother ever get your brother to do anything?" (Jimmy had a strong dislike of authority figures.) I responded, "Chief, she was waiting for you to get hold of him." He walked away disgusted, but at least I got a chance to offer my mother's opinion. Remarkably, Jimmy joined the Navy full time after high school. He trained as an electrician and started his own company when he finished his commitment. He's been successful and has never had to work for anyone else since.

We arrived in Portugal on June 26, 1950, the day after the North Koreans invaded South Korea, starting the Korean War. The old hands on board were telling us that we would probably keep going through the Suez Canal and head straight for Korea, which wasn't welcome news for my brother and myself. We were just there for a month, and hadn't planned on going anywhere else. However, I wasn't too worried by the chatter. As a fire-control man, I had been training in the firing of the guns on the cruise over. I knew we had expended most of our ammunition on the way over and were in no shape to go into a war zone without at the very least stopping to restore our ammunition.

War in Korea or not, we still had leave for a shore visit. I chose to join a daytrip to the Virgin Mary's shrine in Fatima outside of Lisbon, but at the last minute was put on mess duty and couldn't leave the ship. As compensation, I was given liberty to go ashore by myself the following day, the last day before we set sail for home. Since I was the last and only one going ashore, a bunch of guys asked me to get things for them for the trip back. The problem was that it was a Portuguese holiday, and I couldn't exchange the dollars my crewmates had given me because the banks were all closed. As I wandered around Lisbon, I came upon some Portuguese sailors and figured that maybe they could help. We struggled a little with the language, but finally they understood what I needed. They led me down an alley to a black-market operation where I actually got a better rate of exchange. Taking me under their collective wing, the sailors then took me shopping for the items on my list, mostly food the mess cooks wanted to supplement our meals on the cruise back. We covered Lisbon together. In the end, they invited me aboard their ship, which was across the harbor from the *Keller*. They offered me lunch on their mess deck: a fish with the head on it and a big glass of wine. When I finished the wine, they offered me more. I said that I didn't really drink that much wine. When they asked me what I did drink, I said, "Milk." They group of them looked at me and asked incredulously, "*Leite?*" I guess they couldn't believe it.

Before my newfound friends returned me to my ship, they wanted to take me to a brothel. I said, "I don't do those." They gave me a look similar to the one they'd given me when I told them I drank milk. "Why not?" they asked. I pulled out the picture of Anne that I carried with me and showed them. They said, "But she's not here!" They understood that even less than they did the milk. I gave them my address and after a while, I did get a letter from one of them that ended, "Someday we'll come to the United States and see the nice girl too, oh boy, oh boy."

Chapter 3

"I've Got a Diamond Ring You Won't Believe"

After McKinley Tech, I planned to go to college. Since I had only vague ideas about what college entailed, I went to a high school counselor to get some information. She took one look at my grades and told me I wasn't college material. The fact was, on nice spring days when you could see the trees though the windows, I paid more attention to the clouds than I did to the class. However, after my mother had recuperated, I ignored the counselor's advice and entered the University of Maryland, though in the School of Continuing Education as a result of my grades. I spent my freshman year in Continuing Ed as a pre-law student, but I worked hard and decided to try for engineering, as I really wanted to become an engineer. I had decided that if I couldn't do that, I didn't want to work so hard for anything else. As it turned out, I was swimming against the tide: beginning in sophomore year, half the people who had started in engineering were headed back to the School of Arts and Sciences. That scared me, but I decided to gamble it all and was accepted into the engineering program.

Toward the end of my sophomore year, I received a registered letter from the Naval Reserve ordering me to report to Camp Bainbridge, a boot camp near Port Deposit, Maryland. I was a Seaman Second Class, and the letter from the Naval Reserve was to activate me into the now full-blown Korean War. That would be the end of University of Maryland and of engineering, I feared. Then, by a great stroke of fortune, I received another letter about a week later, telling me that I had been promoted to Seaman First. A third letter followed, canceling the order for me to report for active duty: the Navy couldn't send a Seaman First to boot camp. However, the letter informed me that the Navy would reissue my orders soon. Fortuitously, this was when I met a "Father" Flanagan, who wasn't actually a priest, but a major in the Air Force Advanced Reserve Officers' Training Corps (ROTC) and a professor in the University of Maryland's Advanced ROTC program. He had found out about my predicament and suggested that I apply to the Advanced ROTC, which I was eligible for as I was entering my junior year. With Father Flanagan's help, I was accepted for Advanced ROTC and released from the Naval Reserve. This is how I joined the Air Force.

While I was studying at Maryland, I lived at home and commuted to College Park. In those days, they called our Irish ghetto in Brookland "Little Rome." Catholic University was there, and the whole area was spotted with houses for seminarians and priests who were studying or working at the university. To raise a little money, I found a job working at the Franciscan monastery Mount St. Sepulcher, near my home. Mainly I worked for them as a switchboard operator. The Franciscan monastery was special in that it served as the representative of the European Holy Land places, particularly those in Rome and Jerusalem where indulgences could be sought. As travel was so difficult when the monastery was founded in the 1800s, it was granted the privilege of providing indulgences that could otherwise only be obtained by going to the Holy Land.

Place of discharge POTOMAC RIVER NAVAL COMMAND, NAVAL GUN FACTORY, WASHINGTON, D.C.

Authority for discharge BuPers Manual, Art. H-6206 (2)(b) & BuPers ltr Pers-B22-JMS
                                                              QR/P19 of 29 January 1951.

Serial or file number 440 68 47

Date and place of birth 8 April 1929   Washington, D. C.
                                   (Date)   (Place)

Date of entry into active service 15 January 1948

Rating at discharge Seaman

Total service for pay purposes during this enlistment 03 years, 12 months, 26 days.

Service (vessels and stations served on) 1-29-48 to 3-4-48, attached to Organized Surface
Division W-3, PRNC, Washington, D. C. 3-4-48: to 2-14-52, attached to Organized
Surface Division W-6, Washington, D. C. 7-18-48 to 7-31-52, Training duty on
board U.S.S. ROCHESTER (CA-124). 8-29-48 to 9-11-48, Training duty aboard U.S.S.
PORTSMOUTH (CA-124). 7-30-49 to 8-12-49, Training duty on board U.S.S. PC 1168,
6-17-50 to 7-14-50, Training duty on board U.S.S. Robert F. KELLER (DE-419).

Remarks 4-2-48: advanced in rate from AS to SR.

8-5-48: advanced in rate from SR to SA.

10-18-51: advanced in rate from SA to SN.

C. L. BROOKS, JR., LTJG,   U.S.N. (R)

Released from Naval Reserve

Mount St. Sepulcher, as a holy place, received many visitors from all over the country, particularly in the spring. On days when it got crowded, the director of the tours of the church and gardens would send a brother down to spell me at the switchboard, and I would be asked to help lead tours. On certain days, I had to go straight from College Park to the monastery, and some of these were days I was required by ROTC to wear my

Air Force uniform to classes. I got so many strange looks—people didn't appreciate a man in a military uniform leading a tour through a Franciscan monastery—that I started saying at the end of my uniformed tours, "I'm not a religious, I'm just a college student working here." Until one day, a little old lady said to me, "Isn't that wonderful, you're doing this work and you're not even religious."

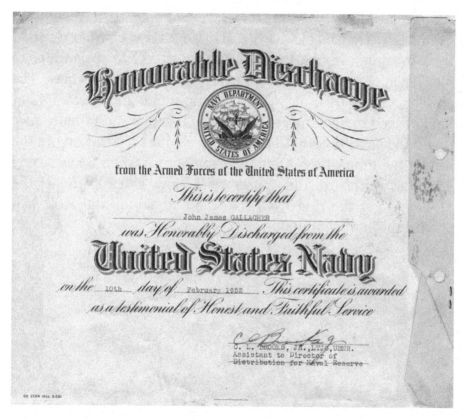

Honorable Discharge from United States Navy, 1952

I was in my junior year at University of Maryland when a friend of Anne's, a Georgetown student named Vincent Ciano, came to me and said, "Jack, I've got a diamond ring you won't believe." I told him I was nowhere near graduating and I didn't have the $900 that his contact wanted for it anyway. Vince kept after me about it. He even had the diamond sent down from New York so that I could look at it. I went to Father Paul Bragy, who was the treasurer of the monastery, and asked for his advice. He told me, "Get it and let's have a jeweler look at it and see what it is worth." A few days later, I got a call while I was working the switchboard. It was Father Paul, who was downtown after riding the train back from New York. He said, "Come meet me at Olmstead's," a famous fish restaurant downtown. That meal was the first time I'd ever tried clams. I tried to smile through them, but they tasted like river water to me. After our supper, he took me to a jeweler he knew. The jeweler told us that, at $900, the ring was a good deal. Father Paul offered to help me get the money together. So I finally gave in, on the condition that Father Paul would keep the ring in the safe at the monastery. After that, sometimes when I was sitting at the switchboard and things were slow, I'd ask one of the monks to get the ring from the safe and I'd sit and look at it against the sunlight outside of the office.

Jack with his parents, L to R Lorraine & James, Jack and Anne

PART II

FRANCE

Chapter 4

Laon-Couvron Air Base

On Monday June 7, 1954, I received my degree in Aeronautical Engineering from the University of Maryland at College Park. Five days later, June 12, I married Anne Ellis.

The Korean War was ending and the armed services were looking for ways to deal with the surplus of officers that they had generated. The Air Force decreed that only graduating ROTC officers who were signing up to fly would be commissioned, while the rest of us would have to serve in the enlisted ranks. Due to my color-perception problem, I had known for a long time that I'd never pass the pilot's physical, as much as I would have loved to fly. But I wasn't relishing the idea of returning to the enlisted men's ranks. Then another bit of fortune sprang up. The Air Force was experiencing an acute shortage of engineers in the Cold War military buildup throughout Europe, so I did get my commission after all, and would expect to be called up in three months or so.

Anne and I had traveled to Indianapolis, where I had found a temporary job working at the Allison Gas Turbine division of General Motors. We all knew the arrangement was temporary, but Allison put me to work supervising the testing of their experimental jet engines. Anne helped find an apartment on North Meridian Street, and I began learning an awful lot about jet engines.

Jack and Anne wed

In late July, I received my orders for processing. I was being activated as an engineer to provide some of the requisite engineering capability for the maintenance of aircraft in Europe. The Air Force gave me two weeks to report for induction. Anne left for Kenwood to visit her parents; I wound down my work at Allison, loaded our Buick station wagon with our possessions, and drove back to Washington. When I reported to the processing station at Camp Kilmer in New Jersey, for some reason my processing went swiftly. One of the airmen in the processing center told me that he hadn't seen anybody pushed through so quickly, and he couldn't figure out why. I had an inkling, though. Before her accident, my mother had been working as a home nurse for children. One of her favorite patients was the grandson of General Emmett "Rosie" O'Donnell, the Air Force chief of personnel. My mother had stayed in touch with General O'Donnell since then. When she mentioned to him that I was being sent to Europe, he told her I'd probably be going quickly. Apparently, his inquiry into my orders was what got me processed so speedily.

I remember the group of us who were being sent out the next day got a night's liberty to go up to New York City. We did our best to paint the town red, calling on every bar between the Bowery and 49th Street. After our evening in New York, a bus took us back to the base, where we were promptly loaded onto another bus and shipped up to an Air Force base in western Massachusetts. Once there, we boarded a C-54 mail plane, a version of the DC-6 built during the war, and took off for Europe, carrying only our uniforms and a duffle bag apiece. We made three stops: the first at Halifax, Nova Scotia, to refuel, then on to the Azores, where we overnighted at an Air Force refueling terminal. The third hop was from the Azores directly to Ramstein Air Base in Frankfurt, Germany.

After we were processed, we were allowed to visit Frankfurt. I was a bit worried at first because the only clothes any of us had to go around in were our uniforms, and here we were in a town that the Air Force had nearly bombed out of existence only ten years prior. I wasn't sure how the natives were going to feel about us. Tentatively, we walked into the first *gasthaus* we found, a sort of bar and restaurant. All of the tables were occupied. I turned to leave, but the bartender came running over and said, "No, no, boys, we have room for you." He sat us down at a table with an older couple. The man had been with the German Merchant Marine and had spent time working in Miami before the war. When he found out that it was our first night in Europe, he started schooling us on the protocols for getting along in Germany. He understood the difficulties of being a foreigner in another country. Finally he said, "Gentleman, I'm sorry but I have to leave now. You boys are like the nice boys from Frankfurt before the war, nothing like those foreigners who came in from Hamburg afterwards." I felt a lot more comfortable in Frankfurt after that.

Two or three days later, an engineer from MIT and I were assigned to Laon-Couvron Air Base in Northern France. We boarded the train to Paris and shared a compartment in the sleeping car. We were to take another train from Paris to Laon, which was up near Rheims, but we timed it so that we could take a couple days in Paris just to see some of the sights. We went to the Folies Bergère and other tourist sites. My travel companion turned out to be a reclusive sort of guy; he was a real engineer, not too much for partying. He was very conservative and, instead of a hotel, he found us a place to sleep at the American Church in Paris, where they had places to put up American servicemen. I didn't realize until later that it was a barracks for enlisted men, not officers, and that we probably shouldn't have been there.

Mural of WWII fighter planes that Jack and a friend painted in the hanger of the Bomb Squad room

Finally, we got on a train to Laon. I was detailed to the 71st Bomb Squadron and lost touch with my travel mate, who was detailed to one of the other squadrons. A few months later, I found out that he was in the hospital. It turned out he'd caught the bug for Paris and had been going down there every weekend, finally exhausting himself. It was quite a change of character from the fellow I knew in the first days of Europe.

There were three squadrons on the base at Laon: the 822nd, the 405th, and mine, the 71st. Each bomb squadron was placed several miles apart on the base, which had been a former German Messerschmitt base after France had surrendered to Germany during World War II. I was immediately installed as the Aircraft Maintenance Officer for about 20 B-26 light bombers of the 71st Bomb Squadron in the 38th Bomb Wing. The B-26s were twin-engine propeller-driven light bombers developed by Douglas during World War II—mature aircraft with a known history and most of the kinks worked out. We were scheduled to get new Martin B-57 jet bombers, but they weren't expected at the base until eight or nine months later, so I spent some time learning the bomb systems.

The base was still in the building mode in some places, with most of the men living in winterized tents. The winters there were very dreary and muddy; you could put your sunglasses away in the fall because there was so little sun most of the winter, even on the tarmac. There were still American Army vehicles left over from the war stored on the base periphery. The bachelor officers' quarters for the 71st were finished, so I didn't have to sleep in a tent, and my office was in the squadron hanger, which was also finished. The officers' club for the base was a temporary building that was probably built during World War II when our forces occupied Laon with P-47 fighters on their way across France en route to Germany. Some of those fighters were probably from the P-478 fighters that I worked with at Dover Army Air Base when I was stationed there.

Mural of WWII fighter & bomber planes that Jack and a friend painted in the hanger of the Bomb Squad room

Jack on duty at the base

Chapter 5

The Château

By November, we were eligible to bring over our family members. As quickly as I was able, I brought Anne to France via civilian air transport. I went to pick her up in Paris, brought her back to Laon, and we set up our first house at the Hôtel Accueil du France in the heart of the old uptown district of Laon. The old part of the city was surrounded by a medieval wall and close to the Laon Cathedral, one of the first of the Gothic cathedrals to be built in Europe, which served as a model for many later cathedrals constructed throughout France.

We wanted to find a more permanent place to live but, as a Second Lieutenant, I was pretty well tied-up during this period with my work at the air base. I had little time to do much in the way of searching for better quarters than the Hôtel Accueil. Fortunately, there was a Major Emil Urban staying in the same hotel. He and his wife, Sue, had more time for house hunting, so Anne joined them in seeking out a better residence. For a number of weeks, they'd go out nearly every day looking at places throughout the surrounding area to see if they could come up with something that met our minimum requirements (indoor plumbing and central heating being two such features). Every night I'd come home to the hotel to find a downhearted group of people who had wasted a lot of time looking at what little was available. They'd been looking up to 50 miles away, and every night there would be much gloom about what they had seen. Then, on one particular evening, they were overjoyed to inform me that they had located an available château, the Château du Bois Roger, which had all the amenities we could imagine—with the exception of round doorknobs. We went out that evening for a look.

Le Château du Bois Roger was a country hotel built on the remains of an ancient château just outside the small farming town of Laniscourt, only 20 minutes from the base. Monsieur Berte, the owner, had been forced by the other hoteliers in the area to give up on running his hotel; he was Belgian, not French, and there was some prejudice about that in the area. Monsieur Berte was looking for some way to keep the place up without losing too much money. We all agreed that it was really a find, but there was one problem: we would need more tenants to be able to pay the rent. The château had eight bedrooms, and between us, we only needed two. Emil and I put our heads together and realized that we might be able to find other officers in a similar situation.

Jack at the back of Le Château du Bois-Roger outside of Mons-en-Laonnois in his jaunty Irish tweed cap

Emil located another officer who also happened to be new to the air base. He was Captain Paul Carlson, the chief aircraft controller, who ran everything to do with operating the base as an airport. He and his wife Norma, brought a dog with them. We still needed one more officer, so we located a couple of short-timers on the base with only a few months left to go. They had been billeted in Soissons, 50 miles away, and were interested in taking up residence with us for the time they had left. They were John Price and his wife, Ellie, a former professional ice skater.

The château was luxurious compared to everything else Anne had seen, and it came with its own chef. Monsieur Berte had a housekeeper at the château who had been with him for years, Madame Marthe de Colanville. The château had a wing for her, with her rooms above the kitchen, but she was packing up, planning to go back home to her family in Mauberge, near the Belgian border. We asked Monsieur Berte if Marthe would like to stay on and work for us. He came back to us with a proposal from Marthe: she would cook a dinner and give us a chance to see her, and after that we could decide if we'd like her to stay. So we went out to the château and Marthe served us a dinner of seven courses, each with a different wine. It was quite a show she put on and we were pretty much taken.

The only things we had to bring were our own sheets and towels. Marthe agreed to do all the cooking, and we'd be responsible for the rest of the upkeep. Most of our fellow residents of the château were career Air Force and had been involved in sharing houses around the world. Emil, being experienced in these things, set up a plan for managing responsibilities so that we would get along. He suggested that each couple take certain tasks for certain weeks each month. The men would feed the furnace and get the ashes out, as I remembered doing as a child, while the women would plan the meals and take care of the shopping for the food. We also had a room with a bar, and through our Class Six store on the base, we were each able to keep the bar stocked. Monsieur Berte had two wine cellars in the basement—he kept his own bottles in one, we kept ours in the other. We began inviting friends out regularly and entertaining. Sometimes we'd play touch football on the 80 acres of land surrounding the château, using grazing cows as blocking. We were leading an idyllic life.

Marthe making American-style pizza in the kitchen

At the château, we also had rabbits, ducks, and geese that had belonged to the kitchen when it was a hotel. At that first dinner, Marthe had suggested menus including rabbits and ducks. Well, I got familiar with the barnyard pretty quickly. One day I went to Marthe and I said, "Marthe, one thing I don't want to see are any ducks or the rabbits on the dinner table." There was a pair of white Barbary ducks, one of which Marthe had named Rosalie and the other I called Patrick. Of the pair, Rosalie ran the barnyard—except when she was sitting on eggs, which never hatched. Marthe finally said to me, *"Patrick n'est pas bon."* In other words, he was impotent.

Jack's birthday party at the château, L to R Mrs. Urbin & Major Emil Urbin, Norma Carlson, Jack & Anne and two friends, April 8, 1955

When Emil and Sue were transferred to Germany, Bob and Nancy Roig, who were also new at the base, replaced them. I'm still in touch with Bob and Nancy, a beautiful woman from Texas, and we would get together occasionally to relive old times. The Roigs had a dog that, after not too long, got hold of Patrick and killed him. Marthe quickly got another Barbary duck to replace Patrick, and the next time Rosalie had eggs, they hatched. The animals were very tame. We'd feed them potatoes that were kept in the barn for that purpose.

Anne with rabbit

When Emil and Sue were transferred to Germany, Bob and Nancy Roig, who were also new at the base, replaced them. I'm still in touch with Bob and Nancy, a beautiful woman from Texas, and we would get together occasionally to relive old times. The Roigs had a dog that, after not too long, got hold of Patrick and killed him. Marthe quickly got another Barbary duck to replace Patrick, and the next time Rosalie had eggs, they hatched. The animals were very tame. We'd feed them potatoes that were kept in the barn for that purpose.

In the time since we'd come to Laon, some housing had been established on the base with trailers. One of the rules of the château was no children, so when Paul and Norma Carlson decided they wanted a baby, they moved to the trailers on the base. Another couple, Bob and Ellie Gordon, took up their room in the château. At about the same time, the Prices rotated back to the States and were replaced by Walter and Gloria Schmuck. Of course, there were occasionally minor conflicts and things didn't always go smoothly with some of the later entries into the château. However, the system Emil created worked very well during the time we were there. I could see the wisdom in what he had set up in the beginning, and it taught me a lot about living management that I was able to use in my later life.

Jack and Annie dressed for formal party at the Château

Anne's father, Dr. George Ellis, came over to France for two weeks both summers that we were there. He brought Anne's brother, George, the first year, and we traveled up through Belgium, Germany, and on into Italy with them. It was beautiful. We traveled in my English Ford and were able to cover a lot of ground with ease. The next summer, Dr. Ellis brought Anne's sister, Catherine, and we traveled a different route, spending more time in Southern Germany and then heading back up into France. From there, we traveled to England and Ireland, where I saw my grandparents' country for the first time. On the vacations that Anne and I took alone, we spent weekends in Holland and visited the war cemeteries in Château-Thierry and Belleau Wood, which, like all American cemeteries abroad, are maintained by the U.S. government. We visited them every Memorial Day and walked the battlefields belonging to both of them.

Jack and Madame Marthe at the château

Chapter 6

The *Engineering Review*

One of my duties with the 71st Squadron was the writing and editing of the Unsatisfactory Report (UR). The UR was a means of conveying back to the prime depots the serial problems we were experiencing with the planes or their parts at the base. The prime depots were the places that were responsible for overall maintenance of aircraft, and if a problem was serious enough, or the prime depot saw it often enough, they would revert with a technical order. At the beginning of my tour, the planes we were flying, B-26s, had been around long enough that most major problems had been resolved, so at first the URs were fairly few and far between.

After I'd been at the base for a while, Colonel Corey, the Commanding Officer of the 71st Bomb Squadron, was transferred up to wing headquarters. He asked me to come with him, and I became the Unsatisfactory Report Officer for the entire base, not just one of its three squadrons. The most significant part of this promotion was that I became responsible for the URs on the new B-57 bombers coming in to replace the outgoing B-26s. One of the first things I did at the wing headquarters was to try and remedy a problem I'd often encountered at the 71st. Each of the three squadrons wrote and filed their own Unsatisfactory Reports to the prime depot, but they never communicated among themselves, even though, as often as not, they experienced similar problems. Because I couldn't change the way the UR system was handled, I decided to set up a publication that I called the *Engineering Review*. The *Engineering Review* was a way for the three squadrons to communicate among themselves the problems they were encountering. To make it more attractive to the maintenance officers, I threw other things in there as well: additional news that wasn't in the UR or the technical reports, scuttlebutt, drawings, and other things that I thought would get the men's attention—even a crossword puzzle with engineering hints.

I also published the names of those who submitted the Unsatisfactory Reports, so that the crews got credit for the work they were doing. When I came across an unusually well thought out UR, I'd give it special attention. I also gave copies to the technical representatives from Curtiss Wright (CW), who began writing articles each month on technical subjects they wanted to convey to all three squadrons. The *Engineering Review* worked pretty well; not only was it popular, but I believe it did a lot of good in minimizing problems that caused crashes. I'm not saying it was due to my newsletter exclusively, but while I was on the base, we had no crashes and never lost a plane. Though I was later to lose one of my best friends from the base, Walter Schmuck, at a base in Germany, and in a plane that wasn't one of ours.

One time, the prime depot sent a report informing us of a malfunction that squadrons on other bases were experiencing that was resulting in crashes. The prime depot ordered a modification for all squadrons to demobilize the movement of each horizontal stabilizer in their new B-57s. We hadn't experienced the malfunction ourselves, but effective immediately all B-57s around the world were grounded.

When the order came down, the entire 38th Wing was down at Wheelus Air Force base in Tripoli, Libya, where they spent the winter, as conditions were too hard to fly and train at Laon in the bleak French winter. I was given the task of taking the engineering instructions from the prime depot down to our B-

57s in Tripoli so that the mechanics there could make the fix and get the birds airborne again. After spending a few days getting my guys started on the repairs, I spent a while touring in the area, which was interesting. For the château, I bought a camel saddle, which was like a small piece of furniture and was all the rage then. I also got a chance to see the notorious artwork hanging over the bar in the officers' club on the base, which had become well known thanks to the units from throughout Europe that cycled through Wheelus. The notoriety of that particular piece had spread all over the continent, and it was worth seeing.

On the flight back, we left sunny Tripoli and returned to deep winter in Europe. We were flying in a C-47 (named the DC-3 in civilian life). I was in the back with a bunch of our base mechanics who were returning to Laon. I was the only officer in the cabin, as the rest of the officers on the plane were flying it. We stopped in Marseilles to refuel and get clearance to head farther north. There was another C-47 refueling there at the same time. We talked together a little as we waited, and it turned out they were Army or Air Force guys heading from Italy to Spain to play some golf. We all left Marseilles at about the same time, they for Spain to the east, while we headed north up the Rhône Valley to Laon in Northern France.

Once we were airborne, I was looking out the window when I noticed that fuel was leaking from a right wing tank. The ground crew had put the cap on incorrectly. I went up to cockpit and told the pilot what I had seen. He responded, "Jack, we've got bigger problems up here. We can't get up to the altitude that we need to cross a pass that's coming up. The gasoline on the wing we can ignore for a while." I went back to the cabin. We were flying through a pretty rough storm and it was bumpy as heck. The mechanics were looking concerned. I tried to look calm, didn't say anything about what I had just heard in the cockpit, and tried to distract them by talking about other things.

Winter at the château

Obviously, we did clear the pass and got into the base in good shape. The next day, the pilot dropped by my office. "Gallagher," he said to me. "I don't know whether you knew it or not, but we came about as close to buying the farm as one can without actually buying it." Thankfully, that was my only near-miss experience in Europe. Sadly, those guys we met in Marseilles flying from Italy to play golf were all killed when their plane crashed on their way to Spain.

While I was in Indianapolis before getting shipped out to France, I had begun thinking about enrolling in law school when I finished my Air Force tour. Now, as my military service was winding down, I started to think about my next steps again. I had a friend, Ned Wilkinson, who was a Marine who had gotten out a year before me and had enrolled at Georgetown Law. I knew that Ned liked it and Anne and I agreed that we wanted to get back to Washington. So I got in touch with Ned and he sent me an application to Georgetown. I filled it out, sent it back to him, and he submitted it for me. Just as I got out of the service, right on time in late October, I received a letter from Georgetown admitting me for the spring 1958 semester. I was also admitted to a special program for veterans that allowed me to finish the courses in two years rather than three by going through summers as well as winters. I immediately accepted the offer. The next chapter was beginning.

Jack, Anne, and Sean

All in all, the time in France was a two-year extended honeymoon for my wife and me, as nobody was shooting at us, and I had a relatively safe billet, except for the usual dangers involved in fooling around with warplanes and weapons. I was sworn out of active duty in the Air Force at the Manhattan Beach Processing Station in New York. As a result of General O'Donnell's special interest in me and the Air Force's special need for engineers, I had managed to spend only two weeks of my entire tour on U.S. soil. Dr. Ellis and my father drove together up to Manhattan Beach to meet us and brought us back to Kenwood so we could set up home in Bethesda.

The château continued on after we left, though I don't know for how long. Finally, the bachelor officers, who at first didn't get allowances for off-base housing, were given such allowances. I gathered that some of them eventually colonized the château after the last of our château-mates had left the base. One of the last to leave was my good friend Walter Schmuck, a B-57 navigator. Walter was the flier who was killed after he and his crew moved to a base in Germany. For a long time we kept up with many of the couples we had lived with and, of course, with Marthe, who used to sign her letters to me, *"Votre grand-mère du France,"* your grandmother of France.

Jack, Annie & kids, Bethesda, Maryland

PART III

STATESIDE AGAIN

Chapter 7

Georgetown Law

Most of the students doing the accelerated program at Georgetown Law were ex-GI infantrymen. Though our military service differed, our Irish heritage didn't. It was really a gang of us: Mulligan, Tierney, names like that. We also had a Bob English in the group, who turned out to be Irish, too. Bob and I looked so much like each other that the professors often confused Bob with me or vice versa when calling on one of us for recitations. I was the only one in the group who was married. My first son, Sean, was born in November 1957, the night before I began at Georgetown, so I had a family to support as well. I got a job at the Naval Ordnance Laboratory, where I had worked as a student-trainee during the undergraduate summers while at University of Maryland. Although I wasn't supposed to be working beyond the enhanced load of the veterans' two-year program, I started working nearly full time as an engineer with the lab. My law classes were all in the mornings, with the last over at 11:00 A.M., so afterward I would hop in the car and go directly to the lab in White Oak, Maryland. I could put in a good part of the day there.

In the summer, my classes were in both the morning and the late evening. At the lab, I was working on the guidance and stabilization systems of what would become the Polaris missile. Incidentally, my grandson is now working in the same buildings where I once worked, which were taken over by the Food and Drug Administration when the Navy moved out. Even though none of us were supposed to be working while in law school, the other guys in the program were doing the same thing, just without the additional load of a wife and family. In the first semester, my grades were good enough to get me into the academic fraternity, but that was the only semester I excelled. I realized that I could spend a little more time with my family and working if I backed off somewhat on school efforts—not enough to threaten anything, just enough to make life a little easier.

The only course I flunked in my whole time at Georgetown Law was Legal Jurisprudence, taught by Father Lucy, a Jesuit priest. The course was mostly gobbledygook to me, since my previous studies were mainly technical. Someone later told me that I should have told Father Lucy that I was an engineer, because supposedly he'd never flunk an engineer. By that point, however, it was too late. Luckily, my brother-in-law had taken a course in legal ethics at Georgetown College, and he lent me his textbook. I re-enrolled for the course and passed it the second time. The rest of my schooling was credible—nothing to brag about, but I got my LLB degree with the ability to pass the bar.

I wanted to become a patent lawyer, so I needed to take certain courses to be able to pass the patent bar as well as the general bar. Those courses, however, were only offered at night and, as a result of my accelerated program, I always had a course conflict with the patent-law classes. Since I finished my requirements in two years rather than three, I still had one year remaining on my G.I. Bill to take the courses needed for patent law after I graduated. By that point, Anne had delivered our second child, Michael, in March 1959. I decided to stay on at Georgetown to get the patent courses I needed. Once I had committed to stay on, I decided to add some extra courses to complete a master's degree in nuclear and international law.

One of the projects I worked on at the Naval Ordnance Laboratory led me to some ideas to improve the things we were working on. In one of our experiments, we fired models of missiles out of a large gun and through a spark shadowgraph to track and record the path of the missile, its motion, and the airflow around it. Firing the missile models out of the gun at tremendous rates of acceleration put a great deal of pressure on the models. To have the correct stability required a distribution of weight across the missile to keep the model in the proper shape, so I got the idea of putting a cylinder with a heavy slug inside the missile. Beginning at the back of the cylinder, the slug would be released at detonation, allowing it to move forward as the gas from the explosion escaped into the cylinder from a small hole created in the back. This improvement was a new invention, and I decided to ask the patent guys at the lab to help me write the patent application so I would learn the process. This induced me to make other inventions. Of course, my inventions only had application to these specific experiments being done on this one missile prototype, but the two patents issued to me were a good training ground. In 1962, I left my position at the Naval Ordnance Lab, which I'd held throughout law school.

In October 1961, my daughter Anne was born on the night before my interview with Kemon, Palmer, Stewart & Easterbrook, a firm in downtown D.C. that principally practiced in patent law, and was looking for an associate. I got the job and went to work for them, initially on searching patents in the patent office. It was a rather dull task, but it gave me a good feel for the subject, and the firm began to involve me in litigation issues. The practice at KPS&E was routine. At one point, I was sent down to Houston to help a client get their patent work up to date. I spent several months down there, working mainly with oil companies. I remember Houston at this time being a town of two-story buildings; the NASA boom had not started yet. I worked in an office on the top floor of a bank building, the tallest building in downtown Houston. The only other tall building in town was the Shamrock Hotel, owned by an Irish oil wildcatter who had struck it rich. Houston was my first introduction to air-conditioned offices and automobiles. One night I was invited by one of the lawyers to dinner at his house. We left an air-conditioned office, got in an air-conditioned car, then dined at an air-conditioned house. It was the first time I'd ever been in so much air-conditioning, and coming from the summers in D.C., it was fantastic.

John F. Kennedy was President at the time I started working at KPS&E. In those days, the President would travel through town in a convertible, and I saw him on numerous occasions from our offices back in D.C. There was an atmosphere in Washington I had never felt before—a tremendous feeling of optimism, a new way of government, a new sense of pride in the city. The creation of NASA led a lot of us, particularly engineers, to look forward to a very exciting future.

My office was near the Court of Claims and one of the senior partners, Carroll Palmer, enlisted me to help him try a suit against the government. It was right at the height of the Cuban Missile Crisis, and people were leaving Washington, terrified by the threat of attack. It was a worrisome time. Once, when I was taking some papers to court, I found myself avoiding the nearby White House, which everyone thought would be ground zero. Later, I realized that a couple of blocks of detour wouldn't have made much difference.

Carroll used to take me sailing with him on the yacht he kept down in Annapolis. He raced often and wanted me to become a crewmember for him, but my wife wanted me to turn down the offer. She thought that I spent enough time away from the family as it was, though the family did get to go sailing together with him once. Carroll was a real taskmaster, but we got along well, maybe because he was an engineer himself and recognized a kindred spirit in me. He let me join him on a couple more lawsuits, write pleadings, and go to court with him, and I could tell that he was intending to invite me to become a junior partner. I didn't want to disappoint him, but I had received an offer from another lawyer, J.J. Byrnes, who was forming his own practice and looking for me to join his firm.

It was 1966 when J.J. approached me. He was quite an operator, having been a captain in the Army during the war, serving in the occupation of Japan. He was forming a law firm with Captain George N. Robillard, who had been the former patent attorney for the U.S. Navy. My first instinct was to refuse, but the offer came with a partnership and an opportunity to get out of the heavy patent-searching part of things at KPS&E, a field that I thought was a dead end. When I told Carroll of my decision, he said, "I wish you could have told me about this sooner, Jack." But I had already committed, and I went with J.J. Byrnes.

We went on for about a year as Robillard and Byrnes. J.J.'s brother-in-law practiced law with Baker & McKenzie, which was a big and prestigious law firm with offices near the White House. Before long, J.J.'s brother-in-law invited him to join Baker & McKenzie and form the patent unit there. Robillard was going to go as well, and J.J. invited me. I was reluctant, as I was looking to get into something I could really be a part of, a firm that had my name on it; there, I'd just be a blip on the roster of a huge firm. But in any event, I did end up going with them, and was soon disillusioned.

It was entirely different from any kind of law I was interested in practicing. They had major partners who I never even met, all running their own fiefdoms in this huge office in this big building, which is still there. I went on for about another year working for them, unhappy with the work I was doing. There was one case against the government that they had me do a lot of the writing for, but at Baker & McKenzie, I was so far down the ladder that there wasn't much of a chance to see the inside of a courtroom.

One day, J.J. called me in and said, "Jack, work is getting scarce here. But, you know, you're a nice guy." I quickly said, "I know, and nice guys finish last, don't they?" His face dropped. But I told him I was kidding. I said, "No, J.J., I know what you're going to say. I'm anxious to get out of here, too."

Chapter 8

Uncle Paul

When I left Baker & McKenzie, I had work that I could get on my own and I knew another patent lawyer down in the Pennsylvania Building, Bill Millen, who had some office space. I joined Bill as a tenant in his office, and we got along very well. Bill turned over most of his mechanical stuff to me—he was more of a chemist. He had a lot of German clients, big outfits. But he had enough mechanical patents coming through that he wasn't adept at and was farming out, so he began farming them out to me. I worked with him for quite some time.

Around this same time, problems at home reached a crisis point. Between law school and being a young associate, I was absent a lot while Anne had three children at home. The strain began to show. Anne's frustration, I think, wore into anger. In her mind, all our problems were related to my drinking. Finally, I agreed to see a physician to determine if I was an alcoholic. He did all kinds of tests only to come back and say, "There's nothing wrong with you physically, but something is wrong in your family and alcohol appears to be involved. It may make some sense to remove it from the equation and see if that doesn't help." He suggested that I observe 30 days of abstinence from alcohol, and I decided to make it ninety. I also agreed to go to Alcoholics Anonymous (AA) for six months. I did go to AA, for more than six months, learned a lot about alcoholism, and agreed that it was a wonderful program, but I couldn't see that I needed it at the time. Later on, however, it would become an important part of my life.

L to R Michael, Anne and Sean visiting Grandma Gallagher

Meanwhile, after ninety days of sobriety, I realized that life at home was not any better. Indeed, it felt worse. We sought professional counseling, but that turned into a waste of time and money. Finally, we saw a Monsignor in the Church. After a prolonged session with him, he suggested that we see if things could be worked out with a "vacation." I decided to take the advice of the Monsignor and try a separation to see if it would ameliorate the difficulties at home.

I rented an English basement apartment in the DuPont Circle neighborhood and continued my solo law practice. For recreation, I decided in earnest to take up sculpting. I also decided to give AA another try. I began to realize its value and started observing its programs, particularly that of not drinking, a day at a time. That began to clear up my thinking about a lot of things. I decided to try to get my family back by gradually trying to make up with my wife. It didn't work. Anne and I divorced in 1967.

When Bill Millen decided to move his office over to Virginia, he invited me along. As I mentioned, we had a good and productive relationship. But by that point, I had clients of my own and had formed relationships with a number of other lawyers. I no longer depended on Bill's referrals in the way I had when I first left Baker & McKenzie, and I didn't much want to move shop to Virginia, so I chose to stay put.

In fact, it was one of these clients I had on my own, one referred by another lawyer, who led to an interesting opportunity. The referring lawyer had warned me at the time that the client was "a little weird." But I guess I go for weird people sometimes, and this was one of those times. It would be the beginning of the biggest change in my career.

Paul Preus, who styled himself "Uncle Paul," was a self-made man and very proud of it. He was great at making friends. Uncle Paul was full of sea stories. He was in the Navy before World War II—the old "White Navy," as he put it. Though many of his stories about those days were pretty tall, he was also friendly with a lot of ex-Navy admirals and other luminaries, and often his stories would check out.

When we first met, Uncle Paul was working for a chemical company specializing in the marine industry. But as a sideline, he had gotten into the oil-spill game, which he had some sense of from his work with a chemical company. One of his good friends was Kenneth Biglane, an officer in the Environmental Protection Agency. Through Ken, Uncle Paul received a lot of opportunities to work with spills in the early days of the Oil Pollution Act and succeeding legislation.

Uncle Paul came to me because he had ideas about oil booms that could be used to corral spilled oil. At that time, the whole oil-spill industry was a new thing. People were using anything and everything—telephone poles chained together, fire hoses filled with air—to try and keep spilled oil from spreading. There were no oil booms around, or at least none in use. Uncle Paul had an idea for a specific type of boom, among other things, but he wanted me to do his patent work for him on spec. I was doing better, but not well enough to work for free, so I told him that I was a one-man show who couldn't work on speculation. We kept in touch, however, and he would look me up when he was down from his home in Toms River, New Jersey. Eventually, he began paying me fees for doing patent work on his ideas.

One day I got a call from Toms River. Uncle Paul said, "Jack, there's been a spill from your alma mater, Georgetown University, into the Potomac River. It's going down the river toward the monuments. They have a Coast Guard cutter at a pier in Alexandria getting ready to go have a look at it. Go down and get on board and see what you can do until I get there." I said, "Paul, I don't know anything about oil spills." Uncle Paul said, "Just go down and keep your eyes open and your mouth shut and hold onto things until I get there." With that, Uncle Paul introduced me into the business I'm in now, and I'm eternally grateful for the introduction.

The Georgetown spill occurred on November 13, 1970, when a power-plant station at Georgetown University was testing a new pumping system. The operator had accidentally released between 2,000 and 6,000 gallons of heating oil into the Potomac River, he claimed because the instructions on the flow controls had been put on backwards: the stop switch was attached to the "on" button (a charge the pump manufacturer disputes). The oil was fouling the river from Georgetown past the Lincoln Memorial, running into several marinas, and going downriver past the Pentagon and the airport, below Alexandria, Virginia.

As soon as I could, I arrived at the dock in Alexandria, got on the cutter, and went up to the wheelhouse, where a couple of Coast Guard enlisted men were stationed. These sailors were just killing time talking and I listened to them as I looked around. The language of sailors aboard ship is legend. There's nearly always an adjective preceding whatever they are talking about. It's usually used for emphasis, and it's almost always unprintable. I remembered a piece Ernie Pyle once wrote during the war on the art of swearing: "Sailors not only know the words, but they also know the tune." These sailors certainly knew the tune. That was my first venture back into the maritime world since my cruise on the USS *Portsmouth* in 1948, and it changed my career.

When Paul arrived, he put me in charge of running the response because I had an AA friend, Richard Kingston, with a yacht-size boat at his home pier in Alexandria. This was the first command center I had ever set up for an oil spill. We had located small workboats in each of the locations where they were working, and they would communicate with me on Richard's boat by marine radio. The cleanup was not a very spectacular thing, it was a fairly standard operation—we did normal booming and recovering of oil floating on the water and manual cleaning of the shoreline. The techniques were pretty rudimentary at that time and consisted of a lot of handwork with suction pumps that we bought at local hardware stores. In retrospect, the spill turned out to be nothing unusual except that it had a lot of coverage in the papers and on television due to its location.

The recovery went well. With the weather cooperating, we confined the damage to areas we could control. It was an interesting learning curve for all of us, certainly for me. With Uncle Paul's connections in Washington, we had a lot of cooperation from everyone in the government, so handling the Potomac spill more or less qualified me to handle the next one on my own.

Around that same time, I moved from DuPont Circle to Arlington Towers, a high-rise apartment building in Rosslyn, VA across the river from Washington. Marie Kelleher, another close friend, had been worried about my living in the dark basement apartment at DuPont Circle and had found the new apartment for me. It had a beautiful view across the river and looking down the Mall, from the Lincoln Memorial to the Washington Monument to the Capitol behind it. I wasn't the only one who wanted the place, and to get it I offered the rental agent a bust of John F. Kennedy I had been sculpting. The bribe worked, and that, so far, is the sum total of my lifetime earnings from sculpting. I found later that the presence of such a view nearly ruined my artistic motivation—it was too distracting for me to maintain my focus.

Uncle Paul had formed a company, Clean Water Inc., which consisted of himself, a secretary in Toms River, and me. The next big spill he sent me out to take care of came in late December of 1970 at a roofing factory on North Carolina's Catawba River. Paul paired me with an ex-sailor in Virginia Beach he knew and the two of us drove down to the factory and surveyed the site. There was quite a bit of oil in the lake where the factory was located, and it was getting into the river.

This really was the dawn of oil-spill response. The ex-sailor and I ended up buying a lot of bales of straw and wiring them together to create makeshift booms. Our creation came to be what is known as an absorbent boom—a boom that not only contains the oil on the water, but also picks it up. The one drawback of our setup was that the bales would get heavier and heavier as they absorbed oil and would sooner or later sink; we couldn't keep them in the water for any length of time or we would lose them. By working around the clock, we were able to finish the job over the course of about a week. As Christmas Eve arrived, we had done nearly everything we needed to do. We worked until 2:00 A.M. taking the last of the booms from the water and putting them in the care of the client's workers, then headed for home. Uncle Paul's ex-sailor drove me as far as Richmond, where I could catch a bus back to D.C.

We got to Richmond at 5:00 A.M. I knew my friend Marie was spending the holidays in Richmond with her family. Marie and I had what one might call a volatile relationship and, for one reason or another, weren't speaking at this time. But hoping I might see her, I had brought along to North Carolina her Christmas present: a fur wrap. I asked Paul's ex-sailor friend to swing by Marie's family's home before dropping me at the Richmond bus station. No one was awake at the house, of course, so I left her gift on the front porch, rushing off to make it back to Washington in time to open Christmas presents with my kids. That evening I received a call from Marie thanking me for the present. In my rush and exhaustion, I'd neglected to leave a note or even any indication of whom the gift was for, but Marie didn't mention the unorthodox delivery. She just knew.

*Jack on LOOP vessel during the development of the Louisiana
Offshore Oil Port, Gulf of Mexico*

I found a new office and continued to practice law solo, hiring Marie off-and-on to type briefs, applications, and contracts. Meanwhile, I kept working spills for Uncle Paul. The next large one came up in the St. Lawrence River in October of 1971. There was a ship called the SS *Singapore Trader*, an old World War II Maritime Commission freighter that had sailed from Hong Kong carrying 74,000 cardboard boxes, mainly goods for the Christmas market in the United States. It was scheduled for New York, but a longshoremen's strike along the East Coast had shut those ports down. The *Singapore Trader* was diverted up the St. Lawrence Seaway to make port in Detroit, which wasn't under union control. She went aground in the seaway near Clayton, New York, and began leaking oil. The response was soon an international operation, since both Canadian and American shores were being impacted.

Paul was contacted to take care of the oil spill, and my first task was to get up to New York City to get a contract signed by the ship's owners, ensuring payment for our efforts in dealing with the ship's needs. (Paul tended to use me either as a lawyer or as an engineer, depending on what the job demanded.) From there I traveled to Clayton, where ship salvors were already taking the cargo off the ship to lighten her. My job there was to control the oil that was spilling from the ship and to clean up the oil that was getting away from her.

Clayton was a summer resort with beaches along the river. The salving was a chaotic process, and locals were being hired to go out and help bring in cargo off the ship. The townsfolk helped themselves much of the time, and Clayton rapidly broke out in an epidemic of rubber spiders and Christmas toys. This was the first time I really got close to salvors, and I found them to be a bunch of characters. Temperamentally, they're just a little bit removed from the condition of pirates and have a swashbuckling way of doing business. They were always at loggerheads with the Coast Guard, but I learned a lot working with them.

Uncle Paul came up to Clayton to have a look around. On the day he arrived, I was aboard ship working with the salvage master. We were talking in the wheelhouse of the *Singapore Trader* when I saw the salvage master's eyes grow wide. He was looking past my shoulder, so I turned to see what he was looking at. Uncle Paul had come aboard dressed in a work outfit that, despite maybe being appropriate, made him look like the Easter Bunny. The salvage master said, "What are you supposed to be dressed up as?" Paul was pretty upset by that remark.

The *Singapore Trader* had its engine room amidships. As a result of that design, it had a long shaft going back from the engine room to the propeller at the stern. The source of her oil leak was damage along the shaft alley, so I began to stop the discharge of oil from the ship by pumping out the oil in the alley. The job went on for several months, giving me time to learn a whole raft of things from scratch—for example, the need to bring in trucks to receive and safely dispose of the oil we pumped out of the shaft. It was my first real maritime operation, and my first experience in working on a ship since my days in the Naval Reserve. The spill response brought back memories of my sails on the *Portsmouth* and the *Keller*, and I began to see that there was interesting science to be explored in what I was getting involved in.

Toward the end of the job, the local men's club—Shriners or Masons—put on a special holiday dinner for us at the hotel where we were staying. The place was one of the nice summer resorts that conveniently offered a view of the stranded ship from the dining-room windows. The Coast Guard captain for the Western Great Lakes, who had been working with us, was invited as well. It was a friendly evening between the locals and the responders, at least until the Coast Guard captain, who was enjoying himself, was asked how he had liked the dinner. In a moment of questionable diplomacy, he told the assembled local gentry, "It's hard to screw up a spaghetti dinner." That led to much consternation, but we worked it out in the end.

Chapter 9

The Birth of the Sea Sentry Boom

After the *Singapore Trader*, Paul told me that he wanted to hire an attorney to do the legal work so I could become his lead guy for oil spills. This was opportune, as I was beginning to enjoy the business of spill response a lot more than practicing law; the spills kept coming, and I was doing things now rather than arguing about them. I turned my practice over to friends of mine who were continuing patent work, gave up my office, and moved to a house in Annapolis on Burley Creek. I wanted to have a place where I could easily reach any responses Paul needed my management on and also where my children could visit me.

Even as the response business grew, Uncle Paul kept coming up with new inventions. A notable one around this time was an oil-absorbent material he named Sorbent-C. The base material was a by-product from decorative boarding manufactured for houses. Mostly it was made from plastic, but it also contained waste-fabric filler. Someone noticed that the shavings created in manufacturing the boarding could both absorb oil and float on water; even when fully absorbed with oil, they wouldn't sink. Paul worked with the paneling company to use their shavings, which had previously been discarded, to formulate his Sorbent-C. He also made a deal with the company who manufactured the material the board was made of to market their own brand of it under the name Fiber Pearl. I obtained a patent for Sorbent-C and let Paul store bags and bags of the stuff in my Annapolis basement.

I was busy running around Maryland and Pennsylvania doing spills for Paul. Sometimes I'd take my boys along when they had vacations from high school. Once, we got a call from a small town on the Eastern Shore of Maryland. They had had an oil spill that went into their sewer system, which emptied directly into the Chesapeake Bay. I hired some fishing boats to help with the job on the water, and found some locals to clean up the shorelines and the boats that had been oiled. My son Michael worked with me along with coastguardsmen stationed in the area, and between them, they ended up doing most of the remaining work.

A large spill occurred in June of 1972 at the Burks Associates, a used-oil processor that kept unusable portions of the waste they processed in large pits on the shore of the Schuylkill River in Pennsylvania, about 10 or 15 miles west of Philadelphia. As a result of Hurricane Agnes, major flooding brought the level of the Schuylkill up so high that it lifted thousands of barrels of waste oil from those pits and began to spread it through adjacent floodwater areas and towns. Usually it was Ken Biglane of the Environmental Protection Agency (EPA) who contacted Paul with the work, and in this case, again, the EPA called Paul, who put me in charge of the initial response. The floodwaters had run so high that there was oil in the trees and black oil bands around the second stories of houses. As the flood receded, the oil settled into places where it became very difficult to recover.

The Coast Guard requested a survey from me on the extent of the damage. I started in places that had not been oiled and moved toward the river to establish a useful perimeter of response operations. What I found was that there were already several different contractors at work in these areas. The work, though, was all being done by hand, with men loading buckets and carrying them up out of the gullies and ravines that had been oiled. One of the guys carrying buckets out on his shoulders asked me if there wasn't some better way to get rid of the oil, and I had to agree that it didn't look like a very productive system.

Paul was very social, and he was always finding people around Baltimore and nearby areas to form teams for me to use when spills occurred. One such subcontractor was a guy named Jim, who raised horses in Baltimore County. I don't know how Paul found him, but he began using him for small spills, at schools and inland locations, for example. There had been one job where Jim used a mule of his, named Soul Music, to carry multiple buckets of oil up out of a ravine in a residential area where oil had spilled and run down into the river below. Jim developed a way to harness Soul Music to carry baskets on either side of his saddle, and later began using horses in the same way, with special saddles he rigged up to carry as much oil as the horses could manage in one trip. In that tough terrain leading down to the Schuylkill, I thought that Soul Music might be a good solution. Paul called Jim and up he came with his horses and buckets.

The Coast Guard had just instituted their Strike Team concept. Eventually, there would be three Strike Teams formed: West Coast, Gulf Coast, and East Coast. But at the beginning of this response, there was only one Strike Team, based out of Governor's Island in New York Harbor. I was supervising a crew with Jim's horses and mules as they hauled oil out of a steep ravine and up to a road where it could be trucked out when a Coast Guard warrant officer from the Strike Team intervened. He asked me what we were doing, and I told him. He decided that it was a pretty archaic way of doing things, and ordered me to stop using the horses until he had checked with the Army

Corps of Engineers, who were standing by to take over the response after we had removed the spilled oil. I stood down for a couple of days until the same warrant officer came back and told me I could go back to work with the horses. When I asked him what the Corps had suggested we do in place of the horses, he said that they wanted to bulldoze the whole place out.

When the emergency aspect of the spill response had been completed, we did turn the rest of the remediation over to the Army Corps of Engineers. Our main directive from the EPA from the outset had been to exercise as much caution as possible, in an effort to preserve the undamaged environment, and we had done a good job of following that directive. True to form, however, when the Army Corps of Engineers arrived, they promptly started knocking everything down.

The Burks Associates spill on the Schuylkill River was the first really big spill I'd been involved in where there was a major environmental impact. Both Paul and I recognized that this kind of response was to be the way of the future. Uncle Paul wanted me to move up to New Jersey to be closer to him, as he had plans to grow Clean Water into something significant with me. I could see the logic of being closer to where the business was located, but I was delayed in joining him, as Anne was preparing to remarry for the second time. She had already married an ex-Methodist minister, a nice, meek man, and divorced him. I felt for him. According to Anne, her new fiancé didn't want the boys or their dog to be part of the equation, so in 1972, my sons Sean and Michael, and their dog, Taffy, moved in with me. By that point, I had already decided to move from Burley Creek in Annapolis to Toms River, so I brought them all along with me.

The move to Toms River was quite a dislocation for all of us. To complicate matters, the jobs were coming fast and becoming much larger in scope and much more complicated. The work had me away from our new home quite a lot. There was a spill at a steel mill in Pennsylvania where oil was leaking into the Ohio and Monongahela Rivers. It was a big spill and a complex one to deal with. Next came a spill in Dover, Delaware, where a power plant that had been burning coal installed tanks so that it could burn oil as well. Before the oil went on-line, vandals got into the tanks and opened the valves. The plant sat on a hill above a residential lake, and when the oil flowed down into the lake, we were called in to clean it up. The client was the power company for Dover, and the manager lamented that he had been running the plant for years and never had a spill—they had always run on coal. Now he had oil, and before he even got to use it, he had this spill. Before long, this kind of large, time-consuming, and complicated spill became routine.

While we were working on the Dover spill, Uncle Paul and I took a break to go up to a conference on oil-spill equipment in Cleveland, Ohio. We had a booth in the show that displayed what we did and some of the products we made. Goodyear also had a booth in sight of ours, and they came over to chat with us from time to time about what we were doing. They were interested in an oil boom I had designed, which was made of fabric-reinforced plastic. It was rudimentary by today's standards, but it was pretty much the state-of-the-art then. The industry of boom equipment design was still in its infancy; in many cases, the boom was made right at the spill site, such as with the bales of straw that I had used on the Catawba River in Virginia.

The Goodyear people were interested in trying some of the specialty fabrics they manufactured for use in the booms we were displaying. We agreed to keep in touch with them and I went back to the Dover spill to resume my work there. A week or so later, I got a call from Paul, who said he'd been talking further with Goodyear. They were serious about working with us on a boom design and wanted us to come down to their plant in Rockmart, Georgia.

I left Dover to meet Uncle Paul at a pre-selected spot in the airport in Wilmington, Delaware. When we finally located each other at the airport, we found that we had missed our flight. Uncle Paul said that we would have to drive overnight to get to Goodyear's plant in Rockmart, so we started off in his car. As we approached Washington, I realized that the flight we were supposed to take from Delaware was connected to the Rockmart flight at Washington's National Airport, and that we had plenty of time to make our connection to Rockmart by boarding there. Uncle Paul said, "No, no, we'll never make it." I knew we could get there more than an hour before the flight, because we'd be driving right by the airport, but I said, "Well, Paul, I've been working at Dover all day and there's no way that I can help you drive through the night to Georgia." Paul readily agreed to drive the whole way, and I slept. Much later, I learned that Paul was morbidly afraid of flying. The whole thing—the mix up at Wilmington and the insistence that we'd never make our connection at National—was a charade. Paul just wouldn't admit to his phobia.

When it got light, I woke up. While Paul continued to drive, I started sketching out ideas of a large inflatable boom to be made from the Goodyear material being fabricated. The boom I was designing would have a 12-inch diameter inflation chamber. But even as strong as the fabric was supposed to be, in the rough uses of oil spills, the boom was still liable to puncture. So I amended my design to insert a diaphragm down the center of the flotation chambers to minimize the danger of the boom sinking in case of puncture.

Paul and I stopped at a motel outside of Rockmart to clean up and change clothes before meeting with the Goodyear managers. We spent a couple of days with them, going over the design I had worked out and the materials they had available. Paul himself selected the actual material: a rubbery textile they used to make inflatable dunnage bags, which are used in railroad cars to separate cargo to prevent shifting and damage of individual pieces in transit. Essentially, dunnage bags were like large balloons the height of the rail car but fairly flat, like a pillow, made out of a very heavy, almost tire-like material. It was probably as heavy a fabric as could be reasonably constructed for this purpose.

To begin, we asked Goodyear to produce a few booms for testing the design in action. After our initial meetings, Goodyear decided to use a lighter fabric with a more intermediate strength. We used that set of booms on a few spills that occurred in some of our responses, but as I had suspected, the chambers were quickly penetrated in some of the more dangerous incidents. When we went back to Rockmart, we specified the heavier fabric and the intermediate diaphragm-protecting flotation. The second design was eventually named the Sea Sentry boom by Rockmart.

PART IV

THE BIG SPILLS BEGIN

Chapter 10

A Tale of Two Captains

The steam tanker *Esso Brussels* and the container ship *Sea Witch* collided in New York Harbor in late May of 1973. The *Esso Brussels* was at anchor at Stapleton anchorage off Staten Island, lightering cargo to the refineries before continuing on toward an Exxon terminal in New Jersey. While the *Sea Witch* was leaving New York Harbor, she lost her steerage and T-boned the *Esso Brussels* amidships, putting a tremendous dent into her port side. The collision penetrated the *Esso Brussels* cargo tanks and caused them to go afire, resulting in an explosion that engulfed the entire ship. There was loss of life on both the *Sea Witch* and the *Esso Brussels*. The *Sea Witch* drifted over into Gravesend Bay and burned there for some time, singeing the under part of the Verrazano Narrows Bridge to the extent that the flames shut down traffic between Brooklyn and Staten Island. The New York Fire Department went aboard and was eventually able to quench the flames aboard the *Esso Brussels*, but the *Sea Witch* continued to smolder in Gravesend Bay.

Uncle Paul's Clean Water was called aboard the *Esso Brussels* to assist in cleaning up the decks and other parts of the ship damaged by fire and spillage of cargo. I was put in charge of the operation, and we worked there for several days with the salvage master from Exxon to secure the vessel and clean it up to the point where they could start doing some salvage work. It was eventually towed into the Bethlehem shipyard in Hoboken, New Jersey, in preparation for towage to Europe for repair. After leaving the *Esso Brussels*, we went ashore to places like Sandy Hook, New Jersey, at the entrance to the harbor, to clean up the beaches there. There were many landings of oil along the shorelines on all sides of the harbor and all along the southern beaches of Long Island. Oil went out of the bay and into the Atlantic, tarring many other places up north and south of the collision site.

A few years later, I became involved with the *Sea Witch* in another way. I was living in Brooklyn at the time and working for Lamorte Burns, a company representing European and other foreign underwriters. My friend Alex Rynecki, about whom I will have much more to say shortly, invited me to a dry dock in Brooklyn to witness a job for which he was consulting at the time. Since it was close enough to the place I was living at the time in Brooklyn Heights, I walked to the dock. When I got there, I found that the stern section of the *Sea Witch* was the subject of Alex's efforts. The contractors in the yard had intended to combine the remaining stern of the *Sea Witch* with a new fore body to make it into a chemical tanker. They had gotten the stern of the *Sea Witch* into dry dock and were ready to start building. Other operations in the yard, however, had interfered, and a barge was brought into the same dry dock for repair first. The dock was a graving dock, a fixed dock with doors on the end to control water into and out of the harbor. When the dry dock was flooded to begin work on the barge, it caused the stern section of the *Sea Witch* to float off the blocks on which it was resting, eventually listing until it leaned against the dry-dock wall. As this was a large section of ship, it was threatening the stability of the dry dock itself. Alex, who was one of the best salvors in the world, was called in to try and fix the mess. The intention was to float the section out of the dry dock and tow it from Brooklyn to Norfolk, Virginia, to complete the rebuilding down there.

Alex had designed bags to stabilize the *Sea Witch's* stern section and had also planned the operation for a day with a spring tide coming so that it would give him the maximum amount of water to attempt the refloat. Alex was successful: not only did he have a spring tide day, but also he had quite a helping wind and heavy rain for more water. They readily towed the stern section down to Norfolk and rebuilt it onto a new bow. The new ship they created was still sailing well into the 21st century as the *Chemical Pioneer*.

A final note about the rest of the *Sea Witch*: Years later, when I was doing some work for Cindy Hudson—another name about which there will be much to say later—some people asked us to go up the Delaware River and have a look at a wreck that was docked in a remote area above Philadelphia. They had an idea of making a hotel out of it. The place was so overgrown by trees that one could hardly identify it as a dock. Anchored there was just the fore body of a ship. The cutwater was badly damaged, with tremendous indentations in it. I asked the people who were offering this thing for sale what the name of this ship was, and they told me that it was the bow section of the *Sea Witch*. This was a good ten years after the casualty with the *Esso Brussels*, and the bow was still floating around. I told the potential client that it wasn't something he wanted to get involved in. As far as I know, the bow is still there.

In 1974, the French-flagged motor tanker *Mobil Athos* was moored alongside the pier of the Mobil Paulsboro refinery in the Delaware River. She was discharging her cargo of crude oil when another oil carrier, the *Notre Dame Victory*, lost control while transiting up river. The *Notre Dame Victory* struck the *Mobil Athos*, puncturing her port-side bunker tank and releasing a substantial discharge of bunker oil into the Delaware. Uncle Paul sent me down to go aboard the *Mobil Athos* and deal with the on-board oil discharged by the puncture. The whole casualty had come very close to causing a major disaster, as the bunker tank was just aft of the aftermost cargo tank. If the cargo tank had become involved, an explosion and serious fire would have been likely to occur.

Our primary task was not only to clean up the oil on the ship, but also to go into the bunker tanks and start cleaning them out. Mobil had decided to put the ship into dry dock at a large shipyard across the river, and since the bunker tanks had to be cleaned before any repair work could begin, the job quickly became a tank-cleaning and oil-removal project rather than just an oil spill. Several other oil-spill contractors were engaged by Mobil to clear the oil that was out on the river, but matters were complicated by the fact that there were no professional tank cleaners in the area. Uncle Paul had identified some in the Gulf and was bringing them up, but in the meantime, he enlisted some high-school boys from Toms River to come up and earn some extra money cleaning the tanks. The boys had no idea what they were doing. They would come out of the tanks soaked in oil, then spread it over the rest of the ship as they wandered around. It made a terrible mess and caused pandemonium with the crew.

The next drama arrived in the form of a federal inspector, who came on board and announced that he was making an inspection of the ship. After canvassing the deck and finding no one who could speak English, he finally located me and demanded that the gangway to the dock be made properly safe. I told him to talk to the captain of the ship. He threatened me with jail before he left, but I had no further trouble from him.

As the crew continued to pump oil ashore, the draft of the ship changed, causing the vessel to list. Thus, the oil continued to leak out of the large horizontal puncture to the hull. I would go up to the control room during pumping and get the crew to try and keep the ship level as they pumped, because if they let the ship sink in the stern we were looking at a much bigger volume of contamination in the river.

Also, the tanks had water at the bottom due to the damage, and since the suction for the ship's cargo pumps is located at the bottom of the tank, the cargo pumps were only pumping water, not oil. We had to bring aboard pumps to use in the tanks to pump the oil. These pumps were air-driven double-diaphragm pumps that we would run with an air compressor on the deck of the ship. We were trying to bring the oil from the tank out and over the top, and into some other container or barge alongside. We had a pretty good program going. We maintained a lookout down in the tank itself to keep the pumps adjusted as they floated in the oil. At one point, one of the lookouts needed to go ashore. There was no one else to do his job, so I wound up babysitting the double-diaphragm pumps down in the bunker. It was a nightmare. The pumps were quite loud, and the echo in the tank was terrible. It was a sort of hell, only cooler. The crew had claimed that there was an inflatable boat to move around from pump to pump to adjust them, but all I found when I got down there was a kid's toy, not a working raft. When I stepped into it, it immediately folded up around my foot. I went on with my tour, but when I came up, I told the usual worker responsible for the operation that he was nuts to be working in those conditions. If he fell in, he would be sucked under the oil and be a goner. I then went straight to Uncle Paul to try to persuade him to make the operation safer. This was one of the problems I had working for Clean Water: I found that Uncle Paul could be skimpy on the people who worked for him and short on their safety.

A local diving contractor, David Stith, worked on the oil that leaked out of the punctured side of the ship. Dave got his training in the Navy during World War II, working on the SS *Normandy*, the passenger ship that had been trapped in New York Harbor at the outbreak of the war. The United States government took over the *Normandy* and attempted to retrofit her at the pier in New York as a troop transport. However, she caught fire during the work and the New York Fire Department, as land-bound fire departments invariably do, started pumping water aboard to stop the fire. All the water aboard caused the ship to destabilize and capsize in her berth. She never sailed as a troop carrier, though the government used the vessel for the rest of the war to train Navy salvage divers. So Dave's salvage-diving training came from there, on the *Normandy* as she lay on her side in the dock.

Dave was quite a guy. He was essentially a competitor to us to some degree, so Uncle Paul, in his usual fashion, had little good to say about Dave or anything he did. As it turned out, I found that people who were Paul's competitors weren't necessarily the bad people he usually characterized them as being. Dave and I later became close friends, and remained so until his death in 2008.

While the cleanup was going on, the ship was being switched from a French flag to the German branch of Mobil Oil. During the switchover, a German engineer was in charge of the operations. He was difficult to deal with, loudly and constantly criticizing everything about America he did not like. When I was in the Air Force, I found Bavarians much more light-hearted and friendly than their compatriots from the north. Not so for this Bavarian. The next fellow who came on board for the Germans was the new captain, who was extremely helpful. He was very specific about his needs and clear in planning. I really got to appreciate him, even though at times he could be pretty brusque and businesslike. From time to time during the spill, we'd have a chance to talk about things other than the operations at hand. He had a lot of stories about ships and ship problems. One of the questions I asked him was about how ships could run into each other at sea. In the situations I dealt with, the reason was clear: they were operating at close quarters. But at sea, the cause wasn't so obvious to me. He explained that some crews tend to get very loose about their discipline at sea. Ships will get closer than they need to be, simply to have a look at one another and maybe exchange some contact. But ships are hard enough to maneuver without asking for trouble by approaching each other too closely.

He had a funny illustration of the point from his childhood in Hamburg. His family was in the ferryboat business in the harbor, and he had a job running a boat for his family when he was 11 or 12. It was a minor job with a small wooden boat for shuttling supplies, not people. He became quite adept at handling the smaller boat, and when he turned 13, his family gave him a steel boat. He was very proud of himself and his new boat, so decided to make a little show of his maritime aplomb when he returned from his first job out to the harbor with the new, bigger boat. As he was docking, he threw the boat in reverse, thinking he would dock it as he had his old boat. But this much more substantial craft, despite its reversed propellers, kept sailing for another half mile past the pier, giving the captain his first lesson in the hard facts of ships and momentum. He had a lot of stories, and I learned a lot from him. We got along well, giving the lie to my assumptions about Germans: the Bavarian captain was a real pain in the derriere, and the one from Hamburg was the opposite.

In the end, it took about a month to get the *Mobil Athos* clean enough that it could be towed to the shipyard. We rode the ship down with a crew following to collect any trailing oil from it, and successfully got it dry-docked with no more oil spilled.

Chapter 11

The Last Straw with Uncle Paul

During the *Mobil Athos* operation, I was on 24-hour call seven days a week. The shipowners were pushing us hard to clean up the ship and get the remaining oil out of the tank so they could move it into the shipyard. At the time, my boys were living with me in Toms River, which wasn't a great setup in the first place, and I had to be on this ship over in Philadelphia all of the time. I told Uncle Paul I needed a little time to take care of them, and he said, "Don't worry, I'll take care of them. You stay on the boat." He didn't do much, though. That was the beginning of the end for Uncle Paul and me; he could treat me how he chose, but I wouldn't let him mistreat my kids.

Paul had always romanced me with the idea that I'd be taking over Clean Water when he got too old to work, which was hard for me to visualize. But he always spoke as if the progression was assured. At some point, his daughter started to date a guy. I believe Paul began to think of this kid as a son-in-law. Pretty soon, I was not being invited to the conferences and meetings that I usually attended with him. I found myself being put in cheaper and cheaper motels and began to get the picture: the son-in-law had become ascendant. By this time, I felt that Paul had decided to continue to use me until he could replace me with his prospective son-in-law or somebody else. As it happened, Paul's daughter died suddenly and unexpectedly before she could marry. She was a lovely girl, and I was very sorry for the loss. But it didn't change the fact that the break with Uncle Paul had begun.

I had learned an awful lot from Paul, but in the process, I began to realize I had a lot more to offer than just cleaning up oil spills. I could be at home on the end of a pier where people were getting covered in oil, but I could also be at home in academia. With my background in law and engineering, I thought that I could serve as the bridge between where academia and industry were headed. Finally, though, it was my family that made up my mind for me. I packed up the boys and we moved back down to Washington, D.C. By this time, their mother had gotten divorced from the man who wanted the kids out. The boys were welcome to move back in with her, be near their friends, and return to the schools they had left the year before. I must say, by the time they left, I had become a pretty good cook feeding them, although the fare was more Navy than anything else.

Paul being Paul, he managed to keep me working for him even after I formally quit. There was still outstanding business regarding the boom I had developed with Goodyear, and Paul wanted me to continue as his legal representative in that matter. After meeting with the fabricators in Rockmart, Georgia, and then testing the boom on our own, Clean Water ordered enough booms to handle large operations. Discussions then began between Goodyear and Clean Water toward an agreement on the marketing. Paul and I went to Goodyear headquarters at Akron to negotiate with them on the division of rights. After I did the patent search, however, I found that Goodyear had obtained a patent on a boom very similar to the one we were building some 15 or 20 years before. Their existing patent didn't have several additional features ours did: notably, a fin on the top of the boom to ensure that it wouldn't fly out of the water in high winds, and an interior membrane dividing the flotation chamber. I told the Goodyear attorneys about the patent, and it was news that came much to their surprise. We then agreed that as long as the boom was made with the additional features that I had come up with, we'd be entitled to royalties from booms made and sold that way.

The Coast Guard applied to us for permission to experiment with some of our boom in a facility that had been set up in Richmond, Washington, at the old Army nuclear-bomb production plants. One of the cooling water tanks in the plants had been converted to a test tank for oil-spill response tools. The Coast Guard could discharge oil into the tanks, which had been fitted with wave generators, and deploy booms to see how they worked. As a result of those tests, the Navy's Supervisor of Salvage and Diving, known universally as SUPSALV, learned about our boom and asked to use it in offshore testing they were doing. SUPSALV was working out of Port Hueneme, south of Santa Barbara, doing their tests in the oily water that arose naturally from the seeps in the Santa Barbara Channel. Principally, SUPSALV was testing their skimmers, but I went out with them on a number of occasions to experiment with the Sea Sentry boom. I got to know SUPSALV pretty well during that testing, and when the Navy asked SUPSALV to put out a proposal for the boom it intended to purchase in huge quantities for its spill-response teams around the world, SUPSALV asked me to consult. As a result, SUPSALV became one of my first clients when I set myself up independent of Uncle Paul.

SUPSALV put up for public bid a large supply of the Sea Sentry. While I had consulted with SUPSALV on the request for proposal, I still had a deal with Uncle Paul that I'd handle the bid process for him. Uncle Paul was a smart guy in many respects, but he could be blind to obvious things. In this case, he felt somehow, perhaps through his connections, that he could win a contract for supplying boom to the Navy against the company that was actually manufacturing the boom that he proposed to supply. He just didn't understand that he couldn't compete cost-wise with Goodyear, which was offering its own product without a middleman. It was inevitable that Goodyear would win that contract, and when they did, I terminated the rest of my contact with Paul.

The Navy ordered and deployed a tremendous quantity of the boom. They ordered it to be packed in containers along with the accompanying required gear, and shipped the containers to depots around the world. I was soon to be involved in one of its first deployments.

In April of 1974, the M/V *Ida Green*, a research ship run by Texas A&M University, and the M/T *Bow Elm* collided in Galveston Bay Channel, Texas. From that contact, the *Bow Elm* then collided with the Army Corps of Engineers' Dredge *A. Mackenzie*. The *A. Mackenzie* promptly sank in the middle of the Galveston fairway. SUPSALV called me down to Galveston to direct the placement of their Sea Sentry around the sunken vessel. The concern of SUPSALV was that certain aspects of their wreck removal would involve (or could cause) a release of oil from the vessel's regular bunker tanks, as they were going to cut her up in place on the bottom of the channel and remove her piece by piece.

I knew that, at the full flow of the tide, the current would be too much for the boom to hold. So my idea was to put in the boom and then make sure that cutting in the wreck would only be done at times of slack tide, away from full and ebb tides, when the currents in the inlet would be minimal. If there was to be a discharge, the boom could contain it under those circumstances. The next job was to determine what sort of anchoring systems we needed and how to lay the boom. I decided to enclose the entire operation area within a circular boom that could be opened up when there was no potential for the release of oil. In this manner, the salvage vessels could go in and out of the work area over the wreck. I designed the layout of the boom and the anchoring system, developing some heavy sinkers that would be in place throughout the operation. Then I went out in the small harbor tenders and supervised the connections of the different lengths of boom to each other and to the anchoring system. In its completed fashion, the boom encircled the entire area where the cutting would be conducted.

The casualty, which kept me down in Galveston for over a month, was the occasion when I first met Alex Rynecki, an ex-Navy salvor. By this point, as I wrote earlier, Alex was known as one of the best salvors in the world. We were billeted in the same hotel on the shoreline, where we learned that we both liked classical music. We became good friends, spending time listening to music together and talking about a lot of things other than the ongoing operation. Alex educated me on salvage, and I educated him on oil spills. He was born in Poland, but left for Italy with his mother and father at the time of the growing Nazi threat. He was raised in Italy, and moved with his family to California when the war started. There, his father became successful in the scrap business, which gave Alex a good education. He then went into the Navy, later moving up to salvage operations as an officer. After his tour of duty in the Navy, he began providing engineering for salvage companies and developed his own business.

Several months after I had finished booming the site in Galveston—the wreck-removal operations went on that long—SUPSALV notified me that the chains I had designed for the boom were stretching. I knew that the high-test steel those boom chains were made of would not stretch: they would break before that. When I asked SUPSALV to send me a photo of the "stretched" chains, I discovered from studying the images that the chains, as I had known, were not stretching. Rather, there

107

was enough wear at the chains' linkage points that, over a length of several hundred yards, it added up to a measurable distance. I found that fishermen who use such chains regularly in their operations know that they must continually watch for chain elongation and shorten the chain length to account for this same wear. As a consequence, I suggested to Goodyear that they replace the chains with Kevlar fabric line from DuPont, which would not wear the way that the steel chains had.

Chapter 12

A Big Spill on the Delaware

Within a few months of finishing with the *Mobil Athos*, in the spring of 1974, there was a nearby incident with a Greek tanker. The *Elias* was unloading at the pier at Fort Mifflin, just across the Delaware River from where we had worked on the *Mobil Athos*, when she blew up, broke in half, and sank at the dock. The *Elias* was an older tanker, with her house amidships, as was the case with the *Singapore Trader*. This was a common tanker configuration during World War II and for some time after, until accommodation eventually moved to the stern, where it has remained on contemporary tankers. The explosions blew the ship apart, collapsed the amidships housings into the tanks, and killed most of the crew.

The *Elias* left a significant oil spill in the river and a lot of damage around the berth. Eleven people on shore were killed, struck by flying debris; parts of the ship had been blown into the terminal parking and smashed cars parked there; as we were cleaning, I found a large section of the deck about half a mile onshore, in the woods toward the Philadelphia airport. The explosion had been remarkable.

This job was the second time that I had the opportunity to work with Alex Rynecki. Alex had been called in by a company that did a lot of maritime work in the Philadelphia harbors. That company, as it turned out, was owned by the father of Cindy Hudson, about whom there will be more to follow. The elder Hudson hired Alex to advise him on running the salvage job on the *Elias*, since the company had no previous experience with salvage. When I first met Hudson, he asked me what I knew about Alex. I told him that he was one of the top people in salvage, which I guess got back to Alex and built a continuing basis for our friendship. Alex ended up running the show for the Hudsons.

After our work together in Galveston and on the *Elias*, Alex became my next client. He was on the West Coast and wanted a consultant in D.C. to help with his salvage business, particularly with the federal government and the agencies that impacted his lines of work. Around the time Alex hired me, I gained another client and good friend in David Usher. David ran a contracting company in Detroit, and I had previously done some work for him on an oil spill in the St. Lawrence River. As with Alex, David needed someone in Washington to help with problems and opportunities in dealing with the federal government. These two friends kept me afloat in my early going as an independent.

In need again of an office, I began subletting space from Alice Bonfield, a friend from AA in Washington who was primarily in public relations. One of her clients was the Alyeska Pipeline Company, which at that time was constructing the Alaskan Pipeline to bring crude oil from the North Slope of Alaska down to Valdez, an ice-free port in southern Alaska. The work was not directly involved with anything I was doing at the time, but it was interesting to me, so I remained interested in learning from Alice what was going on up there.

Little did I know that, in the future, much of my life, including the loss of my love Marie, would involve Alaska. In the early 1970s, Marie and I flew together to Japan to visit her brother, Ed, and his Japanese wife, Kosuco. Ed had ended his tour in the Air Force in Japan and had landed a teaching job in Tokyo that later morphed into a job with a Tokyo newspaper covering American matters. As it turned out, our trip over there included a stop off in Anchorage, Alaska, for refueling. Years later, Marie took off from the Anchorage airport to fly herself down to Kodiak Island and was killed when she crashed on a mountaintop named Devil's Prong while attempting to land at the Kodiak Airport.

In the summer of 1976, the barge *Nepco 140* ran aground in the St. Lawrence River, rupturing two tanks. My friend Dave Usher was called in on the spill, which had fouled quite a length of the river. Dave asked me to go up and assist on the spill response effort. This was at a time when my friend Ann Reid, an opera singer I had met in Washington years before and have remained close friends with since, had returned from Italy to Washington for a period. Ann was originally from Buffalo and wanted to visit her parents there. I offered to drive her up and drop her off on my way to Ogdensburg, where Dave Usher's response center for the operation was situated. It was a fairly complex operation, spilling over a great deal of coast. There were a couple of different contractors on the scene, principally involved in beach-work, cleaning shorelines, and the containment and removal of floating oil. Ann asked me if she might take a shot at working on the spill, since she wanted to do something for the environment before returning to Italy. I decided to put Ann in charge of a wildlife cleanup crew and thought that I'd make her team all women, to forestall any problems. It turned out that none of the women wanted to work with women only, and I later learned that they felt Ann was like a female warden in women's prison. In Buffalo, I met Ann's family, including her brother-in-law Bob Collin. He came up to Ogdensburg with me, and I put him to work running a response gang in the operation as well. After I had finished, Bob stayed on and worked for Dave Usher in Detroit.

After the *Nepco 140*, I heard from Jim Parker—Pappy Parker, as he was known at Industrial Marine Services in Norfolk, Virginia. Jim was a former Coast Guard officer during World War II and had become one of the earliest spill contractors. He spotted an opportunity in New York Harbor with a company named Clean Harbors Inc., which was being formed by a cooperative of the oil companies that had facilities and operations in New York Harbor. Clean Harbors would be financed by the oil companies to provide a system for dealing with spills originating from members of the cooperative. Jim knew that oil-spill responses there had been hit-and-miss for many years, and there was presently a paucity of reliable contractors in the area. He had also approached Bill Holly, President of Sealand Environmental Services in Connecticut, to join forces and try to put together a capability for properly dealing with spills in New York Harbor.

Jim asked me if I knew of anyone else in the area suitable to join them in supporting the proposed new company. I had recently done some work for SUPSALV in the Boston Harbor, assisting with some dredging and boom-deployment drills just off the runways at Logan Airport. SUPSALV had hired a tug to deal with boom deployment from an oil-spill contractor named Bob Dee, who owned the tug belonging to his company, Jet Line Services. Bob had been a professional football player for the Redskins and then the Patriots, after the American League came into being. I was quite impressed with his work team's reputation and their equipment, so I suggested Bob as somebody who might work in the New York Harbor venture. I arranged a meeting for him with Bill Holly and Jim. The three decided to form a new company together, which would be a contractor with their backing and equipment. They asked me if I would come on board long enough to set up the operation and run it for a period. At that time, I didn't want to go in the direction of spill cleaning, but told them I would work with them until it was running well enough for them to replace me with someone who wanted to take it on full time.

I researched the oil companies coming into the cooperative. From there, I developed a plan for building a company that I called Clean Venture, which would be comprised of resources from Parker, Holly, and Dee's businesses. I developed response plans and a working manual. After the producers' cooperative had a chance to digest the prospectus, they signed a contract with Clean Venture. From there, I started working to get it fully manned and began visiting all the terminals we were being paid to protect in the event of a spill.

One day during all of this, Bob Collin called and said he was being let go by Dave Usher. I invited him to come down to Washington, where he could help run my operation. By that point, I was away a lot on jobs and needed someone in Washington to hold down the fort. I hired him and set him up in the space I was leasing from Alice Bonfield. Alice was a women's advocate and had a women's advancement organization as a client. They were going to run a radio spot, but the producers felt it needed to be read by a man, so Alice got me to record a demo. After hearing my demo, everyone agreed with Alice that the voice needed to be female—they said that my reading sounded chauvinistic.

I didn't have any trouble with Bob during this time, My friend Danny Coleman had some space upstairs from the place he owned, the Dubliner on Capitol Hill. I moved Bob there. We were pretty far apart by that point, and Bob had a penchant for screwing up. Whenever my kids came in to work, they would invariably have one story or another about the mixed-up things Bob did. They started calling him "Bebo," because he had applied for a permit for the business under the name "Bebo

Collin." It wasn't intentional, of course; he had just mispronounced his name to the point where it came out sounding like Bebo. Eventually, when I left to go down to New Orleans to do training for the Petroleum Strategic Reserve, which turned out to be an multi-year project, Bebo and I decided that it was the right time for us to finally part ways.

One day, around July of 1977, I was on a beach on the New Jersey shore practicing responses with our Clean Venture team when I got an emergency call from the EPA. There had been a flood of major proportions at Johnstown, Pennsylvania, and the EPA wanted us to provide protection from the petroleum and waste that was coming out of the flooded steel mills. The city was pretty much wiped out. It was one of the worst floods in the history of a place notorious for floods, even making the cover of *Time*, which said Johnstown was "the city whose name is synonymous with floods." There happened to be a chartered helicopter there on the beach with us that I was using to help with the exercises. The pilot didn't mind flying us to Johnstown, so off we went. We landed at the airport to find that the only other flights being allowed in and out were Army Cavalry helicopters. Because none of the phones in Johnstown were working, we then flew the helicopter to the next nearest town. The EPA gave me a contract and I started forming our spill-response group. Clean Venture immediately started flying equipment in and began a response that would last for several months.

The Coast Guard flew in a Strike Team to assist, and they sat with us in our command center. The EPA guys, however, wanted more comfort than was available locally, so they set up their command center 50 miles away, near the Pennsylvania Turnpike. This was fine with us, because we were used to working with the Coast Guard and generally got along well with them. The EPA, though, was a different story. To begin with, they always wanted our helicopter to go down to where they were staying to ferry them up to the site. We were mostly able to comply, except for one notable time. One of the major national news magazines was coming to report when we got a call from the EPA guys, asking us to come down and get them so they would be there when the press arrived. Unfortunately for them, the Coast Guard had the chopper and they were working. The EPA guys didn't like that. The next time I went down to their command center near the turnpike, they confronted me in a meeting, demanding to know why I didn't send the helicopter down when they asked for it. They told me, "We're in charge of this response, Mr. Gallagher, and we certainly can find someone to replace you." Fortunately, the commander of the Coast Guard Strike Team was sitting next to me. He said, "I made the decision on the deployment," which settled that.

There was a lot of interesting work on that operation. Several gas stations had been flooded, and their fuel tanks had overflowed into the sewer system. Their gas and vapors were going into the sewer, which finally caused an explosion that resulted in a death. We formed a crew to go down into the sewer system, knocking down vapors. We also did some work for the police, who were pretty hard-pressed. We had boats, ATVs, and marine radios, so we helped where we could. One of the worst jobs was examining sunken cars to determine if there were bodies in them. Fortunately, we found none. My daughter, Anne, came up to help, and when the mayor met her, he was so impressed that he asked her to be his secretary. She worked with him in the city command center, which was set up in a department store just out of the flood zone. It was a good experience for her. Indeed, bad as it was, the casualty was a fortuitous thing for Clean Venture, which was just a start-up at that point. With that response, the company was launched.

As a result of my solution to the problem with the vapors in the Johnstown sewers, I got a call later on from the company that was building the Baltimore subway system. They, too, needed expertise in the control of petroleum. The tunnel system was being designed in such a way that drainage from the street above would come down into the subway and be passed on for discharge into the harbor. Their question for me was this: What could be done if a gasoline truck was knocked over on the street and then emptied its load into the sewer and thus the subway system? I told them that, aside from ensuring that they had the means to shut the power off immediately, they would need to have on-hand materials, like the ones we had used in the Johnstown sewers, to knock down the gasoline fumes and prevent them from being ignited by any sparks. I guess that was all news to them, so they hired me.

I next told them that, in the same scenario, an additional problem would be with the recent environmental laws. No oil could be dumped into navigable waterways, so if their system dumped into the harbor, they were going to need to work against running afoul of these laws. The best place to start, I suggested, was to meet with the Captain of the Port of Baltimore, as he was in a position to give them a dispensation from these regulations. The engineers and I met with Captain William Kime and explained the potential for a problem. I was really impressed with Captain Kime, who understood the problem right away and immediately identified the best solution. I was glad, because I knew that the Coast Guard could be bureaucratic and didn't want this to become some major stumbling block. However, Captain Kime must have been an engineer. I thought to myself, "This guy is going places. I wouldn't be surprised if he became Commandant of the Coast Guard one day."

Chapter 13

The *Argo Merchant* Introduces us to the Buckleys

The motor tanker *Argo Merchant* grounded off Nantucket Island in the winter of 1976. She was bound for Salem, MA, carrying a cargo of No. 6 Fuel Oil when she missed the Nantucket Light. I happened to be in New York doing some work for Eric Nielson, who had a couple of inventions I was helping with. Because of the environmental threat and proximity to the United States, the U.S. government became involved. SUPSALV, and thus I, were quickly drawn in.

I went out to Cape Cod and found a place to stay in Sandwich. The problem was the ship was stuck firmly aground. The Coast Guard had boarded her and removed the crew when it was clear that there was no way of getting her off her strand. My job was to work with Alex Rynecki and Dave Usher to develop a means of getting oil off the ship—183,000 barrels of No. 6 fuel oil, the heaviest classification of fuel oil, plus cutter stock, a distillate diluent. It was pretty apparent that they weren't going to be able to salvage her in a whole fashion due to the considerable stress she was suffering from the strong nor'easter that was blowing.

We first arranged with some vessels to get us out to the *Argo Merchant* and support us in pumping oil off the ship. Dave Usher's was one of the few companies in the country with access to a submersible salvage pump that could be put down into the tanks of the ship to pump the oil overboard, so we had brought Dave's pump to the scene on the Cape. There was another pump of that type we knew of, owned by one of the oil companies, and we had that shipped up as well.

The issue became one of being able to get on board before the *Argo Merchant* began to fracture and spill oil. We spent several days going over the plan in our command center, the bar of the Daniel Webster Inn in Sandwich. I was in charge of finding the gear for the people who would board the vessel. Our problems increased significantly when the Army Corps of Engineers, who were delivering the borrowed pump on a flatbed truck, managed to drop the pump off the truck. I had them start fixing it, but I knew that we were going to need to go ahead with just one pump. As we were preparing to board the *Argo Merchant*, Alex received a query from the Catawba Corporation, which turned out to be owned by the Buckley family, of Senator James Buckley and William F. Buckley fame. They had an idea for using microwave units in the tanks of vessels to heat oil. Because No. 6 fuel oil is so heavy (it reverts to nearly a solid at room temperature), it is normally heated by steam on a tanker when being loaded, then reheated when approaching port for discharge. With her engines not functioning, the *Argo Merchant* could not heat the oil using anything on board the ship, so we needed some means of getting the oil warm enough to pump it out. Dave's pumps had an external heating system, as did the broken pump. But the Buckleys had an idea (and a patent) on this concept of using microwaves in the tanks, and they wanted to test it on the *Argo Merchant*. I thought it was a good idea, but that we should experiment with the machinery beforehand.

We managed to locate a tank full of cold oil and started working with representatives from Catawba to try their microwave method on this tank ashore before we took it out to the stranded ship. As it turned out, we didn't get a chance to experiment before the *Argo Merchant* broke in half. She sank fairly quickly, and we learned later that within a few days she had come apart so completely that she had broken down into parts no larger than a car. After we canceled the experiment, we got a call from John Buckley from his family compound in Sharon, Connecticut, asking if we would still come up and talk to them about the device. It was too late for me to get home for Christmas, so Alex and I decided to go up to Sharon and meet with the Buckleys.

(Photo U.S. Coast Guard)

The two halves of the Argo Merchant, Nantucket, Massachusetts, July 2000

They put us up in a hotel in Sharon, and for a couple of days we met with the family. As the winters there were replete with snow, tunnels connected all the houses in the Buckley compound. We were taken from one house to another and introduced around; we even spent some time watching a movie in James Buckley's basement, where he had a theater for the family. I remember talking to the Senator, who asked me if I was familiar with the concept of double hulls on ships. I said that I'd heard vaguely about them, but didn't know too much. He wondered if a double hull would have saved the situation with the *Argo Merchant*. I told him the stress had been so great, breaking the ship into such small pieces, that I didn't think a double hull would have made much difference.

Alex and I stayed in touch with John Buckley, who was the CEO of Catawba. Through Dave Usher, we tried to find uses for the microwave device on some projects the Navy was involved in, but we were never actually able to do anything with their product. They even called us later to tell us to stop trying. I never heard anything about the design again, and tankers don't use it today.

The oil that the *Argo Merchant* spilled all went out to sea, with no landfall of oil from the casualty that we ever learned of. Initially, there was a lot of concern that the oil might make it out to the Grand Banks and affect the fishing industry there, but we never learned of any impact there, either. The southwesterly winds were pretty regular in that area at the time, and they just kept pushing the oil to sea. There were other consequences, though. Because it took several years to find the owners of the ship, when the Oil Pollution Act was written in 1990, it mandated the creation of a "Qualified Individual," a party appointed for every ship to be responsible for immediate response in the event of a casualty. Previously, some owners would create layers and layers of companies to protect themselves from having to pay costs associated with casualties. The mandate of a Qualified Individual, which would become central to what we do at Gallagher Marine Systems, was very much in response to what happened with the *Argo Merchant*.

As a gift, Alex bought a book about shipwrecks on Cape Cod for the salvage master on the *Argo Merchant* job. Alex knew about my interest in drawing and asked me to sketch the ship on the frontispiece of the book. That launched my reputation as an artist in the salvage community. I get kidded about it a lot to this day by the salvors with whom I'm close and continue to work.

Chapter 14

The West Hackberry Blowout

Early the next year, I struck up a consulting agreement with Jack Wilson, a government engineer working for the Department of Energy and in charge of building the Strategic Petroleum Reserve. The Strategic Petroleum Reserve was set up in 1975 as a response to the oil embargo of 1973 to 1974, and was meant to serve as a hedge against future oil shortages. "I'd like you to come up with some training ideas for the people who are going to be manning the equipment," Jack Wilson told me. The U.S. government was buying empty cavities along the Gulf Coast: drilled-out salt domes and salt mines that had been mined out. Previously, some of these had been used to store oil or chemicals because the walls were inert and impermeable. But they were also flexible, so they would shift in the event of an earthquake, lessening the risk of spill. This gave the DOE the idea of using them for the strategic reserves.

Because these empty caverns were going to be filled with tremendous amounts of oil, Jack wanted me to come up with spill-response plans and training programs. I worked for two or three months, going down to the Gulf Coast periodically to examine the five projected sites and reporting back. Jack decided that it would be best to bring the teams from each site to the Strategic Reserve headquarters in New Orleans, where I was to teach a course on forming and deploying a spill-response team and on the equipment used to respond to emergencies.

I decided to create a manual, which I typed out and printed copies of on a mimeograph machine. I have always believed that the best way to train is to put people into the atmosphere of a real situation. I therefore made exercises as realistic as possible, with the pertinent choices being made step-by-step, as they would be in a real spill response. In creating my training scenario for the Strategic Reserve, I considered each of the different sites where the Strategic Reserves were being planned, looking for the one where I felt a spill would do the worst possible damage to surrounding areas. I finally decided on the West Hackberry site, in western Louisiana. West Hackberry sat right on a large inland lake named Black Lake, into which any oil escaping from the site could immediately spread. From there, the oil could enter the connected waterways that eventually led into the nearby Gulf of Mexico. I made that my model blowout site and created a response scenario for the three-day course I was designing to teach the upcoming class in New Orleans.

The weekend before the course began, I went down to West Hackberry again just to get a feel for the place. The directors of the team there had scheduled to bring a skimmer out on a forthcoming Saturday to give the hands an opportunity to get familiar with their equipment. Because it was to happen on a Saturday and the crew was not being paid, the director suggested they bring their wives along. He also invited a local woman, the owner of a popular bar in the area. We all went out on the skimmer, and I had the crew work through the drill that I had planned. It all went fine, and I got to meet the owner of the bar. On Sunday, I headed to New Orleans for the start of the course the following morning. The course was being held at the headquarters for the Strategic Petroleum Reserve of Texas and Louisiana. I taught for the three days and thought it all went pretty well.

The Wednesday evening after I had wrapped up the course, the headquarters received an emergency call. The date was

September 21, 1978, and there had been a blowout at West Hackberry, of all places. It was out of control, on fire, and they needed help right away.

Strategic Petroleum Reserve

One of my first impulses was to collect all my manuals. This was the exact type of blowout I had used to set the scene for the spill I had designed for the training—the blowout was at the precise point I had picked for the drill, right at the edge of the lake, and I even had a photograph of the West Hackberry site on the cover. It looked very suspicious to me.

The command at Reserve headquarters dragooned me to go along with them to West Hackberry, making me the only one in the place who had ever even seen a major oil spill. By Thursday morning, we were at the site, responding to a major, 72,000-barrel oil spill.

The only difference between my scenario and the reality of the spill was that the wind was coming from the northeast, blowing over the lake and toward the site. This was somewhat less disastrous than what I had envisioned, as the oil was being held against the shore rather than spreading over the water. That was a lucky break. I stayed on to help coordinate the spill response. I had gone to New Orleans thinking I'd only be staying for a week, but ended up being there for almost a year—that is how big a spill it was.

Strategic Petroleum Reserve

At the end of the response, I had one of those experiences that, in retrospect, are definitive. After we had cleaned everything we could easily get to, the remaining problem was that a lot of oil was still trapped in the vegetation along the shoreline. We simply couldn't get at that oil without removing the vegetation, which I knew wasn't an option. Some people on the response suggested that we build a dyke out beyond the shore to hold the oil and keep it from blowing or drifting back into the lake. I didn't think that would be a good idea for two reasons: First, I thought it would take an eon to get a permit for the construction. Next, I knew that Black Lake had been an oil-producing lake for years and that there was bound to be lot of muck on the bottom. Building the dyke would only stir all that up, very possibly creating more of an environmental impact than it solved.

My solution was to use the Sea Sentry boom. I called Goodyear and asked how much they charged for the boom, and they told me something like $63 or $64 a foot. I knew that much earlier Uncle Paul had bought a whole shot of Sea Sentry boom, maybe 1,000 feet of it, for a spill that had happened up in the Delaware River. He never ended up using it, so he had it in storage. I also knew that, at the time Paul bought his, it was running around $32 a foot. I hadn't had any direct contact with Paul in the years since our parting, but I called him anyway and told him that, if he still had that boom, I thought I could get a buyer for him. We agreed on a price and I asked him to have it delivered. I explained that it wasn't an emergency—we were buying it for remediation. I told him that delivery just in good time would be fine.

Strategic Petroleum Reserve

Within two days, Paul was in West Hackberry with a whole convoy of trucks, boom, and people. I wasn't too surprised since I was familiar with Uncle Paul's way of getting work. He wasn't just delivering the boom—he wanted to install it as well. I knew in advance that putting the boom in would be a tough task for someone who had never worked with it before, so I agreed to let him do it. He got to work and it took his crew three or four days to install it along the shoreline as we directed. In the meantime, Uncle Paul was running around the command center, making a lot of noise. He would talk to whoever would listen, and was constantly suggesting additional things he thought should be done. In reality, he was just trying to get himself more work. Finally, my contact with the Department of Energy said, "Jack, can't you get this guy out of here? He's getting on everybody's nerves."

I took Paul aside and told him that he'd done a great job getting the boom, but we were wrapping up now and needed his guys out of the way. He took the hint, packed up, and left. He made a lot of money on the deal and got rid of that excess boom as well. For me, it finally closed the chapter with Uncle Paul.

Though my training manual had anticipated the incident and used the general characteristics of West Hackberry as it basis, in and of itself it wasn't a specific response plan for a spill at the West Hackberry site. There was, in fact, a spill response plan on hand, but it was so general that to me, it was useless, as though the authors of it hadn't even visited the site. I suspected they had cribbed from other response plans they had written for other sites. A reputable and workable spill response plan needs specific and local information: telephone numbers, locations of nearest airports and their capacities, detailed information about the existing emergency response capabilities in the area. As far as I could tell, none of that stuff was in the existing response plan, which was in fact little more than a drawing of the site. While I had a good idea from my previous visits to West Hackberry what was available and how to procure it, the absence of a reliable plan on site created serious problems in organizing the response. When, many weeks later, we were ending the response, I told my Department of Energy contact that, going forward, real and workable response plans were something that he needed, not just for West Hackberry, but also for all of the Strategic Petroleum Reserve sites. "Well," he replied. "How about you?" And with that, a job that was supposed to last a week would go on for two more years.

I rented an apartment in New Orleans, which, incidentally, I ended up keeping for 35 years. I learned about the apartment, which was on Napoleon Avenue on the edge of the Garden District, from people at the Strategic Petroleum Reserve headquarters. The architect who had designed the building owned the particular apartment I rented, and my office had been his drafting studio. It came complete with a skylight and provided a wonderful place to do my work. I used the office to design the contingency plans for all of the Strategic Petroleum Reserve sites, as doing them correctly required a lot of groundwork. Each site had to be surveyed, and the area around it studied extensively. In sequence, I ended up bringing my children, Sean, Michael, and Anne, down during summer and college vacation periods. Sean helped me survey the Louisiana sites and Michael the Texas Reserve sites and associated systems. West Hackberry was in Louisiana, but the loading port for it was actually in Texas, so we needed to examine the piping system between that port and the reserve in Louisiana. My daughter, Anne, came down and provided secretarial assistance. Sean and Michael were studying engineering, so it worked well for them and gave them a boost as they entered engineering training after graduation. Anne, though not an engineer, picked up things quickly. She more or less acted as the collator and receptor of all the information that we had collected. I had a word processor at the time that was supposedly portable, though it weighed about 30 pounds. As a friend of mine said, "The thing isn't portable, it's transportable." Anne spent a summer inputting what we had collected and turning it into draft form, which was a big help in making our data into something useful.

Computers at that time, the late 1970s, were still pretty stationary, at least on a personal level. But by using the limited computer technology available, I realized that there must be a way to create a program that could generate a workable plan for the most severe spills, the smallest spills, and everything in between. I felt that there had to be a way that, when a spill occurred, you could plug in the parameters of the spill, leaving the program to return the parts of the plan that would be applicable to the casualty according to its characteristics. That was what first got me thinking of what would later on become a company I intended to call Automated Response Systems (ARS).

L to R Michael, Anne, Jack and Sean

My deadline for finishing the Petroleum Reserve plans was December of 1979. In October or November of that year, I got a call from Lamorte Burns in New York City, a company that served as the commercial representative in the United States for several Protection and Indemnity Clubs (P&I Clubs) in Europe and Asia. I knew of Lamorte Burns, having worked on various marine casualties involving its clients. P&I Clubs insure shipowners against liabilities arising out of casualties that might occur to their insured vessels. Their coverage is different from say, Lloyds, which writes insurance against loss to the owner specifically for the ship itself or its cargo. The P&I Clubs, among other things, insure against damage caused by the ship herself—for example, a collision or an oil spill for which a ship is held responsible.

Lamorte Burns was losing their spill guy and a friend had apparently recommended me to replace him. While I was intrigued by the idea, the fact was that I still had a lot of work to do to finish the Strategic Petroleum Reserve blowout contingency plans. They wanted someone right then and there, of course, and wouldn't make any guarantees to me if I couldn't respond immediately. Nevertheless, when I was finished with the last of the plans a little over a month later, I gave them a call. It turned out that they still wanted to talk to me, so I met with them in January of 1980. I was hired by them immediately and began working on the 32nd floor of the World Trade Center South Tower, where their offices were located (these offices were lost in the bombing of the WTC years after Lamorte Burnes and I moved out of New York City). I was given the position of vice president in charge of their operations involving ship casualties, in particular those involving oil spills. Other things came into play as time went on, and my breadth of interest at the firm expanded. The president was Nicholas Healy, a well-accomplished maritime attorney. His father, Nicholas Healy Sr., was probably the preeminent maritime attorney in the country and was highly regarded then as the dean of all maritime lawyers.

My first job was to go to London to meet with each of the P&I Clubs that Lamorte Burns represented in England. I took my children Anne and Sean. After we visited Ireland for a few days, I left them in the Dublin area while I went on to London for my meetings. Once I had met up again with Sean and Anne back in Ireland, there was one more thing Nick Healy wanted me to do:

call on his father, the respected maritime lawyer, who had a summer place in the southwestern corner of the country. When we got down to the southern coast, I called Nick Sr. and was told by the village operator that he was at a wedding in Dublin, but that he would be back in time to meet me. He was, and we all had tea. It was a wonderful place, and Nick and Mrs. Healy invited us to spend the night. The discussions we had on our visit led Nick Sr. and me to work together on a paper about the wreck of the M/T *Zoe Colocotronis*. She was a tanker that had gone aground on a reef off the southwest coast of Puerto Rico, and the captain had jettisoned some of his oil cargo to try and get her off the strand. He didn't get off the strand, and actually caused a lot of problems with the resultant oil spill. This was in the late 1960s, when there wasn't nearly so much concern about spills and the damage they caused; there were very few penalties in place then. I spent quite a lot of time with Nick on that piece, and it was published in the *Maritime Journal of Law and Commerce*.

Chapter 15

Lamorte Burns

The *Akaterini* was among the first major casualty jobs I did for Lamorte Burns. I was called in through the P&I Club to keep the vessel owners apprised of what was happening, making sure they were up to speed on the severity and potential damages. The ship had been up in the Delaware River, where she had discharged her crude-oil cargo, and was on her way toward the Caribbean when her engine rooms and accommodations caught fire. The fire began roughly off Maryland, where she dropped anchor as the crew tried to fight the fire. SUPSALV offered support, but the crew finally had to abandon ship when the flames approached the pump room.

The salvors, in this case SMIT Salvage out of Rotterdam, were called in. SMIT had a salvage vessel in the Caribbean, the *SMIT London*, which they intended to dispatch to aid the *Akaterini*. My involvement began in New York City, where the *Akaterini* owners had an office. We met there to negotiate the salvage contract between them and SMIT. I'd already spent the better part of an afternoon and that evening with them when I got a call from Nick Healy, asking me how we were doing. We had most of it worked out, but SMIT had one requirement in the contract that represented a sticking point. They demanded that I be on site during the salvage operation, which wasn't normal and stemmed from a previous salvage issue with the M/T *Burma Agate* in Galveston. As that salvage had gone from bad to worse, SMIT had wanted to change the contract, but Lamorte Burns had not been authorized to make changes on behalf of the P&I Club involved. As a result, for this salvage, SMIT wanted a

Lamorte Burns representative onsite for the whole salvage, one who would have the authority to change contract issues depending on any changes of circumstance. The problem was that Lamorte Burns couldn't change terms on behalf of the P&I Club it was representing, whether it had a representative on site or not. Only the P&I Club itself could alter the contract, which was where we were stuck. I explained the circumstances, and Nick said that he would send a lawyer over from the P&I Club's law firm to see if he could help. Unfortunately, the lawyer who came turned out to be the same lawyer who had irritated SMIT on the *Burma Agate*. The feelings were mutual, and this lawyer wasn't about to give SMIT any relief on this deal. In fact, he started trying to undo the concessions that I'd already made in our negotiations. Fortune intervened in the form of a cocktail party that the lawyer needed to attend. He left it up to me to finish the matter. After he left, I told SMIT that if they would agree to the contract as I had previously written it, they could forget all the retrenchments the lawyer had suggested. We signed. To this day, my friends at SMIT tell a different story, always claiming that I was the one who convinced the lawyer to go to his cocktail party. That wasn't the case, but I did seize on the opportunity of his leaving to close the deal.

I went down to Norfolk, Virginia, where the SMIT Salvage vessel was standing by, and we went out to the *Akaterini*. SMIT had hired the shore-side firefighting team of Les and Dwight Williams, whose specialty was oil-well fires and blowouts. They were a father-and-son team who had worked the West Hackberry blowout, though I hadn't met them there. By this time, they had founded their own company, but were still contracting with Boots & Coots, the well-control company, to respond to maritime fires. Shipboard fires were a little out of Boots & Coots' experience, but Les knew shipboard firefighting. His background was fighting fires set by kamikaze attacks in the

Navy. Dwight, his son, though quite young at the time, had already gotten great fire experience.

Les and Dwight took me under their collective wing. Dwight would board the vessel to direct the firefight and Les would stay aboard the salvage tug, where I helped him haul hose and put gear together. Once, when I was driving with them down to the salvage ship, we came into port to resupply and pulled up to some folks on the pier. Les asked them if they had seen any coon-asses around, by which he meant fellow Cajuns. I quickly got Les to lay off that, particularly since a lot of the people around were black stevedores who were certain to misunderstand what the Cajun slang meant.

We established a position off the *Akaterini* for the salvage ship and its firefighting operation. A Coast Guard cutter began sailing a three-mile perimeter around the two ships to establish a no-entry zone. One day, while I was up on the bridge of the SMIT Salvage tug, the cutter kept calling in, asking for updates. The firefighting was still going on pretty hot at that point, and everyone on the tug was working like hell. Finally, the captain of the SMIT tug, who was Dutch, lost his patience. "You've got a hundred men out there to run that ship," he replied to the cutter. "I'm here by myself and I don't have time to answer all your fool questions."

By the time the operation was over, I had gotten close with Dwight, Les, and the rest of the salvors. It was an uphill climb, getting close to them, for as I've said already, salvors are a strange bunch. But it was worthwhile. Looking back, I sometimes think that I've been a half-salvor on many of the jobs that I've been on since.

When we had finished the salvage operation, the Italian owners of the *Akaterini* wanted the ship for scrap. The lawyers in New York became suspicious. The P&I Club had spent a lot of money salvaging the ship, and now her owners wanted to scrap her, probably thinking they could make more money that way. The Italians were within hours of closing the deal with a ship breaker in Texas when someone at Lamorte Burns got the idea of asking a guy from Zim, a large Israeli shipping company that maintained a desk on the floor at Lamorte Burns, if he had any ideas. He was a pretty big man who rode everywhere around New York on a bicycle and was always telling us stories about trying to keep his bike safe in New York in the early 1980s. The biker knew of a program where, if a certain amount of money was spent repairing a foreign-flagged ship, that payment eased the way for the ship to get an American flag. The P&I Club had met that threshold, and Zim had some need for such an American-flagged vessel. To the advantage of the P&I Club, the biker worked out a sale to Zim only moments before the Italians could sell the *Akaterini* to the scrapping people. She went into service as a tanker under an American flag.

My next really significant salvage for Lamorte Burns came in a casualty on the Columbia River between Washington and Oregon in 1983. While carrying a cargo of black oil to Portland, the tanker *Mobiloil* lost her steering coming up the Columbia. She came aground near Warrior Rock on the Oregon side of the river. In going aground, she opened several of her cargo tanks along the bottom and lower side of the vessel, discharging a large quantity of oil into the river. With the flow of the river being to some extent tidal, the oil was being moved up and down the river. As a result, oil managed to contact quite a bit of the Columbia River shoreline all the way down to the mouth of the river, where it empties into the Pacific. One of the twists in this response was that Mount St. Helens had erupted nearby only a few years before. As a result of that massive eruption, there was a huge amount of fallen timber in the river that ended up piling in certain areas, often the same places where shipping companies were mothballing their unused vessels. Several of these vessels were large tankers that had been moored there for long enough to have built up quite a concentration of the knockdown between them and the pier front. The problem with all this was that oil managed to get into these flotillas of logs, making already large and cumbersome timber harder to get to and completely oiled.

Mobil had assembled its own response team. Though they would call in outside contractors, they ran the operations themselves with their trained responders. The Mobil response team performed essentially the way that, as a result of OPA 90, the Unified Command team operates now. My role there was not in the response. Instead, I served as a representative of the P&I Club, reporting back on the length and expense of the spill cleanup. However, because I was there and because the people I was working with knew my background, I ended up offering response assistance as well.

Ken Fullwood was the primary person directing the spill response for Mobil. Ken and I became fairly good friends during the operation. For several months, I was out in Oregon, traveling up and down the river and out to the ocean with the Mobil team. Alex Rynecki was also on this spill, working on board the ship as the engineer of salvage. When the ship, fairly well pumped of her cargo, was finally taken off her strand down at Warrior Rock, the problem that next arose was how to bring her into dry dock in Portland. Although they had pumped oil from the ship as best they could before moving her, they were bound to lose oil from the ship when she came up into dry dock. The dry dock in question was a floating dry dock, meaning it was sunk to allow the ship to come in. Once the ship was in, they pumped out her ballast water, and whatever water was in that dry dock would then flow out into the surrounding water. Any residual oil in the *Mobiloil's* tanks would be discharged and certainly get into the surrounding waters, including the water surrounding the nearby Coast Guard station.

On the *Singapore Trader*, my first really big job with Uncle Paul, he had taken that ship up to a dry dock in Canada. She wasn't a tanker, but she had punctured her bottom at her stranding and was, like the *Mobiloil*, going into a floating dry dock. Uncle Paul had gotten the idea from somebody to design what he called a dry-dock filter box. He claimed it was his idea, though he did let me know that he'd picked it up in a shipyard in the Norfolk area. I must have taken out a patent for him, because I did the drawings for the application. As such, I had a clear understanding of the device, even though I hadn't been to Canada for the dry-docking of the *Singapore Trader*. I told Ken Fullwood that I was familiar with a system for dry-docking ships leaking oil that might be of help with the situation we had with the *Mobiloil*. Ken was interested, so I called Uncle Paul and told him the situation. He said I could use the idea of the filter box so long as we used his Sorbent-C, the material I had stored in heaps in my Annapolis basement.

The idea was to build wire-mesh containers to fit between the dry-dock blocks and the damaged portions of the ships, filling a layer of Sorbent-C in each of the boxes. In this way, when oil and water started coming out of the holes in the ship, they would filter through the boxes before draining out into the dry dock and the water beyond. I got the system into place, working with the dry-dock engineers. As they sank the dry dock, the cages would flood, lifting the Sorbent-C in the cage. When they raised the ship, the waterline would drop, allowing the water flowing through the breaks in the hull to pass through the

Sorbent-C-filled boxes. Thus, the boxes would form a floating barrier to absorb any leaking oil.

I was on the wing of the dry dock with Ken as the ship was coming out. It went swimmingly, with the dry-dock boxes keeping the oil discharged from the ship securely in the dry dock. I stood by and assisted with the continued pumping of the remaining contents from the cargo tanks so that they could do the repair work to get the ship to float again. As it turned out, the *Mobiloil* ended up going to the scrapyard afterward. It was one of only two remaining domestically flagged ships owned by Mobil, and Ken, the manager of the Mobil Oil fleet in the United States, liked to tell me he had lost half his fleet in this incident.

The operation on the Columbia River continued for quite a bit of time. As I mentioned, one of the biggest problems turned out to be the old timber trapped between the neglected ships and the docks. It was tough to see the oil mixed in with the timber, and we weren't going to send anyone into these rafts; they would be too dangerous to work on. The only real option was to take the logs out. The State of Washington had determined that anything coming out of the river with oil on it would have to go into a specialized landfill at a cost of about 100 times the price per ton of a regular landfill. Luckily, Oregon contacted the control center, saying that if we could get the logs to them, they would landfill them at their normal landfill rates. We sent cranes down to pick up the logs, put them on barges, and shipped them up-river to Portland. It was expensive, but cost a lot less than if Washington had had its way.

Chapter 16

The *Aquila*, Bill Milwee, and an Israeli Captain

While loading crude oil from a refinery, the motor tanker *Aquila* suffered a hull penetration and subsequent cargo leak off Dos Bocas, Mexico, in 1983. The ship was leaking oil from the penetration while at anchor at an offshore buoy. I flew down through Mexico City and on to Dos Bocas, an industrial port on the southern Gulf Coast in the state of Tabasco. There, I met with some of the shoreside personnel who were supporting the vessel. The penetration had occurred some days before I got down there, and by this point, there was a team of divers working underneath the vessel to locate and stem the leaks. I met up with William Milwee, a former SUPSALV veteran from the Navy, who was a diver and team leader on the repair. The anchorage was at least three or four miles offshore, well out of sight of the shoreline. Transportation to and from the ship was by launch from the shoreside terminal. The Mexican authorities were quite concerned about the spill and wanted a representative from the ship to come ashore and meet with the captain of the port. This presented a problem, however. The ship, though it had no markings or obvious flagging, was Israeli and had an almost entirely Israeli crew. The captain's name was Ashkenazi, and he was quite a nice guy. His normal job was to captain cruise ships in the Mediterranean. He had been called in on this trip because the usual captain of the *Aquila* was ill.

The Israeli-Lebanon conflict was pretty hot at that point. Captain Ashkenazi feared for his safety if he went ashore; he was afraid he might be arrested on political grounds. Understanding this, I went on his behalf to meet with the captain of the port.

"The captain of the *Aquila* is reluctant to come ashore," I told the captain of the port as diplomatically as I could. "He is afraid that he might be arrested." The captain told me in response, "The one thing I can assure you is that if he doesn't come ashore he will be arrested."

I relayed all this back to Lamorte Burns in New York. Zim, as I have mentioned, maintained a desk at Lamorte Burns. Zim Shippers was connected with the *Aquila*, so my communications with them were direct. Finally, I received permission from Zim for Captain Ashkenazi to go ashore with me and meet with the port captain. As we were going down the ladder to get in the launch, we heard a racket at the top of the ladder. We looked up to see a group of women and children coming down the ladder after us. Captain Ashkenazi made a remark under his breath, something I don't believe was in English, and then went back up the ladder, chasing all the women and children back onto the ship. When he got back, he told me, "I wish I'd never gotten involved with this job. These families that sail with the officers on board the ship are a bigger pain in the neck than anything I ever dealt with on cruise ships."

We went ashore and met with the captain of the port. Captain Ashkenazi was delayed in the outer office by something unrelated to the spill, so I went in first. The captain of the port came into the room wearing a Sam Brown belt and a pistol on his hip. Fortunately, he took all that stuff off and hung it in a closet before Captain Ashkenazi entered. I was glad, because the captain was antsy enough about going ashore as it was.

One of the things that the captain of the port wanted to know was an estimate on the amount of oil spilled against an estimate on the amount of oil remaining on board. The terminal gave us their estimate of the oil delivered. Captain Ashkenazi then wanted me to make it clear that, according to the records, he had more oil on board the ship than the terminal claimed to have discharged. I didn't think that was the appropriate thing to do, but I followed his instructions. The captain of the port glared at me and asked, "Do you mean you're going to tell me that you haven't spilled any oil?" "No, Captain," I said. "I didn't say that. It's just that that is what the numbers show. We're not denying that oil was spilled from the ship." He settled down, but I was thinking about that gun in the closet.

After that, the meeting went smoothly, with no arrests made or shots fired. The spill had been cleaned to everybody's satisfaction. I agreed on behalf of the P&I Club involved to take responsibility for the automatic fine for spilling oil in the port, which I believe was about $13,000.

An odd thing happened on that job. One day, I was on board the *Aquila* and it came up that I needed to contact Lamorte Burns. Captain Ashkenazi sent for his radio officer and told him, "Mr. Gallagher would like you to call his office in New York." I gave the radio officer the number and told him that my name was John Gallagher. He interrupted me when I started to spell it. "I know how to spell Gallagher," he said, smiling. It turned out that he was Irish. He took me back to the radio shack, where we got the call through and then got into an extended conversation about Ireland and such. I was talking with him for so long that when I got back to the captain's quarters, Captain Ashkenazi said, "Boy that was a long telephone call." I told him that the call hadn't been that long, that I had just gotten into a conversation with the radio officer. "That's funny," Captain Ashkenazi said, "because he never says much to us. We were wondering about that, an Irishman who doesn't talk." I had to smile. "Maybe he just needed another Irishman," I replied.

From there I went across the bay to Cancun, where I had been invited to spend a couple of days with Bill Milwee and his crew. Cancun seemed as good a place as any to stand by for any final problems from Dos Bocas, but Milwee's team ended up getting sent straight from Dos Bocas to another salvage job. The *Aquila* sailed, and I headed back to New York. Over the ensuing years, I began to use Bill a lot when we had salvage problems. He was instrumental on both the M/V *New Carissa* and M/V *Selendang Ayu* spills, and continues to be a friend with whom I've swapped a lot of stories. After the Dos Bocas job, he sent me a wooden plaque with a carved saying on it: Murphy's Law, but from the salvor's perspective. I've kept it all these years, and it's now in my office at GMS in New Jersey.

That same year, 1983, saw a major and very interesting casualty. The *Coastal Corpus Christi* was an Ultra Large Crude Carrier supertanker—the highest level of classification. She was carrying strategic petroleum reserve oil for Japan. However, Japan did not have the resources to pump the reserve oil into the ground as the United States did in Texas and Louisiana, so they hired very large tankers to carry the oil offshore and move it into storage ashore when room was available. These tankers would cruise in the waters proximate Japan to be on hand when the cargo could be landed. The *Coastal Corpus Christi* was one of the vessels doing this, sailing in the South China Sea, when she encountered two or three typhoons in short sequence. The storms caused some damage to the steel on the deck of the ship, which at first appeared to be nothing serious. The ship continued to operate, but after some further inspection, the crew discovered that the ship had developed cracks in her wing walls and in the hull along her side. The cracks were actively spreading, and she began losing oil at a significant rate.

The *Coastal Corpus Christi* was carrying different types of crude oils as part of the strategic reserve. The oils had been segregated into different tanks aboard the carrier, but the crew decided they would have to move oil from the damaged wing tanks into undamaged tanks, thus blending their reserves. As they did this, however, they found that the existing cracks were growing faster than they could move the oil. The crew realized that they were going to need to offload some of the oil they carried, so they chartered another tank vessel to come in and lighter off some of the remaining oil cargo.

An empty tanker came out and the crew tried to set up a lightering operation in the South China Sea. Though we were far offshore in fairly moderate seas, due to the size of the ships involved—this would be the largest ship-to-ship transfer ever done—the seas were just too rough to safely accomplish the transfer without endangering the ships themselves. A diplomatic request was made to the Philippine Authorities through the U.S. Embassy in Manilla, and the *Coastal Corpus Christi* was granted permission to enter Manila Bay and attempt lightering into a tanker.

On board the *Coastal Corpus Christi*, the officers were British and the deck crew was Barbadian. The only other American on board with us was a pilot by the name of Hank Johnston, who had been sent to manage the *Coastal Corpus Christi*'s part in any transfer made to reduce the cargo remaining on board. Hank was a professional Federal Pilot, regularly operating out of New York and New Jersey at that time, and was as feisty as could be expected of a man with his pedigree. He came off as a bit of a know-it-all at first, but as I got to know him, he provided me with some of the most stellar memories of my life. I went to bed early most nights and didn't hang out with the vessel's British officers. In those days, there was a lot of drinking that went on aboard British-flagged vessels, and in the mornings, I'd hear some of the officers talking about how Hank Johnston was a "funny bloke." Their comments were always about Hank's jokes, so I started calling him our "esteemed Cruise Director." He appeared to be in charge of the ship's entertainment in the evening, and I assumed he was up there drinking and entertaining the British officers with his humor each night.

One day, when I was heading up to the bridge, Hank came up behind me on the ladder. "Hey, Gallagher," he called up, "are you a friend of Bill Wilson's?" That's a code phrase for guys in AA when they want to find out if someone else is in the group without blowing anyone's anonymity. Bill Wilson and "Doctor Bob" were the two men who founded Alcoholics Anonymous in the 1930s. I said, "I sure as heck am, Hank." He practically threw his arms around me. This was his first time away from home since joining AA about nine months ago. At that stage in recovery, one really needs the support of the group, and here was Hank trying to stay sober in the middle of all this drinking. He couldn't believe his lucky stars to find a fellow member. We started having our own AA meetings, walking up and down the decks of this thousand-foot-long ship.

As a result, Hank Johnston and I became lifelong friends. When we both got back to New York, we began to get together for lunch meetings in the city. Hank had been a Master in the U.S. Merchant Marine during World War II, making numerous voyages bringing weapons to the battlefronts. Vessels under his command were never sunk or even sustained serious damage, but he did witness numerous strikes and sinkings in the convoys he traveled with. Hank continued on afterwards as a Panama Canal pilot, raising most of his family while working there, before becoming a Federal Pilot. Later, when I became involved with the Massachusetts Maritime Academy, establishing the Center for Marine Environmental Protection and Safety for its president Admiral Cressy, I'd have Hank come up and lecture to the maritime students. His maritime experience was unmatched. We stayed friends until Hank passed away in 1997.

Another interesting outcome of the *Coastal Corpus Christi* casualty was that, a little after my work on her, I saw an article in the magazine for the Society of Naval Architects and Marine Engineers (SNAME) concerning this same class of supertankers built in Northern Europe in the 1970s. I knew from the casualty that Harland & Wolff in Northern Ireland built the *Coastal Corpus Christi* in 1978. The magazine article was about cracks that had been developing diagonally across the hulls of many of these tankers. As an aeronautical engineer, this made me think of aircraft flight stress, which in turn suggests that a twisting of the hull in severe storms could explain the diagonal cracking. I had thought a lot about that during the time on the *Coastal Corpus Christi,* but I had no technical input on my theory. Further investigation revealed that there was indeed some fault in the general construction of almost all of these ships of that size built in Northern Europe during that time. The construction techniques being used resulted in stress concentration in the hull. In a callback to my days editing the *Engineering Review,* I was able to write a note about my experience with the *Coastal Corpus Christi* and send it to the P&I Club I was working for to give them some idea of what might have caused these hull failures. They thanked me very much for the information, but I heard nothing more from them on the matter. I assume the information was of no use to them, since the costs involved would have fallen on the underwriters at Lloyd's, who were in line for payment of losses such as hull failure, rather than the P&I Clubs, whose cover is for losses coming from such things as improper operation of the vessel itself.

Chapter 17

The Hot Coal Problem

Around this same time, there arose another endemic shipping issue, which came to be known as the "hot-coal problem." It all started in the early 1980s, when coal miners in both Australia and Poland went on strike. These countries were two of the world's major producers of soft, or bituminous, coal, so the result of the strike was a major depletion in worldwide soft-coal supplies. Soft coal is a tarlike substance that is of a lesser quality than anthracite coal, and requires special handling. While the United States had shipped soft coals domestically in the past, the coal industry had not shipped any soft coal abroad for many years. The result being that the methods for dealing with soft coal had atrophied, but because of the strikes, shipping U.S. coal abroad had become lucrative again.

The most alarming issue in the learning curve for international shipping was that shiploads of coal were increasingly found to be overheating during transport. A year or so before this problem became generally noticed, one of the P&I Clubs had a ship request attention for a coal-heating situation aboard a ship in Norfolk, Virginia. Our ship was taking soft coal from another ship that had carried it from a port on the Mississippi River. That ship had been originally headed for Europe, but had experienced engine trouble and had put into a port in Florida to try to fix the problem. The problem couldn't be fixed in Florida and the ship was towed up to Norfolk for offloading the coal cargo onto our ship. In the process of the transfer, our crew noticed that that coal was smoking hot. The owners of the discharging ship were furious about the offloading being delayed, and our client adamantly refused to continue the transfer. Everyone recognized the immediate danger, and I was called down from New York to try and figure out what was going on.

To digress for a moment: Jimmy Kelley was a good friend of mine as I was growing up in Washington. His father, Augustine Kelley, was a congressman from Pennsylvania and an owner of a coal mine. I knew that Jimmy's brother, Regis Kelley, was a lawyer who had worked for the United Mine workers. As I was quickly trying to figure out what was going on with the smoking coal, I thought of Regis. I got hold of Jimmy, who put me in touch with Regis, who was immediately able to tell me what was going on. The coal being shipped from the Mississippi Valley, in other words the soft or bituminous coal, is oxygen-starved when it comes out of the ground. When exposed to air, it rapidly begins to oxidize, and the oxidization process generates heat. This heat then generates further oxidization, and so forth until the load of bituminous coal heats up and eventually bursts into flame. This is well known at power plants burning soft coal, where the oxidization is controlled by continuous aeration of standing coal piles to prevent uncontrolled rise of temperature. Piles of soft coal need to be continually worked to keep them cool and to prevent ignition. As soft coal had not been shipped abroad from the United States for 20 or 30 years, the shippers had apparently forgotten the dangers inherent in handling the cargo.

In Norfolk I enlisted a couple of local lawyers to enforce the stoppage of the loading of the coal. I knew for certain that, if the loading continued, it would endanger the ship taking on the cargo. Well, a fight broke out over our standing, and as we were going back and forth over the marine radio, I realized that we were at anchor in Hampton Roads in the Chesapeake Bay, the same harbor where the USS *Monitor* and the CSS *Merrimack* (now CSS *Virginia*) had fought each other during the Civil War. We were on the verge of having our own Civil War over the marine radio. As we were on an open frequency, we were overheard by many maritime operations in the area, which induced them to start sharing their two cents. Finally, we prevailed and were able to have the transshipment of hot coal onto our ship stopped and the contract for transport vitiated. In essence, I had been given a quick education in coal, but at the time didn't expect it to be of much value in the future.

The amount of American coal being shipped abroad continued to increase, however, while the shipper's knowledge remained static. What we now expected continued to occur. The P&I Clubs that Lamorte Burns represented realized that there might be an embargo placed on coal coming out of the United States if something wasn't done about the problem. So, based on my training on the subject in Norfolk, I was selected by the P&I Clubs to head up a program for identifying and rectifying the problem. New Orleans was the main port of contention, but Mobile, Alabama, also had heavy coal exports. Before I left, I spent some time with Regis Kelley and hired him to assist in our efforts to find an industry-wide solution to the problem.

There were two ways that coal was loaded in New Orleans. Either it came in by rail car, in which case it was piled on the dock to await loading, or it was brought down the Mississippi by barge to be loaded directly aboard ship. Regis concluded that the heating cycle was exacerbated on barges because they carried so much more coal than a single rail car. Further, the coal brought by barge was loaded directly onto ships, rather than being offloaded onto the dock before transshipment to cool. Finally, the structure of the barges themselves contributed to the heating, with the hull of the barge having almost a Thermos-bottle effect. Regis cautioned me that the cargoes coming down by barge needed to be examined before being offloaded. If the coal appeared spotty or warming, it needed to be removed from the barge and aerated before it could be loaded aboard ship.

I was called to London to meet with the P&I Clubs and other interested parties to brief them on the situation. At this London summit there were representatives of the different P&I Clubs concerned, representatives of the surveyors who had been hired to examine the coal as it was prepared for shipment, and lawyers for the shippers themselves. One of the funny things that came out was that the coal-mine operators were suspicious of the P&I Clubs. The P&I Clubs were mostly based in England, and the coal-mine operators had gotten it into their heads that the whole hot-coal issue was a plot by the English coal mines to block the import of American coal, because it was interfering with the export of "coals from Newcastle." However, by that time, it had been many years since such coal was shipped abroad from Newcastle, so the fear was ungrounded. We were able to convince the coal-mine operators that the P&I Clubs had exactly the same goal as they did: they wanted to ensure the continued export of U.S. coal.

After our meeting in London, I returned to my apartment in New Orleans and set up to work on this hot-coal problem there. I hired Therese Guderian to assist me in setting up procedures for safely transporting coal on the Mississippi and in nearby Mobile. I continued to meet with the attorneys in New Orleans who had been to the London meetings. By that point, having come to an understanding, they had taken over the process of hiring surveyors to check the barges that were coming down the river. On the basis of Regis's theory, I did a review of coal shipping nationally. There was a lot of coal coming out of ports like Baltimore and Norfolk that was not having this problem. I took a look at the method of transportation to these two ports: by rail in both cases. Each rail car carried about 100 tons of coal per wagon. The wagons were open, allowing any heat to escape. On the other hand, the barges coming down the Mississippi carried many times that amount of coal and were packed in a hull that was largely submerged below the waterline, unable to transfer any heat through the hull into the water.

Increasingly, we had cases of shipmasters panicking about loading coal. Local river pilots were regaling the captains with horror stories as they brought them up the river to various ports and points of transfer to waiting ships. A lot of the incoming captains were almost ready to jump ship before they even got to the coal. Therese was a great help, making it her job to get out and educate the masters about the situation. Our surveyors checked each barge load of coal coming down the river. If it looked hot, it would be put on the shore and raked. We also arranged for tractors to be put in the holds to tamp down loaded coal so that the oxygen flowing in would not be sufficient to produce conditions for heating. We shared this information with Therese, who spread the word among the shipmasters, and we encountered little further distress on any of our ships. Where there were specific problems arising on a ship that needed further attention, I usually boarded it to work things out with the master myself.

Gradually, our operations in the Mississippi Valley began working smoothly. We had the occasional problem with the coal shippers who objected to our rejection of their cargo, and we also had to keep a close eye on the monitoring of the cooling of the cargo before it went on our vessels. But, the operation was a success overall, and the feared shutdown of coal export from the Gulf of Mexico never materialized. Still, some of the coal companies remained convinced that the whole thing was a plot on the part of the English, which was ludicrous, but shows how rumors spread and interfere with solving problems.

I wrote a paper explaining what had caused the hot-coal problem and the ways in which we had sought to remediate it. In the end, many of the things we did to solve the problem went on to be adapted in international maritime law. The solutions we introduced continue to be enforced to this day.

The hot-coal problem and my experience on some other casualties around that time gave me the idea of creating a manual that would help masters of ships and their first officers in the event of a casualty. Nick Healy at Lamorte Burns liked the idea, so I put together a rough prototype with the help of some of the people at the P&I Club Britannia. What I created was fairly rudimentary and written in pretty plain English, as I wanted the manual to be as accessible as possible. Nick sent a copy to Robert Seward, the chairman at Britannia, asking his opinion. Robert wrote Nick back, saying, "Jack has a lot of energy, but we've got to channel it." His largest concern was that with this manual we were edging into work that was more properly in the domain of the shipping agent. Robert ended the letter by saying, "I don't want to be too hard on Jack." Nick gave the letter to me and said, "Answer him."

Though Robert Seward and I ended up becoming close friends, I was a little miffed at first. Still, I could see where he was coming from: here was this Yank coming in and rewriting the way P&I Clubs have done business for a long time. I wrote him saying that I agreed with him on many points, but if a major casualty occurred, it wasn't the agent who was going to go to jail over the situation—it would be the captain. At this time, pre-*Exxon Valdez*, there weren't any protocols for what to do in the case of a spill. Often, a captain wouldn't even let anyone know that a spill had occurred. At other times, as was the case of the

Zoe Colocotronis in Puerto Rico, a captain would just dump his cargo.

I explained that there were two precepts that absolutely needed to be conveyed to captains: the first was to be honest with the authorities when a spill occurred; the second was to get in touch with us. In effect, I laid the foundation for what would later become the "Spill Response Plan."

As for the inelegant language, that tickled me. I believe Robert thought that perhaps I was a little simple myself. I explained to him that for many of the people who would be reading the manual, English was not a first language. Plus, in an emergency situation, I had found that instructions needed to be as simple and clear as possible. Elegant prose was not very effective in these cases. We cleared up our misunderstanding, and more importantly, I had developed another important kernel in what would eventually grow into Gallagher Marine Systems.

Chapter 18

Oil Spill Jack

We didn't have any major spills at Lamorte Burns in 1983 or 1984, and I began to feel that I was wasting their money. They had just installed a computer mainframe, and I spent my time creating a response-manual prototype and computerizing spill response plans. Nevertheless, I felt that they were paying me too much to not be working on spills. I made them this offer: I would stop working there as vice president and would open my own company, in which they could be partners, if they wished. In this way, Lamorte Burns could continue to have access to my specialty with spills and also share part of my work in developing automated response plans. Nick Healy supported me in this plan. At the time, Lamorte Burns also wanted to open a branch office in New Orleans, where I had kept my apartment. I'd spent a great deal of time there while working on the hot-coal problem, and I was comfortable with moving there permanently. So we agreed on terms and I went down to New Orleans to open a small Lamorte Burns office. We had just one claim settler and some support.

Around this same time, Nick let me know that he was leaving Lamorte Burns. He felt that he had made his mark, his children were grown and finished with college, so he decided to turn the management of the company over to Harold Halpin, the vice president. Hal was a maritime guy, not an attorney or someone with a technical background; his experience was mostly with claims adjusting for cargo damage and injury. He did not have the people skills that Nick did, and I felt this might be a problem. Sure enough, once Hal took over, he canceled the deal that Nick and I had made. Under my deal with Nick, my

Lamorte Burns stock options served as collateral against the company's investment in our business. It wasn't a great deal for me, but I agreed to it because things like these don't matter much to me when I feel the work I'm doing is important. Hal, of course, reclaimed my Lamorte Burns stock options when he killed the deal. He was a look-over-the shoulder type with a combative personality that aggravated many people. In my early days at Lamorte Burns, Nick said that he realized he had to keep Hal away from dealing with the European P&I Clubs at all costs; Hal really aggravated the Europeans and the English. Instead, Nick let him handle the Asian clubs, to whom his manner was less obvious. In the end, Nick's observations were right: the English and Europeans weren't inclined to put up with Hal's gruff and short-tempered ways.

The severing of our contract didn't keep Hal from calling me when he really needed me. I was in New Orleans, in February of 1986, making progress on the Automated Response Systems project, when I got a call from Lamorte Burns about a big spill in the Virgin Islands. The refueling barge *St. Thomas* had struck an underwater obstruction in Charlotte Amalie Harbor. I flew there, arrived in the middle of the night, and found a hotel room near the West India dock, which was close to where the cruise ships docked. When I opened the window of my room, I smelled the heavy odor of No. 6 oil in the air. The casualty had occurred on the other side of the harbor, in the industrial area, and I wondered how the spilled oil had made it so far across the harbor, because No. 6 oil was highly unlikely to have moved that far across the water in that short of a time. The oil, it transpired, hadn't moved—the damaged barge had.

The initial responders had no pumping capabilities and no place to put the oil even if they could pump it, so they put a patch on the hole in the barge and towed it over to the West

India dock. A cruise ship was there waiting to be rebunkered, and the *St. Thomas'* crew hoped that they could pump the oil onto the cruise ship faster than it was coming out of the barge. However, they had blown the makeshift patch on the hull of the barge in the tow, and now the *St. Thomas* was discharging its oil straight into the waters of the eastern, or tourist part, of Charlotte Amalie Harbor. Oil was everywhere in Charlotte Amalie Harbor and also all the way back to the industrial harbor where the spill originally occurred. Though I wasn't there to take direct charge of the cleanup, I tried to assist where I could. In the morning, I made contact with the attorneys representing the owners of the tug and the barge. They were having trouble finding enough labor to deal with the spill, as most of the locals in the Virgin Islands were not interested in getting involved in the problem. In the end, we had to go to Puerto Rico to find workers for the cleanup.

(Photo NOAA's Office of Response and Restoration)

Barge St. Thomas incident, Crown Bay, St. Thomas, U.S. Virgin Islands, February 1986. Booms are placed off the shoreline to protect vegetated beaches from the oil.

An attorney representing the P&I Club for the barge arrived and asked me what I was going to do about the spill. I was representing the P&I Club covering the tug, so I pointed out that the responsible entity was the spiller (the barge), and that nothing had spilled from the tug. He backed right off. Further, I maintained that the only liability on the tug was in the towing it did at the time of the collision. The *St. Thomas* hadn't participated in the ill-fated tow of the barge over to the West India docks, where the major part of the spill had settled. I suggested that we draw a line across Haulover Cut, which separated the tourist part of Charlotte Amalie Harbor from the industrial harbor. I'd take the industrial side and he could deal with the rest. It put the majority of the load on him.

The *St. Thomas* job was the first time I met Michael Garnett. I knew of him by his activities and record, but had never personally worked with him. Mike was the Royal Naval officer on duty when the infamous tanker *Torrey Canyon* went up on the rocks at Land's End off the coast of the United Kingdom in 1967. It was the biggest spill of its kind at the time (860,000 barrels into the water) and the beginning of the oil-spill industry. Mike had since retired as a captain from the Royal Navy and by that time had been made the technical director of International Tanker Owners Pollution Federation (ITOPF) in London, an oil-spill response consortium that had grown directly out of the *Torrey Canyon* spill.

Mike was quite a character. He stayed down on St. Thomas for several weeks and began to work with me sketching out our responsibilities relating to the spill. My responsibility was to protect the rights of the tug, and his was to protect the rights of the towed barge *St. Thomas*. Since I already had made the basic agreement with the lawyers on the division of responsibilities, my dealings with Mike were entirely amicable. I learned a lot

157

from him on this job and we had enough time together for him to relate a number of his adventures. It was the beginning of a good friendship.

One of the things I learned about the *Torrey Canyon* spill from Mike was that no one had any notion of how to respond. They tried blowing up the ship, which, much to the embarrassment of the English, took quite a number of tries. This was in the spring, with the beach resorts of both England and France in a panic that the oil was going to ruin their tourist season. Mike was running a meeting where they were debating what they could possibly do to stop the spreading oil slick. There was a cleaning lady working in the back of the room who, after listening to them talk, finally interrupted, holding up a bottle of detergent. "That," she declared, "is what *I* would use." They did indeed try dumping detergent on the oil, and with that, the idea of oil dispersants was born. Unfortunately, in this case, they dumped barrels and barrels of detergent into the water, in one instance, just throwing entire barrels over a cliff onto oiled beaches below. As it turned out, the detergents had ingredients that ended up doing more harm to the environment than the oil would ever have.

The use of the detergent at the Torrey Canyon spill led to the banning of dispersants in the United States for a long time. Even after the industry had developed dispersants that were non-toxic and specially adapted to oil-spill response, environmentalists often protested their use. When the *Exxon Valdez* spill happened in 1989, many of us at the command post, from Exxon, U.S. Coast Guard, the state of Alaska and assorted technical experts, agreed that dispersants would be a good way to approach the spill. However, the state of Alaska maintained a strong prejudice against the use of dispersants and banned their use in state waters. A lot of damage and subsequent work could have been avoided had the state government been better educated.

In March of 1986, six weeks after the *St. Thomas* spill, I was still in Charlotte Amalie when I received another call from Lamorte Burns. The tanker *Intermar Alliance* had rammed a pier on the Delaware River and had punctured her bunker tank. They asked me to get up there as quickly as possible to appraise the situation. I had gone from New Orleans directly to Charlotte Amalie, so I didn't have a winter jacket with me. Winter jackets weren't something they typically sold in Charlotte Amalie, and it was still quite cold in Philadelphia, so I went all over town looking for a heavy jacket without any luck. Finally, at a fancy men's shop, they found a jacket stored in their attic. It was probably the only winter jacket on the whole island. I promptly bought it and flew with it in hand up to Philadelphia.

The *Intermar Alliance* incident became a large job. The motor tanker had been putting into a pier in the Delaware River, near the refineries below Philadelphia, when she lost her steering and rammed the pier at the BP terminal. The collision opened up the hull of the ship, spilling crude oil from her port No. 1 wing cargo tank into the river. One of the first things I did when I arrived at the BP terminal was recruit a response team of people I had worked with on the *Mobil Athos* and *Elias* spills. Though there were contractors on the scene, there wasn't any organization set up. Foremost among the contractors was David Stith, who had been on the *Mobil Athos* spill with me. On that job, we had given each other a wide berth. David had been in competition with Uncle Paul, and Uncle Paul never had anything good to say about anybody who was competing with him; he'd denigrated David to me repeatedly. As far as Uncle Paul was concerned, if David wasn't a flat-out criminal, he was, at the very least, not a good person. However, having been away from Uncle Paul for some time, I had found that people who were Paul's enemies weren't necessarily bad people. In this case, I had little choice, so reluctantly, I brought in David Stith to provide the foundation for the team that accomplished the response for the *Intermar Alliance*. It was to be the beginning of a long and great friendship that lasted until his death.

David was a real salvage type. He started out as a Navy diver, earning his stripes training on the wreck of the *Normandy* in New York Harbor. Later, he was wounded by Japanese sniper fire while riding in the back of a Marine Corps truck in the South Pacific. When he recovered, he got out of the Navy and began a career in salvage. He was a guy who worked with his hands and his brawn. He was a really honorable and nice person, one of the absolute stars of the oil-spill industry.

We had a lot of oil in the river and had essentially shut down the BP refinery by tying up its dock. With the spill right up against their dock, oil was getting under the docks and coating them from beneath at high tide. We had a lot to do. David and I came up with an idea for getting the ship away from the dock, but the Coast Guard wouldn't let us do it unless we proved that we could contain the oil trapped against the pier. David designed a bubble curtain that, with the air on, held anything under the dock that might tend to come out when the ship came off. It worked very well.

We finished with the *Intermar Alliance,* and I went back to the Virgin Islands to finish the job in Charlotte Amalie. This job lasted for almost half a year in total, between negotiating with the government and working with the Coast Guard on the cleanup. As a result, I got to know St. Thomas island fairly well. My 18th year of sobriety came while I was down there. After I'd been working for several weeks and we were out of the emergency phase, I started going to AA meetings I'd found in downtown Charlotte Amalie just about every evening. Most of the regulars, who I got to know pretty well, were people working in the tourist trade on St. Thomas. The rest were tourists and others passing through. On the evening of my 18th anniversary in the program, we had a spill meeting that had been called to review our progress. The work meeting conflicted with the timing of the AA, but was taking place only two blocks away. As not everyone had arrived on time for the meeting, I told those who had to that I needed to run up the street and asked them to hold everything until I got back.

I made it inside the door of the AA meeting just as they were starting the announcements. I raised my hand and said from the back of the room, "My name is Jack, I'm an alcoholic, and today is my 18th anniversary!" They cheered and applauded, and then I said, "Now I've got to go."

Some weeks later, at another meeting, I got to talking to the captain of a sailing yacht that had put into Charlotte Amalie to drop off some passengers. We got along, and he invited me to sail over to St. John's with him, telling me I could catch the ferry back. It sounded like fun, so I got aboard, and we sailed over to St. John's. We arrived around 10:00 in the evening, and after putting his passengers off, he said he was sailing down to St. Croix and suggested that I stay on. We'd leave around 2:00 A.M. and would arrive at St. Croix about dawn. From there, I could catch a plane back to Charlotte Amalie. Again, I said, "Sure, that sounds like fun." A girl from the AA meeting, who I hadn't met but who had also been on the trip to St. Thomas, overheard the captain and asked if she could join. So, at the appointed time, the three of us started off for St. Croix. Because the captain knew I'd been in the Navy, he asked me if I wanted to take the wheel for a while. I did, but I noticed that the light was out on the binnacle and I couldn't see the compass. He said, "See those stars? Just keep them a little to the port of the bowsprit and use that as your compass. That will get us close enough by daylight to see St. Croix." After a while, he disappeared, and it dawned on me that he had only invited me along because he needed some crew. Though I'd been shanghaied, I enjoyed sailing by the stars. Once we arrived in St. Croix, I went to mass and then an AA meeting, and took a plane back to St. Thomas later that day.

The young woman from AA flew back with me to Charlotte Amalie. She ran an inter-island sales business that provided imported goods for the people who serviced the visitors to the Islands. I saw quite a bit of her while I was in the islands. After a year or so, she came back to the States and eventually got in touch with me when she came to Washington, D.C. It turned out that she was also a composer, singer, and dancer, and was wrapped up in that business in Utah and points west. I've since lost track of her, but I still have copies of the work she sent me over the years.

After the *Intermar Alliance* spill in Philadelphia, I learned that there had been a couple of spills related to Lamorte Burns P&I Club clients that I hadn't been called for. By asking around, I found out that Hal had hired most of the crew I had assembled on the *Intermar Alliance* casualty and had created a company he called ECM. I still don't know what ECM stands for, but it was my crew he was using, and he was using them on P&I Club spills. Still, Hal may have poached a lot of my team, but he didn't get David Stith. David was a man of principal and fiercely loyal to his friends. ECM eventually grew to become a competitor of mine.

Despite the unfortunate ending of my relationship with Lamorte Burns, I kept in touch with Nick Healy over the years. Not long ago, I read in the Maritime Law Association newsletter that his father, Nick Sr., with whom I had written the paper on the *Zoe Colocotronis* and whose cottage I had visited with my children in Ireland, had passed away. I looked Nick up and found that he was the president of Ave Maria University in southwestern Florida. I called him to express my condolences about his father. We had a nice talk, and he invited me down to visit. I'll make a special trip some wintery day.

As a coda to the job on St. Thomas: Years later I was on a trip down to Charlotte Amalie, where I was consulting with a manufacturer of spill response equipment. I thought it might be fun to drop in on my old AA group, who were still meeting at the same time and same place. I went one night, and as soon as I walked into the room, someone stuck his head up and announced, "Oil Spill Jack is back!" I said that I hoped I was remembered for other things as well!

PART V

ORIGINS OF Gallagher Marine Systems

Chapter 19

Clean Seas, the *Pac Baroness*, and New Orleans

As I was finishing up with the *Intermar Alliance*, the captain of the Port of Philadelphia, who was overseeing the cleanup of that spill, asked me if I would speak with a woman in Philadelphia whose father owned a big maritime contracting firm in the area. As it turned out, he was the same contractor I had encouraged to hire Alex Rynecki on the *Elias* spill. The Hudson family had long been involved in the maritime business around Philadelphia, principally in construction, and the daughter was considering getting into the oil-spill business. The captain of the port hoped that I might give her some advice, and I told him that I would be glad to. My plan was to tell her to stay out of the oil-spill business—as my experience with Hal Halpin had demonstrated —it was a dog-eat-dog world.

However, when I met the contractor's daughter, she told me that she didn't want to start an oil-spill response business. Instead, she wanted to start a woman-owned consulting firm that would provide advice to mariners for any particular problem they might have: oil spills, ships run aground, repairs—anything you could think of. Her plan was to identify experts in the field and then organize them to provide advice to her clients. She wanted to know if I would consider being available to help her begin. I told her that I would be glad to help her get started, but that I intended to retain my own established clients. And that's how I met Cindy Hudson.

Back in New Orleans, I continued working on my Automated Response Systems programs. I gained a couple of new clients, one of which was a group of Canadian oil companies that liked my idea of automated contingency plans. For better or worse, however, the spill-related business kept coming in. The jobs were getting bigger and more complex, and I just didn't have the time to work those and program my response system. To a degree, the idea was finally abandoned. That said, I did incorporate a number of my automated-response innovations into the GMS response-plan system for our ship clients. Automated Response Systems still lives on in the way we keep all our shipboard information available.

I took Cindy Hudson to London and introduced her to the P&I Clubs, which I thought would be ideal for her all-inclusive consulting. In anticipation of our trip, I'd called Mike Garnett, the ex-Royal Navy captain and ITOPF representative I had met down in St. Thomas, to set up a meeting with him as well. But when I had mentioned Cindy to him on the phone, Mike had misunderstood me to be saying "Sidney" Hudson—he thought I was talking about a man. So, when I first introduced the two, he was surprised to find out that Cindy was a "bird." It was a story Mike used to like to tell a lot. By this time, Mike was semi-retired from ITOPF. He and Cindy hit it off, and they went on to do a lot of work together until he died.

After the London trip, in September of 1987, I was consulting in Houston when I saw news of a big casualty off the California coast. The news footage was of a ship foundering and getting ready to sink. The *Pac Baroness*, a bulk cargo ship carrying copper ore, had collided with a Panamanian freighter, the *Atlantic Wing*, in high and foggy seas off the coast of Santa Barbara. The next day, one of the P&I Clubs contacted me: the *Pac Baroness* was one of their ships. Though flagged Liberian, she was a U.S.-owned vessel belonging to a company in

Washington State. The P&I Club asked me to go out to Santa Barbara and represent the owners on the matter.

In Santa Barbara, I found that there was nothing for me to do in the way of response and prevention, because the *Pac Baroness* wasn't spilling any oil. The ship was three or four miles offshore and out of sight, but still within the limits of the Clean Seas Oil Spill Cooperative, which patrolled the oil drilling fields off the coast. Clean Seas had been established after a fracturing of the formation in the drilling zone caused a major blowout. As a condition for continuing to drill in that area, state regulators required that a cleanup cooperative, with a fleet of response vessels large enough to be continually stationed offshore, remain available to respond immediately in the case of a spill. Clean Seas is still a major co-op on the West Coast.

I made contact with the Clean Seas operation, enlisting them to handle the spill, should it arise, and then began working with the attorney for the *Pac Baroness* owners to set up a response contract. There was a lot of back and forth to get the contract written to the company lawyer's standards. This was a problem, because while we were negotiating, the ship had gone down and, sitting on the bottom, began leaking from her bunker tanks. The closest landfall was the Channel Islands, which were under federal protection for the wildlife and flora there. The lawyer could not understand that the ship, although not responsible for the collision and sinking, was still responsible for cleaning up any spill resulting from the collision. Subsequent litigation has ameliorated the level of the owners' responsibility by shifting it to the vessel causing the sinking, but in 1989, the ship that spilled the oil was, by law, the one responsible for cleanup. Worse, its owners could be held further accountable if they did not properly respond to Coast Guard direction. Still, despite the tremendous risks he was taking by not acting immediately, it was difficult to convince the lawyer. In the end, he was probably the biggest problem we had dealing with the casualty.

In the meantime, I had established a command center of sorts, though at that point, I was there by myself. Clean Seas and I established a plan to protect the Channel Islands, if the necessity arose, and to be prepared when the owners finally capitulated, which I knew they would. I chartered an aircraft to fly over the site and found that there was oil in the water and that it was spreading with the wind and the currents. It wasn't in heavy or large quantities, but nevertheless, there was a lot of pressure from the Coast Guard and the California government to demonstrate protection for the Channel Islands. Next, I went to inspect a Clean Seas vessel, as our response plan involved chartering one. These vessels were said to have quite a lot of spill control on them, skimmers and boom, for example, and I wanted to examine the equipment. I went with the chief of Clean Seas and was introduced to the crew of the vessel. To my surprise, I found out that the boom that they carried was the Goodyear Sea Sentry, the boom I had designed. I also found that the rest of the vessels for Clean Seas—probably half a dozen or more—carried the same amount of Sea Sentry boom.

The chief of Clean Seas introduced me to the crew as "the man who designed the Sea Sentry boom that you guys need to lug around." Though later versions of the boom had hydraulically driven rollers for deployment, in those days, there wasn't a lot of equipment for moving it—the boom had handles designed for manhandling, and that was about it. You can imagine the crew's response.

The contingency of a spill at the Channel Islands went on for quite a while. I had a nice hotel room on the beach in Santa Monica. The rooms were all outfitted with an unusual amount of telephone equipment—multiple phone lines and faxes. It turned out that these were the rooms used by Ronald Reagan's press office whenever the President was in residence at his ranch northwest of Santa Barbara. As this was little more than a waiting game by this point, I had time on my hands and got to reconnect with some of my West Coast friends. One close friend, Patrick Stewart, had once been engaged to Sharon Gless, who played Cagney in the *Cagney & Lacey* television show. I had gotten to know Sharon through Patrick, who had lived with me in New York when I worked for Lamorte Burns. I let Sharon know I was in town, and one afternoon she called. We met and had dinner and spent a long time catching up. She invited me to come down and see her house in the San Fernando Valley, which would have been nice. But Sharon was shooting *Cagney & Lacy* at the time, which meant she had a very early call, so I passed.

The operation went on for a good month before we finally closed it up. The Coast Guard called a stop to the ongoing operation. In the end, there wasn't a lot of oil spilled, as far as we could tell. But we couldn't be certain as long as there was fuel oil leaking from the sunken *Pac Baroness*. To compound the uncertainty, the weather and the tides were erratic. Some attempts were made to apply oil dispersant on the water in what was more or less a dry run. They dropped some dispersant, but there was never enough oil to tell how well it worked. Over the course of my stay there, I spent a good amount of time flying back and forth over the site of the wreck without seeing much of anything, other than the drilling operations out there. There certainly was no damage or impact to the Channel Islands.

As I was leaving Santa Barbara and heading back to New Orleans, my plane flew over the campus of University of California, Santa Barbara, which is right on the coast, and then out over the gigantic and natural oil spill that has been going on in those waters from time immemorial. Oil comes up out of natural fissures on the ocean floor and seeps slowly but continuously into the ocean. One of these seep sites lies below the ocean just off Santa Barbara. This was the site where the Navy had done some initial testing of the Sea Sentry boom as I was developing it. I hadn't been there for that testing, but I while I was staying in Santa Barbara during the *Pac Baroness* casualty, I did go down to the beach near the university to view the patterns of spilled oil hardening on the shores.

The *Pac Baroness* casualty gave me the opportunity to observe the Clean Seas Cooperative. I also got to meet most of the officers in the Southern California Coast Guard. Unfortunately, manning in the Coast Guard is for limited times, and guardsmen are regularly rotated in four-year segments. In a spill, it is best to be working with a Coast Guard unit with experience in spill response operations. The less experience and knowledge they have about spill response, the more tense and difficult they can be about working with civilians and the media. A stellar example of such difficulty happened a few years ago, in a rather simple spill response in a Texas waterway. The job was assigned to a reserve Coast Guard officer who had been activated after 9/11. Although the response was in all measures routine, the Coast Guard officer complained to the press that she "had never seen such a badly managed response." No one mentioned that the Coast Guard officer had, in fact, never seen *any* live response. Happily, however, in most cases, the Coast Guard officers were pros, and we could fairly quickly get the principal to mesh successfully with their efforts.

Sometime after the *Pac Baroness* casualty, the Government Accounting Office asked me to review and critique four or five spills that had been handled by the Coast Guard. My evaluation was pretty straightforward: the ability of the Coast Guard to respond to a spill was directly dependent on the level of experience of the Coasties responding. The only problems we ever had occurred when the Coast Guard lacked experience and relied on us to educate them. It takes real diplomacy to get a Coast Guard officer to go along when they lack experience.

Throughout my career, I have tried to cultivate working relationships with all parties involved in a given situation. In terms of my relationships with state-level officials, I've usually been able to create good rapport. The people working in state environmental departments tend to stay there for a long time. One particular state employee had a big personality, and his office was continually competing with the Coast Guard in the Unified Command. As was often the case in these types of situations, a lot of it was simple showboating; he wanted to demonstrate his power as a minor functionary. But, even in this instance, we were aware of how it was going to be ahead of time and could anticipate. We knew that at the end of the day, everybody had to go along with what the Coast Guard wanted, so there was a premium placed on getting their cooperation. However, if we couldn't get the state's environmental agency to listen to reason, we had to do it their way, which made for the most difficult operations of all.

All of these issues arose on the *Pac Baroness* matter. During the post-mortem, it came out (as it often does) that every group involved felt that they should have been in charge of the response. Often there are groups who feel that the shipowners and their P&I Clubs shouldn't be involved at all. Usually it is the environmentalist groups who demand that they run a spill, which would be a disaster in every case, because they might not have the experience or expertise to remedy the oil spill itself.

From Santa Barbara, I went back to New Orleans, where I was working on an interesting project for the Louisiana Offshore Oil Port (LOOP). In the mid-1970s, I regularly attended the

Offshore Technology Conference in Houston, Texas. One year, I met a man named Ken Wehmuller at the conference who represented Zodiac inflatable rafts. We were both living in Annapolis, Maryland in those days, and came to be friends. At this same conference, I also met a representative of the Whittaker Corporation of California, which specialized in enclosed lifeboats and Expandi inflatable oil booms, which was a specialized boom made in Sweden. After several discussions with Whittaker, they asked me to become a salesman for their boom. I didn't want to be a salesman for anything, but I was reluctant to turn them down out of hand. I contacted Ken, a successful salesman himself, and asked him if he would be interested in Whittaker's offer. He was, and he appreciated the introduction. In thanks, Ken took me out to the Grand Tetons on a camping trip he had arranged for some of his clients. I spent about a week camping with Ken and the other people he had invited. We slept in tents and cooked by fire—all of that woodsy stuff. I had a fairly good time, but realized that, never having done anything like that so far inland, I felt claustrophobic; I was ocean born and raised. With the exception of Ken, the other people on the trip were westerners or Californians, and they did a lot of trout fishing during the week. What they caught only looked to be the size of a Chesapeake baitfish, as far as I could see.

At another of the Offshore Technology Conferences, I met up with some of the people I had known at Goodyear when I'd worked there developing the Sea Sentry boom. The Goodyear blimp was in Houston, as usual, flying around above the conference, and my friends from Goodyear asked if I'd like to go for a ride. I said yes, and got my first and only blimp ride. While up there, I asked the pilot what would happen if the engines stopped. "Well," he said, "I can stop them right now and show you." I wasn't too sure that was a good idea, but I figured that the pilot knew what was he was doing. He shut the engines off and we just started drifting backward at the same altitude. I learned that it was the balloon that was keeping us up there, not the engines.

It was at these same conferences that I met some people from LOOP, which was still in the process of being built. They invited me to come down to Galliano, Louisiana, to talk about oil-spill response technology. LOOP was to become an offshore platform on the Gulf Coast. It would handle and pump oil discharged at three single-point mooring platforms around the pumping platform, allowing offload of the biggest ultra-large tankers. Underwater pipes would bring the oil from the ships to the central pumping platform, where it would then be pumped through a very big pipeline to salt-dome storage ashore, and then continue on to refineries. I went down and met with the president of LOOP, and we talked about oil-spill response, which was a fairly new idea to them at that point.

As LOOP neared completion of the facilities, they asked me to come on board and help train the people they were hiring to run their spill response team. I did it on and off for a while, as the requirements dictated. I became close to their team and ended up helping them write their contingency plans and design and conduct drills practicing spill response. We spent a lot of time preparing, but there were no spills during my time with LOOP. In fact, it turned out to be a very safe operation. By 1993, LOOP calculated that they had pumped 2.9 million barrels of oil, with only 893 barrels spilled. Unfortunately, those 893 spilled barrels involved a ship that I was responsible for through the P&I Clubs, with whom I continued, and would continue to have a good working relationship with long after leaving Lamorte Burns. So on that one particular spill, I found myself caught between the continuing friendships I had at LOOP and with the lawyers for the P&I Club, who were trying to pin the blame on LOOP.

Chapter 20

The Big One

In March of 1989, I was busy working on training programs for LOOP in New Orleans when I received an emergency call from two of the P&I Clubs I worked with, Britannia and IDIA, to report to Valdez, Alaska. The Exxon tanker *Exxon Valdez* had experienced a casualty. The P&I Clubs wanted me to get there as soon as possible, by whatever means available. Britannia was involved in case the *Exxon Valdez* became a wreck-removal matter, while IDIA had the oil pollution policy for the ship. I immediately got tickets and boarded a plane. The first leg of the trip was from New Orleans to Dallas. By coincidence, my seatmate on that flight was an employee of one of the oil companies. He was coming up from assisting with a drilling operation in the Gulf of Mexico and was headed for California, where he was overseeing the setup of a rig. He asked me where I was going, and I said, "I'm heading up to Alaska. The *Exxon Valdez* has had a casualty there." He looked shocked and told me, "I'm a member of the board of directors of Exxon, and I haven't heard anything about it." I gave him what details I had.

We parted company in Dallas, where I boarded an Alaska Airlines flight for Anchorage. Up in first class, I found a bunch of Exxon officers and Jim O'Brien of O'Brien's Oil Pollution Service (OOPS), though this was before Jim founded OOPS. Jim was someone I'd known throughout most of my career. For the most part, we'd been friendly competitors after he got out of the Coast Guard. The last time I'd seen him before this flight, he had been the commander of the Coast Guard Strike Team on the West Coast. But he had recently retired from the Coast Guard and had been hired by Exxon to go up to Anchorage as a consultant on spill response matters in Alaska. We were seatmates, so we exchanged what information we had and did some speculating on what response might be called for. Particularly we talked about oil-spill dispersants. From what we had heard so far, the size of the spill was such that we agreed dispersants would probably be needed. We had no hard or fast figures, but it sounded big.

My primary remit was to represent the P&I Clubs on the scene and keep them aware of what was going on. As a rule, the Coast Guard did not tend to listen to the P&I Clubs' advice on how to deal with spills, but the P&I Clubs were allowed representation at the site, as they were the ones, ultimately, who were going to pay. I got off in Anchorage to overnight there. This was late March in Alaska, and I was coming from New Orleans with no winter clothing. I bought some heavy-weather gear and contacted the local correspondent for Britannia and IDIA, a law firm called Bradbury, Bliss & Riordan. Doug Davis was with Bradbury, Bliss & Riordan in Anchorage and handled most of the firm's P&I Club work. Doug quickly got me a rental car and a motel room in Valdez, a move that was fortuitous because within a few days there were no more rooms or rental cars to be had anywhere in Alaska. The influx of people into Valdez was that great.

On the flight from Dallas to Anchorage, I'd been able to see the ship aground. When I flew into Valdez the next day, I got a much closer look. By that point, another tanker was aside her, lightering off her cargo. This was March 26, and the grounding had occurred on March 24, so I was among the first people getting to the scene. As it happened, the accident had occurred on Good Friday, exactly 25 years after another terrible Good Friday disaster struck Valdez: the tremendous offshore earthquake that caused a tsunami that wiped out the town in 1964. Valdez of 1989 was fairly new and had been rebuilt on higher ground to the west of the original waterfront.

When the Trans-Alaska Pipeline was built, in 1977, Valdez was chosen as its terminus. The *Exxon Valdez* had loaded her cargo at the Valdez Marine Terminal in the Valdez Arm, and was on her way to refineries in the lower 48 when she entered Prince William Sound. She then deviated from the usual course under the direction of traffic control. It was springtime there, and the glaciers to the starboard side of the pathway through the sound were shedding ice, which produced small icebergs floating into the fairway. Vessels were being ordered to avoid the calving ice. The *Exxon Valdez* did that, though there has been a lot of speculation as to what got the *Exxon Valdez* so far over to the port side, where she grounded on Bligh Reef.

(Photo U.S. Coast Guard)

Exxon Valdez grounded in Prince William Sound, Alaska, March 24, 1989

Apparently, there was some mismanagement of the vessel, for which the captain, Joseph Hazelwood, received the full blame and was fired by Exxon. What happened was that Captain Hazelwood, once he cleared the Valdez Arm, had gone down to his office to work on the paperwork they had to submit to leave Valdez. While he was below, he left his third mate in charge of the wheelhouse. Obviously, there was inattention of some sort, or they would not have encountered Bligh Reef. The ship went aground there, and Captain Hazelwood took over attempts to get her off. At that time of year, the tidal range was about 12 feet. She had gone aground at high tide, and the tide was going out. Every minute that passed after the grounding, she was continuing to lose support underneath. As the tide went out, it brought her down harder on the rocks, to the point where they punctured a good bit of her underbelly.

Exxon mounted a full response. Despite their mobilization, I think that they retained their usual suspicion of the P&I Clubs' involvement. As I entered Jim O'Brien's office for the first time, he said, "Here come the spies!"

The International Tanker Owners Pollution Federation (ITOPF) soon had a presence in Valdez as well. Because they arrived later in the response, there wasn't any place in Valdez for them to stay. I was friendly with the ITOPF people, so I invited them to stay with me, and we turned my single hotel room into a bunkhouse. We worked together as a team, as they were there to perform similar things for their offices in London.

One ITOPF person who wasn't there was my friend Mike Garnett, the ex-Royal Navy captain of *Torrey Canyon*-spill fame. The fact was that Mike had more experience than any of the other ITOPF people, who tended to come directly from academic or environmental-science backgrounds and had rarely dealt with actual spills. Mike even had more experience than I did, having a few years on me. However, ITOPF is a consortium of tanker owners, and one of those owners was Exxon. Mike had had a falling out with Exxon over the *Burma Agate*, a major spill down in the Galveston Fairway, in the Gulf of Mexico. (Incidentally, the *Burma Agate* casualty was the reason that SMIT Salvage had given me such a hard time negotiating the contract on the *Akaterini* when I was first with Lamorte Burns.) On *Burma Agate* spill, Exxon wanted to use a dispersant product that they had developed and sold. Mike disagreed with the suggestion. Consequently, he had been in bad favor with Exxon ever since. Though it was the P&I Clubs that made the decision as to who should represent them, the oil companies held a lot of sway with the Clubs. Essentially, I was sent in on the *Exxon Valdez* spill as a substitute for Mike Garnett, because I was acceptable to Exxon.

(Photo NOAA's Office of Response and Restoration)

Tanker Burmah Agate incident, Galveston Harbor entrance, Texas, November 1979. The burning of the Burmah Agate.

Jim O'Brien was working for Exxon, and I was working for the P&I Clubs. We got along pretty well. Due to the tremendous amount of work that needed to be done, I did a number of things that, strictly speaking, were under the purview of Exxon and not the P&I Clubs. For example, they asked me to attend a lot of meetings with various segments of the affected population. But that was all part of the response.

In one case, we were picking up all this oil and Alaska would not permit any of it to be disposed of in the state—it had to be taken elsewhere. To do that, Exxon had come up with a good idea. There was a pumping station at the Valdez terminal that took ballast water off incoming tankers as they loaded cargo. Because it is illegal to discharge ballast water into the pristine waters in Prince William Sound, a ballast treatment center had been set up at the pumping station to clean the ballast water before discharging it. Exxon engineers came up with the idea of taking what was being skimmed off the water, about eighty percent water and twenty percent oil, and processing it in an upgraded ballast treatment center to leave only the oil for transport, rather than the oil and the water. Exxon gave me the paperwork and asked me to keep an eye on the meetings going on to get the state's approval for this scheme. I sat through most of those meetings until I realized that it was a waste of time. Alaska was never going to approve it.

Another set of meetings that Exxon asked me to attend were being held with the commercial fishing fleet to establish their concerns. These turned out to be significant. The fishermen were worried about Jack Bay, which was adjacent to the Valdez Arm. They brought up the fact that Jack Bay was prized as a nursery for a lot of the fishing stock that came out of the Prince William complex, and they were particularly concerned about the spill getting up in there. The flow from the casualty was outward, and we weren't encountering any currents that could carry oil back up toward Jack Bay, nor was it likely that winds could blow oil in that direction. We were fairly well covered against the oil getting there on its own, but we had to reassure the fishing fleet of that.

Not long after attending one of these meetings, the Exxon salvage master began thinking about moving the *Exxon Valdez* off Bligh Reef to a place where she could be cleaned and readied for tow down to the West Coast, where she could be repaired. When I realized they were talking about moving the ship closer to Valdez, into Jack Bay, specifically, I knew we had a problem. As a result of my meeting with the commercial fishing fleet, I was aware that this was a very soft spot for the fishermen, and the commercial fleet was probably correct: it would be a catastrophe if they moved the ship back up there. I asked the salvage master if he had realized that he'd be moving the ship to a place where there hadn't been any oil at all. He looked at me and said, "Jack, would you mind doing a survey of the entire sound and recommending the places where we could safely take the ship without the danger of polluting clean areas?"

(Photo U.S. Coast Guard)

Exxon Valdez cleanup, Prince William Sound, Alaska,
March 28, 1989

(Photo U.S. Coast Guard)

Exxon Valdez cleanup, Prince William Sound, Alaska,
March 28, 1989

I didn't want to condemn another clean place to more oil, so I looked for an area where there already was at least some oil. We needed a place away from maritime traffic, where the ship wouldn't be at risk of another collision while being cleaned, and a place that had sufficient protection from significant wind speeds and other threats from Mother Nature. I looked around and studied the charts. I'd been in Valdez for over a month and it seemed to me that the winds were coming predominantly out of the northeast. I needed an anchorage with sufficient depth and scope for the ship, as she would be swinging on her anchor chain with any changes in wind direction. I also needed a place generally shielded from the winds by mountains so as to tone down stresses on the moorings. I suggested Naked Island, as it had more of the required features than any of the other places I canvassed, and that was the site eventually decided upon.

Before moving the *Exxon Valdez* off Bligh Reef, as much oil as possible needed to be pumped out of her. Exxon hired my friend David Usher, among others, to help with the oil removal job. As part of our partnership some time before, I had gotten David involved with a Swedish pump manufacturer, and he had developed with them a cadre of power pumps that could be dropped down into ships to pump oil out of them. This was something that grew out of our experience together up at the Daniel Webster Inn in Sandwich, when we were working together on the *Argo Merchant* casualty. After the microwave scheme patented by the Buckley family failed to pan out, David and I had continued to look for ways to handle the problems we would have faced with the *Argo Merchant* had she not broken up the way she did. The pumping system that David and the pump manufacturer had come up with was something new at the time, and Exxon was grateful to have it on the *Exxon Valdez* response. David was on board quite a bit during the time she was stranded on the reef.

The Britannia P&I Club had been slated to take over the oil-spill cover for the *Exxon Valdez*, but hadn't done so by the time of the casualty. In this, they got lucky. They did have the wreck-removal cover, however, so one of my jobs for Britannia was to keep a close eye on the ship for them. The last thing the P&I Club needed was for her to sink. As a result, I developed a good relationship with the salvage master for Exxon. I would consult with him regularly, as he was the one who would know best if there existed any danger of further loss to the ship. As a precaution, Britannia wanted me to go out and board the *Exxon Valdez* before they moved her from Naked Island to wherever she would go for repairs. They wanted me to check the towing plan and ensure that the correct towing gear—gear that was not normally on board—had arrived and been properly installed.

I took a camera with me to the ship and was taking pictures of the arrangements—the way the line was flaked out, where the hard points were—so I could have visuals for the report I was going to forward to the Britannia. This was the moment that one of the crewmen came up to me and asked, "Mr. Gallagher, don't you want to have your picture taken on board the *Exxon Valdez*?" It had never occurred to me to get a photo, but I'm glad I accepted the offer.

I brought my son Michael up to work for me after a few weeks. He was assigned to follow the Coast Guard and the SUPSALV operations with their equipment and to get some idea of how much money they were spending. Based on his observations and material reports, we estimated what we called the burn rate—the amount that the cleanup was costing on a daily basis. I then reported this to the P&I Clubs to keep them cognizant of what was being spent.

Michael and I were up there for long enough that we really lived the Alaska lifestyle. It was all very interesting. We saw eagles, which were all over the place, as well as killer whales and other wildlife. I met quite a few people on the response, including some who would eventually help us start Gallagher Marine Systems. One individual I met, named Judy, was working as a waitress in a hotel there when I first encountered her. She was pretty savvy, and I learned that she'd moved to Alaska straight out of college and had gotten work doing a number of odd jobs, as many people up there do. She was married to a guy working on the pipeline and had become a landowner. I tried to help her get work with the response people I knew, and eventually she landed a job with Exxon, something involving the waterfowl response. That led to another job: Judy had her own airplane (one of her many jobs was as a bush pilot), and she began flying scientists around to different islands to monitor the recovery and clean up.

Judy and I stayed in touch. I had more casualties later on in Alaska, and she often came and helped on those. When I first founded GMS, Judy came down and helped us set up our first contingency plans and subsequently joined responses to spills on the West Coast and in Alaska. She was one of the keys in forming the company. She is still in Alaska and has worked for Alyeska and various Aleutian tribes.

Another problem we encountered with the *Exxon Valdez* casualty came when pupping season began and seals started going up on the rocks to deliver their offspring. A lot of those rocks were covered with oil, and there was very little chance of getting the oil off of them in time for pupping season. Pete Lane had the idea to cover the rocks with an oil-repellent plastic sheeting made for construction operations so that seals and other animals could be protected from stranded oil. We deployed the plastic over fouled rocks, and the oil didn't touch the seals.

These were just a few of the things that happened in a spill that was, at that time, the largest casualty and casualty response to ever take place in U.S. waters. We had thousands and thousands of people working on it, from Valdez all the way through the Aleutian Islands and down to Kodiak.

Finally, the question arose as to where exactly to tow the *Exxon Valdez*. The salvage master suggested the National Steel & Shipbuilding yard in San Diego, where the *Exxon Valdez* was built, and which they knew could handle her. But Exxon was looking for something closer to avoid any complications that might result from a longer tow. I recalled the dry dock in Portland, where I had helped dry-dock the *Mobiloil* tanker using Uncle Paul's dry-dock filter boxes to prevent oil from leaking out of the ship's hull. I told the savage crew that if we could get her to that dry dock, some arrangements would need to be made to prevent oil from leaking from the ship. I described Uncle Paul's dry-dock filter box system, and Exxon was interested. So once again, I contacted Uncle Paul, who agreed to let us use it under the same condition as with the *Mobiloil*, namely that we use his Sorbent-C. Exxon was willing to go along with this arrangement, but in the end, they had to take the *Exxon Valdez* to San Diego after all, as the dry dock at Portland turned out not to be big enough for her.

Years later, in the ensuing litigation surrounding the cleanup, I was subpoenaed to testify in a trial. Exxon had claimed that the spill response cost $2 billion, and they were trying to get additional compensation from underwriters, as the P&I Clubs liabilities had stopped at $250 million. How Exxon reached the $2 billion it claimed was beyond my comprehension, and I testified to that effect. On cross-examination, the Exxon attorney asked me if I had any monetary interest in getting the *Exxon Valdez* into the Portland dry dock, and I said no. I suppose he was trying to suggest that I had been profiteering in some way. Maybe his strategy was to impugn my overall testimony. I told him that I hadn't tried to sell Exxon anything, and then repeated my testimony that the very size of Exxon's claims were wildly unrealistic—they went far beyond any previous response costs in the United States and were, in fact, far beyond anything I had seen in spill responses in the United States since. He and I rode an elevator down to the lobby together. He congratulated me on my response to his questions. I considered asking him, out of curiosity, what he had been thinking of in asking me that last question, but I let it go at that.

Chapter 21

Enter the Dragon Lady

Almost immediately upon returning from Valdez, I got a call to go up to Newport, Rhode Island, where the M/T *World Prodigy* had run hard aground on Breton Reef while bound for Providence, carrying home heating fuel. In grounding, a number of her cargo tanks had opened up and started spilling oil into the Narragansett Bay. The spill was slicking the surrounding shoreline. By the time I made it to Newport, the captain of the port for the Coast Guard had created a forward command post in a Coast Guard station at the entrance to the harbor. When I arrived, I found that he had taken over the operation. (Again, this was before we had codified the Unified Command structure.) I approached him and told him I was there representing the shipowners and he told me the Coast Guard was handling the response. He kept holding me off, and in fact, I never did manage to have much input on the operation. But there wasn't much to be done; the spill response had been activated.

I stationed myself in the advanced post and wound up hanging around with a group of reporters who were trying to get information from the Coast Guard. It wasn't such a large spill, but there was the potential for problems. The weather was good and the vessel was taken off her strand, so there was no trouble getting salvors in. In fact, there was even a bit of time to offload some of her tanks. I went aboard the ship to assist or at least observe. At this point, I had no official duties, as the Coast Guard was in control. I observed and reported to the P&I Clubs, but I had very little operational involvement. Though things were mostly under control, the Coast Guard wasn't saying anything and the gathered reporters were hungry for information. When they saw that I had a minor role in the response, they started interviewing me. When I couldn't tell them much of anything, they started interviewing each other. This shows how rumors get started when reporters are hard up for information.

I took care of whatever problems I could. I got information from people whose property was damaged by the spill. Newport Harbor is a prominent place, filled with important historical sites and much valuable property. It's also the sailing center of the Northeast. I surveyed to see if there was much damage, but there wasn't a lot of oil on the scene. One thing the captain of the port asked me to do was establish a tow of the ship to dry dock down in Brooklyn, New York. Once they decided exactly where they were going to take the ship, they asked me to set up an escort down the coast for her and I went about doing that. Meanwhile, I was still keeping up with the progress of the *Exxon Valdez* down the West Coast, as the P&I Clubs had asked me to do. This was in June of 1989, and at this point the *Exxon Valdez* was underway from Alaska to her dry dock and repair in San Diego, California. The salvage master was accompanying her, and I had arranged with him to get daily reports on the progress of the ship for the Britannia P&I Club. So, while I was accompanying the *World Prodigy* down the East Coast, I was at the same time monitoring the progress of the *Exxon Valdez* as she headed down the West Coast. It was an interesting coincidence of big-ship versus little-ship casualties: both grounded and caused some oil pollution, both under tow to shipyards for repair and each of them moving down its own coast at the same moment.

Jack at sea

I hired a boat to go out to the entrance to New York Harbor to accompany the *World Prodigy* in. When we arrived at the outer light off New York Harbor, several miles over the horizon from the harbor itself, we stopped to await the arrival of the *World Prodigy* in tow behind. It was June and sunny, and the *World Prodigy* was late. My roommate in Brooklyn Heights at the time, Patrick Stewart, was on board with me. None of us had thought to bring sunscreen, and we all got a good dose of sunburn. When the *World Prodigy* arrived, we set up alongside her, boomed her off to control any leaks that might work out, and escorted her into the harbor.

I was consulting for Hudson Maritime out of Philadelphia one year later, when the M/V *Nautilus* foundered in June 1990 in the Kill Van Kull, a busy channel that separates the shore of Bayonne, New Jersey, from the shoreline of Staten Island. She had been making for a terminal to deliver a cargo of black oil when she struck something large enough to rip a hole in the hull (it was never determined what). The tear caused her to discharge part of her oil bunkers. The *Nautilus* casualty would be the first casualty that our future GMS president David Barry was to become involved in. It also involved the attorney Steven Candito, who went on to become the president of the National Response Corporation, or NRC, one of the two major countrywide Oil Spill Response Organizations (OSROs).

Because the Kill Van Kull separated two states, we had cross-state attendance in the *Nautilus* response, which complicated matters considerably. The current through the Kill Van Kull, although tidal, was generally outflowing, so the spilled oil, besides contacting the shorelines of both Staten Island and Bayonne, also went into New York Harbor. I arrived at the terminal where the ship had docked after having the casualty. I tried to set up some sort of command center, starting out with just a radiotelephone that worked on the marine frequency. Soon I had found a telephone booth that sat at the edge of a parking lot at the terminal, and that became my office. I started contacting people to come in and man the response activities.

Fortunately, the surrounding area was mostly industrial, so there wasn't much of a populace to worry about. Along the channel itself, there were mostly tug operators, with several pleasure-boat operators among them. The channel opened up into a large container port, one of the major recipients of containers for the New York area. There was a lot of traffic entering the channel from either end. The spilled oil was tending to flow more toward the northern mouth of the channel, because the tidal flow predominately went in that direction; but the net tidal flow coming in around the island from the other side was a factor too. Thus, on both a flooding tide and an ebbing tide, the discharge would tend to travel into New York Harbor. A more adverse factor to the flow and direction of the oil was the wind, which varied all around the compass during our operations there. We stayed on that response for nearly eight months before we got to a point where we were ready for inspection by Coast Guard and state officials.

One of the interesting memories from this otherwise routine, if lengthy, operation was the role of the Frank family and their matriarch, Evelyn Berman, otherwise known as the Dragon Lady. Evelyn, both of her daughters, and her son were lawyers who headed maritime businesses of one sort or another all over New York Harbor. At one point, one of her daughters was appointed to the post of maritime commissioner for New York City. Evelyn's headquarters were on Staten Island, just across the Kill Van Kull from the terminal where the *Nautilus* was docked. She was well known for commenting over her marine radio on all the maritime traffic operations going on nearby. She was a real hell-raiser and often wore leather miniskirts, even at the age of 75. She talked like a sailor, and on the maritime radio, her handle actually was the Dragon Lady, a nickname taken from the old comic strip "Smilin' Jack." Evelyn even had a yacht in Palm Beach named *Dragon Lady*. To say the Franks were infamous in New York Harbor would be an understatement. *Business Week* once dubbed them "The First Family of Pollution."

My experiences with the Franks began as a result of some oil they were "recovering" as part of the spill cleanup. We had hired one of their businesses to clean up the oil that was coming from the *Nautilus*. After skimming it, they would put the recovered oil into their waste-oil storage tanks, and then sell it. Between billing us for the skimming and billing buyers for the oil they had collected off the *Nautilus*, they were profiting twice off the same oil. One day, Susan Frank, one of the two daughters, came over to meet with me at the command center offices we had established next to their waste-oil operation. She handed me an outrageous bill for the cleanup that they had done. I took one look at the bill and told her that it was so far out of line that I couldn't settle or discuss it myself. I told her that we'd have to take it to the attorneys for the P&I Clubs in New York, across the river near Wall Street. She became obviously indignant and told me that she was going to bring her attorney over to talk to me about it.

I immediately called up the P&I Club representative, another Gallagher, and told him what was going on. He told me to make sure somebody was with me to help back up whatever went on in the meeting when Susan Frank came back. David Barry was sitting with me in the office at the time, so we waited.

A short time later, Susan Frank returned, accompanied by a guy she introduced as her lawyer. As it turned out, he was also her husband. They began cross-examining me on why I wouldn't pay their bill. I told them that I wasn't saying that I wouldn't pay the bill, just that I wasn't authorized to negotiate a bill of this size, and that it would have to be sent to the P&I Club lawyers for settlement. By this time, I'd heard enough about the Franks to know that this type of behavior was typical of them. We went on for quite a while, until they finally accused me of reneging on our contract. "We could bring a suit against you," they told me, not knowing that I was an attorney as well and knew the nature of their shenanigans. I suppose they thought they could intimidate me. I told them, once and for all, that I simply wasn't authorized to negotiate with them, and they left unhappy.

Shortly after that, I heard that they were going to make a presentation to the P&I Club's attorney in New York, and that I needed to be there. Susan and her husband did not participate this time. It was Susan's attorney brother, Peter Frank, who appeared. Peter was something else. He was wearing a double-breasted suit with two-toned shoes and a bow tie. He looked like a standup comic in the Borscht Belt. Immediately, he launched into a long disquisition on the stellar reputation of the Frank family in New York Harbor. He carried on this way until one of the attorneys for the P&I Club proposed a settlement. Needless to say it was quite a bit lower than what the Franks were asking. Peter, becoming indignant, exclaimed, "You're hondeling me, and I won't be hondeled!" Nonetheless, the negotiations went on until they reached a settlement. I went up to Peter afterward and said, "I know some Yiddish but I've never heard of the word 'hondel.'" He told me it meant to negotiate in bad faith. Later, I checked with Dave Usher, my Yiddish translator, and he told me that it didn't mean that at all.

The *Nautilus* spill response went on. As we were doing our final cleanup of oil off the riprap located along the shorelines of New Jersey and Staten Island, there came another spill, this time at a repair yard down the Kill Van Kull toward the container port. As it happened, the yard was run by Peter Frank, and the spill featured a barge named the *Sara Frank*. The Franks had moved *Sara Frank* from the Dragon Lady's waste-oil place to Peter's operation for some hull work. The barge sank right in its berth, spilling oil. As the Franks were involved, a predictably odd situation ensued. The Dragon Lady's boats weren't covered by the P&I Clubs, but apparently she had been able to get some coverage at Lloyd's, which was unusual because the underwriters at Lloyd's had stopped issuing P&I cover for vessels in the 1860s. Since she had Lloyd's cover, they sent the oversight of the cleanup to the Salvage Association, who would analyze what was being done and keep the insurers apprised. In this case, the Salvage Association contacted Hudson Maritime. Cindy Hudson then contacted me to do for Lloyd's what I would have done for the P&I Clubs under usual circumstances. We still had crews working on the final touches of the *Nautilus* cleanup, so we just continued working in the Kill Van Kull, re-staffing the response so we could go on to deal with the results of the *Sara Frank* spill. We set up our command center in Peter Frank's shipyard, and that turned out to be quite a lesson for us all. Compared to our first Frank-family encounter, this was a whole new world: a yard run by the Franks, for the Franks. We ran into a lot of interesting shenanigans that we had not seen before, or since.

The space for our command center was beneath Peter's office. He had a man named Nobel "Buzzy" Darrow working for him as a yard boss. Buzzy Darrow was one of the slickest operators I have ever known. One Saturday, federal officials descended on the yard. Somehow, both Buzzy and Peter left the yard just before the agents appeared. The Feds did a thorough search of the offices and walked off with some files. Buzzy returned after they were gone and for some time took control of the operation for the Franks.

Later, the federal officials stationed themselves in our command center to keep an eye on things. We went ahead and did what we could to get the oil out of the water. But, with Buzzy in charge now, things got even more complicated. Rather than hiring a salvor for the sunken barge, Buzzy decided to set up his own salvage effort. He fiddled about with that for almost two weeks, while oil continued to come out of the barge. The government finally told him to get a real salvor in there.

Buzzy came from an Irish family. His father had worked with the Franks on a lot of jobs and on his deathbed, he had asked Evelyn to take care of his teenage boy for him. So, although Buzzy was born into an Irish family, he was thereafter raised in a Jewish one. He was a tough customer and had learned a lot under Evelyn's tutelage. One summer evening, I was sitting in the command center with a couple of young female FBI agents when Buzzy came in carrying a television, a video player, and a bunch of VHS tapes. He said, "This is for the night crew, to provide you with some entertainment when it gets late and things are slow." As he was leaving, he turned around and said, "Now, I don't want the television left alone in here, because that's how I got it." And he then took off. That was the general tenor of the way things worked with Buzzy.

It was Arnold Witte, a longtime salvor and a lawyer himself, who came in to relieve Buzzy. Arnold ran a company, Donjon Marine, on Staten Island, and operated a scrapyard that his father had established in the early 1900s where vessels could be brought in for restoration or scrapping. He had gathered a whole fleet of outdated ships and ferryboats there. At one point, Arnold was in business with the Dragon Lady and her brother, Morris Berman, doing tugs in a joint venture. Morris was running a fueling facility in the harbor, and one day Arnold took one of his tugs into Morris's facility to refuel and got a bill for more fuel than the vessel could hold. Arnold went to the Dragon Lady with the bill and said, "Evelyn, look at this: Morris is charging me for more fuel than my vessel can hold." And Evelyn replied, "Arnold, you know how Morris is." To which Arnold said, "Yes, I know Morris, and knowing that, I'm out of here." That ended his partnership with the Franks.

We continued our cleanup, but with this circus going on, it was a challenge.

When Peter returned to the yard, I remember him saying, "Well, it's good to be back." He wasn't back for long, however. The Franks had contracts to deposit sewage in an ocean dump 100 miles out at sea, but to save on time and fuel they would sometimes dump it into coves and streams around New York Harbor. The resulting lawsuits eventually forced the family out of New York Harbor and spelled the beginning of the end for the Dragon Lady.

Exiled from New York, what was left of the Frank family operation resurfaced in the Virgin Islands. The barge *Morris J Berman*, named after her brother, was passing by San Juan, Puerto Rico, when the towline broke. They couldn't reattach to the barge, and it went aground, on a coral reef off Escambron Beach near San Juan, where it started blanketing the surrounding shoreline with oil. The barge was insured for something like $5 million and subsequent clean-up/response costs above this amount (~$125M) were paid for by the National Pollution Fund Center (NPFC) Once that money had been spent on the cleanup, the U.S. government pursued one of the major U.S. life insurers for recovery of monies spent by the NPFC. Ultimately, that insurer got hornswoggled (negotiated settlement) into reimbursing the NPFC for a significant portion of the monies the NPFC had spent on response costs. Unfortunately, that insurer had underwritten a loan on the barge and/or towing vessel (*EMILY S*) and as a condition of that loan, was holding ownership until the loan was paid back. This made them (technically and unwittingly) a vessel owner and thus a "Responsible Party" under OPA 90, with liability.

Prior to settling with the U.S. Government, that insurance company hired GMS through a law firm in Seattle to do a review of the case. David and I spent three months studying the documents and the bill for the cleanup and its legitimacy. We went down to San Juan and toured the area, actually walking the shorelines and examining where the oil came in. We discovered a lot. The NPFC had created a wonderful money making opportunity with little controls on costs. In one instance, we noted that the NPFC had issued a contract to a Norfolk, VA Company to clean two barges used in the response at a cost of several million dollars. Upon closer examination, we found that the operation had been under the direction of none other than Buzzy Darrow and many of the workers names we recognized as being the same as workers at Standard Tank in Bayonne, New Jersey. It appeared that the USCG had unwittingly hired and paid a Frank company handsomely to work on their own spill.

At the Coast Guard's instruction, the salvors had taken the barge out and, after offloading a portion of the remaining cargo, sunk it into what was supposedly a deep trench, even though they were still losing oil. By that point, this had become a government cleanup, and Donjon, Arnold Witte's company, was working for the government. We came to the conclusion that the oil that had leaked from the sunken barge had moved off to the west , and greatly expanding the scope and scale of the clean-up as the oil eventually came ashore, oiling beaches that otherwise likely would have seen little or no oil.

Eventually, three Frank companies were convicted of felonies in connection with the spill. After Peter Frank failed to appear for the sentencing, he was cited for contempt of court. Hearing this, Peter got on a plane to Puerto Rico. He landed on a Friday and was greeted at the airport by a marshal, who promptly jailed him for the weekend. We got a kick out of that: Peter, with all his bravado, ending up in a Puerto Rican jail, unable to talk his way out of it. That was more or less the end of the Frank businesses. The Dragon Lady even spent nine months in prison for violating probation on an earlier suspended sentence.

Buzzy resurfaced in Norfolk, where he owned/operated a tank cleaning company. I ran into him a couple of times at International Oil Spill Conferences. At a recent meeting in Washington, D.C., I learned that he had died. That was the end of a colorful career, for the Franks and for Noble "Buzzy" Darrow, the Jewish Irishman.

Jack purchasing his ships wheel at South St. Seaport

Chapter 22

Desert Storm

After I finished with the *Nautilus* casualty in New York, I was invited down to Houston to meet with an attorney at one of the large law firms there. He had a client who was interested in my consulting services, but wasn't forthcoming with much further information. When I arrived, I learned that the prospective client was Saudi Aramco, the oil company of Saudi Arabia. Saudi Aramco ships most of its oil in Saudi-owned and Saudi-flagged ships. They were looking for help developing spill response scenarios for Houston, where most of their cargo ships berthed. They wanted plans, skills, and training that could address shoreside problems that might arise for their operations.

I was still consulting with Cindy Hudson, and my friend Mike Garnett, the retired Royal Navy Captain, was very involved in her operation. When I let her know about my talks with Aramco, she suggested that she and Mike sit in. I agreed, which was a mistake, because Cindy saw Saudi Aramco as a big fish for her to land. By the time Cindy and Mike got through with them, Saudi Aramco didn't want to have much to do with any of us. Cindy had tried to steal my pitch and expand it, to poor effect, and we wound up not getting much work out of the meeting.

The principal breach, however, was between Cindy and Aramco. I continued to do some work for Aramco, but it was substantially less than what we had talked about initially. However, I must have remained somewhat in their good graces, because in 1991, when Desert Storm began with Iraq invading Kuwait and threatening Saudi Arabia, I received another call from Aramco asking for my help. By this time, there had been a large, purposeful discharge of oil into the Arabian Gulf from Kuwait by Saddam Hussein. This oil spill was massive, the largest man-made spill in history, far exceeding even the size of the later BP Deepwater Horizon spill in the Gulf of Mexico. Hussein also sank several tankers to add to the spill.

Saudi Aramco wanted me to go on the McNeil/Lehrer News Hour, which had asked for a representative to appear for an in-depth segment on the Arabian Gulf spill. I told the Aramco people I knew in Houston that I didn't know much more than what I'd seen on TV, but if they really needed someone, I'd go on for them. Admiral John Costello, recently retired from the Coast Guard and newly hired to run the Marine Spill Response Corporation (MSRC), was the other guest for the segment. It was a fairly long segment, and Jim Lehrer questioned both of us. At one point, he called Admiral Costello "Admiral Gallagher," and I saw the look of pain on the Admiral's face. That was the first and only time that I've been called Admiral. The segment gave pretty good oversight of what was happening in Kuwait, and our shared opinion was that the people working on the spill had a tough job.

After my appearance, I received another call from Saudi Aramco asking me to fly out to Saudi Arabia and help protect their water intakes. Since Saudi Arabia has no potable ground water, all of their water comes out of the Persian Gulf, for the eastern part of the country at least. The oil coming down from Kuwait was a threat to those water intakes; if it reached them, it would imperil not only the country's drinking-water supply, but also the water used to process oil in their refineries. I believe this was the real reason Hussein released so much oil into the Gulf—to sabotage the country's economy as well as the welfare of its people. Saudi Aramco wanted me to consult with them on setting up the defenses against the massive oil spill heading their way.

The next Saturday, I was on flight to New York to pick up a Saudi transport all the way to Dhahran. Less than one week after my appearance on the McNeil/Lehrer News Hour, I was in Saudi Arabia.

I settled first at the Saudi Aramco headquarters and then moved up to Ras Tanura, on the Gulf Coast, to set up barriers around the water intakes for the refineries there. I worked via phone with my friend Dave Stith back in New Jersey as my team and I spent a couple of weeks installing the same type of bubble-curtain barriers Dave and I had developed during the *Intermar Alliance* casualty around the intakes for the Ras Tanura refineries.

The refinery in Ras Tanura had a golf course on its grounds. The fairways were made of sand, and the greens were given a coating of oil. The floors of the restaurant in the refinery, where we ate lunch quite often, were therefore always decorated with oil from the golfers' shoes. Everything was highly guarded, and only the Aramco employees and their guests could use it. Most of the upper echelons of the refinery operators were foreigners, Americans or Brits for the most part. The Saudis preferred Americans, but employed Brits as well. The Saudis had some angst about the British, as they had been a colonial power that had ruled Saudi Arabia in the 18th century.

While I was designing the barriers for Ras Tanura, the Saudi Aramco engineers came into our offices to design a barrier for a large water intake at the desalination plant in Aziziyia, south of Ras Tanura. The intake was great distance offshore and very large. The Saudi engineers were planning to place floating oil booms around structure. However, I knew that the ebb and flow of the water with tidal changes would be strong enough to allow underflow of the booms, the way they were configuring them. As I was explaining this to them, one of Saudi engineers looked at me and said, "You seem to know what you're doing. Why don't you design it for us?" So I wound up designing and supervising the boom installation at Aziziyia as well.

The Aziziyia intake provided all the desalinized water for the region. Among its clients was the King's palace, which looked like something out of the Arabian Nights. I didn't enter the palace itself, but I was tasked with providing recommendations for keeping oil off the palace grounds. I studied the palace waterfront. It had a curious arrangement consisting of an arcuate barrier curving out into the Gulf for about a quarter of a mile. This barrier had a large pipe-like upper-structure, supported by tripods every 30 feet or so, with a gate in the center that could be opened and closed. It was probably two to three kilometers long and had a stainless steel net hanging down its face.

Proper oil booming would assure that the boom didn't take water flow exceeding 3/4 knot or more in velocity perpendicular to it; velocities above this figure will cause oil entrainment and failure of the boom to provide protection. I was trying to come up with a design for placing and securing the placement of the boom to insure that the water velocity perpendicular to the boom was below that causing failure. I looked up the waterway to the north of us and there was the palace of the King's brother, who was also the Secretary of War for Saudi Arabia. His palace was situated such that I could hang a boom from the palace down to the circular barrier protecting the King's waterfront.

I explained my plan to the King's palace managers and told them that it might be expensive and difficult, but if we could run a boom along the stainless steel curtain, it would probably work when oil arrived. The engineers went away to talk about it, and when they came back, they had been told by the King's people, "There shall be no oil of any kind in the King's water, period!" This is when I realized that this was the first job I'd ever had where I could lose my head.

I began looking seriously at the King's brother's neighboring palace, figuring that the King had the power to use it to support the structures necessary to protect his own palace. If we could incorporate the King's brother's estate, the protection provided would keep the oil off the King's installations. I designed the system and put it out for bid. My next job was to get the proposals in and indicate the ones that made the most sense. I wouldn't choose the winner but would suggest eliminating the ones I found unsuitable. I had the contractors come back to the palace and took them around the grounds and waterways to look at the proposed path layout of the boom. As it turned out, only one of the bids for the booming work made any sense at all. I gave Saudi Aramco my opinion to that effect.

At about this point, things came to a standstill on their part. The King wasn't at the palace more than once or twice a year, and his palace managers were indecisive as whether to go to the effort and expense that the plan required. While they procrastinated over the situation, we became involved with some hot work further up the coast. A Marine Corps detachment was located just south of the Kuwaiti border, and the Iraqis had made a thrust toward them. At one point, I was slated to visit the Marine base from which they were leading the response to the invasion. Some other Americans working for me did go, but I had to stand by to see what the contractors at the King's palace were going to do. It was just as well, as some Scuds hit close to where my guys had gone.

Jim O'Brien had been hired by the Saudi Arabian Royal Commission, which had control over several refineries in Al Jubail. He was working through a different arm of the Saudi oil industry and could get better service on equipment and supplies because he was stationary. I, on the other hand, was continually being moved up and down the Coast, responding to quickly moving events of different kinds. He therefore had obtained a lot more boom than I could readily get. Flying over the coastal area one day, I was so impressed by how much boom Jim had gathered I began referring to the place as the Jim O'Brien's Boom Store. Word got back to Jim via scuttlebutt, and his response was, "Tell Gallagher to keep his hands off my boom." Jim and I had jocular encounters like this throughout our careers. It got heated from time to time, usually when one of us thought the other wasn't acting strictly according to Hoyle, but any real flare-ups were the result of third-party misunderstandings, rather than any animosity between us. Jim died in February of 2014 from cancer.

Just to the north of Al Jubail, there is an island called the Abu Ali. It juts out diagonally from the coastline, with one end close to the shoreline and the other extending out into the slipstream of the currents off Abu Ali. It resembles a catcher's mitt, and I was curious as to whether this could be of any value to us in holding the oil coming down from Kuwait. I wanted to do a close inspection of the causeway connecting Abu Ali to the mainland, to see if there was any penetration. I couldn't tell from the air, so I asked for a flyby close to the causeway and saw that there were no openings underneath. Anything that came down west of the island would be directed into this area, a catch called Dawat Ad-Dafi at the lower end of Abu Ali.

We began taking daily flights out over the Gulf, but we could only go as far north as the southern side of the combat zone.

Nevertheless, I could get far enough to see the oil coming down from Kuwait. As oil weathers with exposure to oxygen and the sea, it turns an orange color. This oil coming down was so thick that the only orange that could be seen was along the very leading edge of the spill at the waterline itself. I charted the progress of the oil as it came along the coast, my hope being that it would drop into the Dawat Ad-Dafi and finally enter the lake behind the Dawat, where it could be held. When the oil first arrived at the mouth of the passage to the Dawat, it started moving out around the side of Abu Ali, bypassing the Dawat and continuing on south around the receding shoreline toward Al Jubail. I feared that the jig was up and the oil was going to reach Al Jubail and beyond, and reported this situation to Saudi Aramco headquarters in Dhahran.

I received a frantic call from the head of the office we were working for. He sent over a map of the Arabian Gulf and wanted me to add the location of the oil we'd spotted. He was preparing for a meeting he was having with the King's brother, the Secretary of War. We gathered our reports together and, as best we could, marked the map with a black marker to show the distribution of the oil as viewed during our flights over the area for the past week. When the Secretary of War's retainer saw the map, he said, "Oh, no, no, there's not enough oil here." I told him that this was what we'd been seeing. He took my pen and started enlarging the recorded areas of the oil spill on the map. I thought to myself, "What are we doing here?" As it turned out, they had been continually exaggerating our reported spill sizes and totals in this manner in their press releases, doubling the volume in many cases.

The next day, something miraculous happened: the oil reversed itself and started going back into the Dawat Ad-Dafi. All I could figure was that the oil had reached the mouth as the tide was receding, and the flood current kept it going in. Jim O'Brien then had the responsibility of picking up the oil held in the Dawat. A couple of years later, back in the States, I decided to enter a paper for an International Oil Spill Conference on this phenomenon. I titled it "The Dawat Ad-Dafi and the Mother of All Oil Spills." I asked Jim if he would co-author it with me, as I could only write about what I had seen from the air and wanted him to write about how he had dealt with the cleanup. He agreed to share his story, but Jim prides himself on never writing anything, so the actual writing fell to me. Among his strategies were some techniques he had picked up from rice farmers in Louisiana. There they build barriers around the rice fields with sluice gates that are opened when the tide comes in and closed when it goes out, keeping the water inside. Jim set up a similar system to allow the oiled water in with the incoming tide but keep the oil there when the tide fell. When the time came, I let him make the presentation at the conference, and he didn't refer to the paper once. Instead, he told a long and hilarious story about his time in Saudi Arabia. They only allocated 15 minutes to present the paper and five more to answer questions; Jim took all 20 minutes with his story. Nevertheless, the paper was published, and I recently got a call from a Bloomberg reporter who had heard of it and wanted a copy as background for her reporting on the Deepwater Horizon spill in the Gulf of Mexico— so it ended up doing some good, I guess.

The biggest danger I faced while I was in Saudi Arabia was the Scuds the Iraqis fired on us during the last days of the war. In Dhahran, I was in a hotel in the industrial compound for what they called the Aramcons, the Aramco Americans. When I checked in, I learned the emergency drill. Sirens sounded the alarm that Scuds had been launched. If you didn't hear Patriot missiles launching within 15 minutes of the siren, then you knew that the Scuds were going someplace else. These sirens invariably sounded around 2:00 A.M., since the Iraqis had no way to protect themselves in daylight hours. Though the alarms came, there was never actually a Scud.

One night, however, I went over to Al Khobar, a town about ten miles from my billet in Dhahran, to have dinner with David Usher, who was working through the U.S. Coast Guard as an advisor to another branch of the Saudi Arabian government, providing environmental protection advice. Dave and I had shared a lot of history in the oil-spill business since the early 1970s and we shared a mutual regard for each other; we remain friends today. That night we met at his hotel. It was a quiet night, but later, when I got into a cab to return to Ras Tanura, I saw a large fire in the civilian area along the road home. I didn't think much of it at the time, but the next morning, I heard that a Scud had hit right near the road where I had been driving. The strike was within half a mile of where Dave and I had been having dinner, but we hadn't heard the explosion as it was on the other side of a fairly large hill. When specific details of this event were published several years later, I learned that this particular Scud strike was the next-to-last fired in the war and that it had caused the single largest number of casualties of any of the Scud attacks fired by the Iraqis during the whole war. It had hit an apartment building full of American National Guardsmen recently arriving from Pennsylvania, killing over 30 of the guardsmen and injuring over 100. It showed that, if you're operating in a war zone like that, you are as likely to be killed as anyone else there.

The next night, before we knew that the Scud attacks were over, I remember walking outside around the time the Scuds usually started coming, pausing for a second, and thinking to myself: Uncle Paul, you really got me into something this time!

I stayed in Saudi Arabia for a few days after the war was over. The spill response had changed from prevention to cleanup, and I was no longer needed so I packed up to go back to the states. Before I left, I received a plaintive call from the King's palace. They wanted to know what was happening with the boom system I had designed for them. I told them that the contractors who had signed up for the contest had submitted their bids and that I had reviewed them and submitted my opinions about their efficacy. Since I had heard nothing from the palace after they had received my opinions, and since the war was essentially over and my contract with Saudi Aramco was coming to an end, I turned the selected plans and the responsibility of completing the boom installation over to the Saudi engineers. I went out commercial on British Airways and flew over the pyramids of Giza en route to London, where I caught a plane for the States.

Because this job had come together so quickly, Cindy Hudson had offered to handle my payments from Saudi Aramco, and I had agreed to let her, since I had no other means to ensure proper movement of the funds across the ocean. The agreement had been for me to be paid about $1,500 per day, which Cindy was to receive, bank, and hold on to until I got back to the States. In return, Cindy would get a percentage of my earnings.

When I returned, Cindy immediately told me that the IRS had frozen her bank account, so she couldn't access any of the money, including mine. She gave me a check for $25,000 until the rest of the money due to me could be transferred.

The $25,000 check bounced. After several weeks of malarkey, I consulted with some lawyers in Philadelphia. Several of them informed me that Cindy Hudson spent more time in court these days than they did; with lawsuits either by or against her in the various courts. The experience was another one pushing me to launch Gallagher Marine Systems, and I decided to put my focus there. I still have the bounced check. Over the years, I have come to realize that I owe people like Cindy Hudson, Hal Halpin, and Uncle Paul a thank you for their treatment of me. Each of those disappointments led me to succeed on my own with more fruitful associations.

An ex-Coast Guard captain named Tim McKenna subsequently went to work for Cindy. I ran into Tim at a meeting in California. I said, "Tim, I'm really happy to meet you. I just want to give you one word of caution." He said, "Jack, I know what you're going to tell me. I know all about it. I have decided that I am going to change things there and make something out of this company." Two years later, when we next met, Tim said: "I know what you said to me, but it's just that I had never met people like that. I didn't know they existed." I said, "Well, it's a hard lesson that I learned the hard way, too."

PART VI

THE BIRTH OF Gallagher Marine Systems

Chapter 23

OPA 90

Another key to the founding of Gallagher Marine Systems was the passing of the Oil Pollution Act of 1990, known as OPA 90. The legislation stemmed from the *Exxon Valdez* spill and did much to tighten restrictions on the way oil is transported. As I mentioned earlier, I had brought David Barry to work with me on some of the jobs I had done for Cindy Hudson. My good friend Bob Driscoll was David's brother-in-law, and after David got his master's degree in environmental engineering from the University of Maryland, Bob came to me and said, "Jack, we've got to find Dave a job or he's going to be a grad student for the rest of his life!"

Though David had no background in the spill business, his chemical engineering and environmental engineering degrees made him a quick study in what we were doing. We started knocking around some ideas about how OPA 90 was going to change the oil-spill response industry overall. Sitting around the kitchen table, we began thinking about how GMS might help shippers comply with the raft of new regulations. Prominent among these was a provision that required the development of spill response plans for all individual tank vessels detailing how a catastrophic spill could be handled from the moment it was identified. Remember, in the very beginning of a casualty, the spilling vessel is responsible for the organization and implementation of the response. The new provision also required that each vessel have available a Qualified Individual— an agent entrusted by the owner to immediately authorize mobilization and the spending that came with it, in the event of a casualty.

Slowly, we began to see the two important functions GMS might serve: The first would have to do with the drafting and maintenance of oil-spill response plans for shipowners and their vessels. Here, all the work that I had previously put into my Automated Response Systems came to fruition and grew into our GMS system. The second function would be to define the role of the QI. We were early enough in the whole thing to play a significant role in this, and today it is an important service that GMS provides many of our clients.

While we were developing our plan for GMS, however, the oil spills didn't stop. Our next really big one came in October of 1991, in the Aleutian chain. The Motor Vessel *Hyundai 12*, a South Korean bulk carrier, ran aground in the Twelve Fathom Strait in the Shumagin Islands, Alaska. The vessel had entered the pass to get out of the weather and secure itself from a storm that was passing through the Aleutians. At the end of the storm, when the *Hyundai* got under way again, it became evident that Twelve Fathom Strait was a misnomer—the ship ran aground in much less than 12 fathoms. As it turned out, recent earthquakes had changed many of the underwater formations in the area, and the name Twelve Fathoms wasn't up to date with what the depth had become when the vessel took shelter there.

The ship was carrying soybeans to Asia and about 750 tons of bunker fuel oil in its bottom fuel tanks. The vessel was stranded aground, and though there was no immediate report of any leakage of oil, I was called in on behalf of the Britannia Club to set up a response to a potential spill. The closest place to set up was Sand Point, which was some distance, maybe 30 miles north, from the location of the stranded vessel. Sand Point was a commercial fishing plant that had stopped operating for the season. They had various buildings that were available for our use and a landing strip. As I was the only one representing the ship there at this point, under the terms of OPA 90, I became the QI. After a bit, Bill Milwee, the ex-Navy diver I had met on the *Aquila* spill in Dos Bocas, Mexico, arrived to run the salvage. Bill went aboard the *Hyundai* to try and help break her from her strand. Doug Davis, the lawyer I had worked with on the *Exxon Valdez* spill, also played a role, first by finding me a place to stay in Sand Point. By that time Bradbury, Bliss & Riordan had been merged into a larger firm out of Long Beach, California, called Keesal, Young, and Logan, and Doug had gone with them. There was no need for a pilot on location since the fishing season was over, so Doug found a billet for me in the pilot's apartment. It was fairly good housing, with telephone communications and so forth.

Bill was housed primarily on the *Hyundai*. The operation lasted about a month, and every once and a while, Bill would have a chance to get off the ship, where living conditions were not too good, and put up with me at Sand Point. Rather than thanking me, he started ribbing me about it. Here I had the cushy job, just sitting on shore and telling everybody what to do, while he was out there sweating it out under adverse conditions. By that time, Bill and I had developed a pretty good relationship. He would go on to become a key partner in a couple of big casualties in the future, the *New Carissa* and the *Selendang Ayu*.

For the *Hyundai* casualty, we had access to a minimal number of people who could manage an oil-spill situation and assist in the response. We were chartering fishing boats to get people around. A Coast Guard cutter had been on scene from the beginning, and eventually we had two long-range cutters there as well. The Coast Guard brought down its Sea Sentry boom, stored in Kodiak, on a Coast Guard buoy tender that stood by to assist with the deployment and recovery of the boom around the *Hyundai*. The Coast Guard was treating this as a search-and-rescue operation, which required that all unnecessary crew get off the ship and that all those remaining be provided exposure suits.

Doug had arranged for us to have helicopters come down to aid in surveillance and in moving people and material around. Up until this point, we had had no sign of any oil leakage. The Coast Guard Pacific Strike Team arrived, and one of their officers worked with me to go over potential plans for responding in the event of a spill. Early one morning, around 1:00 A.M., I got a call from the Strike Team watch. A storm had come in and caused the *Hyundai* to start working on her strand. She was still aground, and with the turn of the ship on the pinnacle, or the grounding point, we began to see oil coming out of her.

The Coast Guard had wanted me to be ready to use dispersants in case of a spill, particularly in the event of a massive release. I had questioned the efficacy of using dispersants on heavy No. 6 fuel oil at the temperatures we were experiencing in October in Alaska. Now that the *Hyundai* was actively spilling oil, the Coast Guard captain requested that I go forward with plans to deploy them. I contacted Alyeska, the pipeline service company, and established that they had at the Anchorage airport a dedicated C-130, the big turboprop cargo aircraft the military uses to ferry troops and equipment. It was configured to deploy dispersant and it was available. It was 2:00 or 3:00 in the morning by this time, and we were really beginning to see oil coming out. I hadn't brought my viscosity tables with me from home (today, I carry them around in my computer, but we weren't that sophisticated yet), so I called

ITOPF in London and asked them to send me a viscosity-versus-temperature curve for No. 6 fuel oil. The fax came and I saw that there was no way that the oil that was spilled on the water was going to be anything less than semi-solid. It would not, therefore, be penetrable by dispersants. I sent a message to the captain of the port later that morning: "Captain, we've arranged for Alyeska to turn over the C-130, and we're preparing to deploy dispersants, but I'd like you to look at this viscosity curve and confirm that you still want to go that route."

The Strike Team officer asked if I really didn't think dispersants would work. I said, "Let's get some of the oil, drop it over the side, and see." I went and got a sample of the oil, which proved to be thick, practically solid. Once the Strike Team officer took a look at it, he pretty much agreed with me that the oil wasn't going to disperse at these temperatures.

That day, I started dealing with the problem of removing the bean cargo from the ship. The Strike Team had come prepared to pump the oil off the ship, but the pumps they brought were submersible hydraulically driven pumps designed to be dropped into a tanker cargo hold. On the *Hyundai*, the tanks were located on the bottom of the ship, beneath the cargo compartments, so there was no way to reach them with the pumps without jettisoning the cargo. The Strike Team had already started shoveling soybeans out of the holds and over the side manually, but that wasn't very productive, and now with the ship spilling, time was of the essence.

I had once heard that huge fans were often used to blow cargo on when loading. We figured that if you could blow it on, you could probably blow it off. Unbeknownst to me, when I had received permission to use the C-130 at Anchorage, I had started getting charged for it, so I offered it to the salvors to haul the fans from the port at Portland to Anchorage. They jumped at the offer, which worked out well for me, as I was able to get the plane that I didn't need off my books and onto theirs. Someone got the Alaska National Guard to use two of their big helicopters to bring the fans down from Anchorage and onto the *Hyundai*. I was on board the ship with the Coast Guard, who were still shoveling away, when they arrived. The first helicopter came over the horizon from Sand Point with this huge thing hanging below it, a giant grain pump swinging from a line. Two more helicopters followed, more or less in formation. We got the fans into place on the deck of the *Hyundai* and began to blow the grain overboard.

Nearly as soon as the discharge of the cargo had begun, we got an order to shut down. The word from shore was that some environmentalists had found out what we were doing and were suspicious that there might be rats in the cargo. They claimed that if we pushed the grain overboard, any possible rats on board might follow, get into the water, and swim to the islands. These nearby islands provided a large bird refuge, and the thinking was that the rats would decimate the bird population. So there we sat for two days, in October in Alaska, with our window of opportunity for saving the ship quickly narrowing. The people who were worried about the rats had no idea how we were putting the grain over, nor did they care, particularly—they just wanted to voice their concern. But the fact was, these fans worked like a turbine, and if there were any rats in there in the first place (and nobody at that point had seen any) when they came through the fan they would be diced to the point where they'd be no threat to birds. Later, I used this as an example of ill-advised interference by environmentalists. The title of the paper was "Are Environmentalists a Threat to the Environment?"

We finally sorted things out, got the fans running again, and offloaded enough cargo for the ship to be removed from her strand. We had skimmers follow the ship around to the harbor at Sand Point. The salvors had managed to stop the outflow from her, so there wasn't any substantial amount of oil-spill response needed, other than the booming of the ship. They then towed her to her final destination with her remaining cargo and, I assume, had her repaired. There was never enough damage to the ship to suggest scrapping it.

As we were winding down, I was getting all of the bills together for submission to the P&I Club and working with Doug Davis in Anchorage. Doug never ended up coming out to the site, though we were in contact almost daily by telephone. As it turned out, we never needed most of the equipment that we had called on Alyeska to provide, and we managed to get rid of the C-130 fairly early, which was a boon to our pocketbook. Doug had sent two helicopters, a single engine and a twin engine; I used the single engine for my reconnoitering, and the salvors used the twin for carrying things back and forth to the ship.

I talked to the helicopter pilot who was flying me back to Anchorage and asked if we could fly by way of Kodiak. Seven years earlier, my dear friend Marie Kelleher had died when the small plane she was flying crashed as she was preparing to land on Kodiak. Marie had overcome a great deal of fear and obstacles to become a pilot. While we had been out of touch for a couple of years by the time of the accident, I had always assumed that one day we'd be back together. I told my pilot the story and said I would like to fly over the spot, if it was possible. He was sympathetic, but he was flying a single engine and didn't want to take the chance of flying it out over the sound. With only one engine, he would have few options if we lost it, so he wanted to stay over land as much as possible.

So that was that. I knew exactly where the plane had gone down. In Alaska, this happens quite often, with bush pilots crashing here and there. Generally, the remoteness is such that they don't do much to try and retrieve the plane itself. I assumed that her plane would still be right where it was when she hit the top of that mountain.

Chapter 24

Massachusetts Maritime Academy
and Spill Response Simulation

I was back in Maryland and working out of the family cottage at Plum Point, when I got a message from what I thought was Maine Maritime Academy. I called them, and they said they hadn't called me, but maybe the Massachusetts Maritime Academy had, so I tried them. It was their president, Admiral Peter Cressy, who had called. He and their dean of students wanted to invite me to discuss setting up a Center for Marine Environmental Protection and Safety (CMEPS). Basically, their idea was to train people on the new laws and regulations in the OPA 90. They had some ideas they wanted to run by me, and wanted me to appraise a potential oil-spill simulator some Norwegians had developed. I told him it was an honor to be asked, but at that point, with my starting up GMS as an emergency response company, I didn't have the time.

Admiral Cressy and his dean, Geoffrey Mott, were persistent. They wanted me to come up just for a talk. The Coast Guard had offered the Academy money to set up something along the lines of the Norwegian simulator as well as some funds to help start training for OPA 90. He couldn't move forward without some advice. I finally agreed and flew up to Providence, where Geoffrey Mott picked me up and drove me out to the Academy. A lot of the presidents of the maritime academies have the title of admiral as an honorific, but Admiral Cressy was actually a retired Navy Rear Admiral. He was quite a fireball. He and Dean Mott laid out what they wanted. Again, I explained that I was trying to build GMS, and had little extra time. But they kept asking, saying, "Would you just go to Norway to look at the oil-spill simulator?" until eventually I gave in.

In Oslo, I went to the SFT, which is the Norwegian Federal Environmental Agency. The SFT had a training system that used a sand table, a standard way of training that dated from the pre-computer days. But their neighbor in Oslo was a company that manufactured training simulators for ships, so SFT asked if they could come up with one that would simulate oil spills. Their idea was to create a visual simulator that could be used by various participants in a spill. The teachers would manipulate the spill, and the trainees would be required to react based on the way the spill evolved. I was quite impressed with it. Not only did it provide the ability to organize the training simulation, but you could also add a degree of realism that heretofore had been lacking in the relatively sterile scenarios normally used. As I have written, I have always preferred as much realism as possible when training.

When I returned from Norway, I went back to MMA to see Admiral Cressy and Mott. After I gave them my recommendation, they said, "So, are you coming with us?" They wanted me to be the director of a new program, Marine Environmental Protection and Safety, with the Norwegian simulator as its centerpiece. Again I told them I just didn't have time, to which Admiral Cressy and Mott's responded, "We've talked this over. What if we let you bring somebody with you. That way, you'll have a back-up to take over if you have a spill and must go suddenly."

By that point, at the behest of his brother-in-law, Bob Driscoll, I had succeeded in getting David Barry out of academia. Since GMS wasn't actually a working entity yet, David had continued working for Cindy Hudson, which wasn't a long-term solution, as history had repeatedly shown. David had his B.S. in chemical engineering, his master's degree in environmental engineering, and now he had some real spill experience. So I proposed him as my assistant director, and Admiral Cressy and Mott accepted. With that in place, I agreed to come to MMA. Admiral Cressy and Mott turned to each other and shook hands when I gave them the news. They told me that, in their minds at least, it was never a question of whether I was coming—it was *when* I would come.

In the beginning, we got a lot of assistance from former MMA students who worked with the American Bureau of Shipping (ABS) in Houston. They were very anxious to see MMA get into the spill response training business. The person behind the interest was Frank Iarossi—the former head of Exxon shipping who headed up ABS at time. This was after the *Exxon Valdez*, and Frank had been the chief of the Exxon fleet when the accident occurred. As the president of Exxon Shipping, he was an obvious target of animosity for just about everybody up there in the early phases of the spill. I never met him formally during the incident, but when I met him at MMA, he said he knew who I was from seeing me around the command center during the response in Valdez. He told me, "I noticed you were often in critical places and that you kept your mouth shut, so I made it my business to find out who you were and what you were up to."

Frank liked the idea of a training center for prepping students about spills. With the MMA alums leading, he decided to formulate a reserve of Qualified Individuals within ABS and he wanted our newly formed Center for Marine Environmental Protection and Safety to create a course to train them. ABS offered financial help, along with Mobil and some other oil companies. We agreed that the first two classes we would teach at the Center for Marine Environmental Protection and Safety would be offered solely to ABS investigators for the purpose of creating the qualified individual corps, which they could then market to the industry. So we based our courses on what the investigators wanted to see and what they needed to know. We launched our first course in 1992.

David and I had a lot of wonderful experiences during the ten years that we ran the Center for Marine Environmental Protection and Safety at MMA. In the end, we were able to manage the program and build GMS at the same time pretty effectively, with each benefitting the other. For example, when David was running the *Bouchard Barge 120* spill in 2003, as the response moved down the Massachusetts coast, the command center moved with it, and its second stop was MMA. We ran an actual spill response in a place where we were usually teaching them theoretically.

Likewise, during the *New Carissa* response in 1999, whenever David or I left the spill to go back to the center, we'd bring with us media documenting the spill response as it was actually going on. The connection between the field operations and the coursework really enriched the program. There were several direct benefits for GMS as well. Shipping companies were sending their people to the center, and those who studied with us were impressed with what we were doing and how we were doing it. As a result, a number of these companies ended up hiring us as their Qualified Individuals and spill managers. Those interested were mostly foreign-flag firms who needed to have people in the United States, and we fit the bill. They liked us and helped us build the company's size and reputation. This wasn't the purpose of our involvement with the center, but it was a happy result.

Another thing that benefitted both GMS and the Center for Marine Environmental Protection and Safety was the work we did with the Norwegian simulator. At first, to work on the simulator, you needed to go to Buzzards Bay. After word about it spread, we had a request from the Coast Guard to do some simulation training in New York Harbor. We wanted the simulator to be part of that, so, in those very early days of the Internet, we learned how to use the simulator remotely. Pretty quickly, we were able to transmit our simulations from the mainframe at MMA to New York and, eventually, as far as Alaska, where we did remote simulation training for Alyeska, the company that runs the terminal in Valdez. A funny thing about the training we did for Alyeska was that they always had us go in the winter. Finally, I asked them why they never had us go up there in the summer, when it was warm. They said it was "because things are slow in winter, and we like to see people from the outside."

Soon we had acquired the capability to run the simulations over the Internet anywhere in the world (we even took it to Singapore once on behalf of MMA). We used to watch students in the mock command center over closed-circuit television during drills. One day, we had a Coast Guard officer who was assigned as the telephone operator to take the incoming calls. This Coast Guard officer took a call and we could see that he was getting increasingly agitated, to the point where he started banging his fist on the desk. He finally slammed down the phone, looked around the command center, and said: "I didn't know the Coast Guard could be such a pain in the ass!" That was the kind of realistic scenario we were providing. From our standpoint, we were creating the sense of urgency that comes in a real spill, when your stomach sinks as you realize that you don't know how bad it is or how much worse it can get. I'd seen people freeze in drills and knew it was better to get through that in your training; you need to know how it feels, because on a real spill, it is very likely to happen.

After Admiral Cressy left MMA, there was a period of uncertainty, which was resolved when the MMA appointed as its president former Rear Admiral Maurice J. Bresnahan, who had been commander of the 7th Fleet in the Pacific before he retired from the Navy. He was an alumnus of the MMA as well. He and I got along. He had big plans for expanding our program internationally. Sadly, Admiral Bresnahan developed brain cancer and died in 2004, which was a big loss for the MMA and a disaster for our center. The new administration, which I believe did a lot of good for the Academy, unfortunately wasn't interested much in the center. The funding dried up, and the Norwegian simulator became the property of the computer-science department. They didn't know what to do with it. That spelled the end of our involvement. David and I have gone back to the Academy from time to time, when asked to give talks, but since the academics took over, interest in the center has petered out. My ten years there were wonderful, and it worked out well for us. David Barry and I are still supportive to MMA whenever asked, and perhaps someday will work with MMA to establish and support future industry training for managing and responding to oil spills. I still think it's the best way to train people.

Jack after receiving an Honorary Doctorate from Massachusetts Maritime Academy

Chapter 25

Richard Kingston and the Borrowed Swim Trunks

In August of 1993, the *Balsa 37*, a dry cargo ship loaded with phosphate rock, was outbound in Mullet Key Channel, Tampa Bay, Florida when it collided with the *Ocean 255*, one of two inbound-towed barges, causing an immediate explosion and fire of the *Ocean 255* cargo of jet fuel. Within a minute or so later, the *Ocean 255* and the second barge, *Bouchard 155*, loaded with No. 6 fuel oil, collided. The *Bouchard 155* was holed in the port side and began spilling oil into the bay. I was asked to monitor the response operation on behalf of the *Balsa*, which was insured by one of the P&I Clubs that I had a continuing relationship with.

The evening of the spill, I went down to Tampa. The casualty impact covered quite an area, and the Marine Safety Office had closed the port. The ship had gone aground near the point of the casualty, but the barges, particularly the one that was on fire, had started drifting in the harbor. The fire on *Ocean* was burning quite spectacularly. There was no real situs for responding to the casualty when I first got there, so I set up an office in a hotel room on St. Petersburg Beach, above the entrance to the harbor, where oil was starting to come ashore in large amounts. I got in touch with the Coast Guard and was recognized as a contributing entity to the casualty. They still hadn't developed a Unified Command, so the captain of the port essentially ran the whole operation from his office.

There were also representatives there from the two companies involved with the barges. One was the Bouchard

Barge Company, for the *Bouchard 155*, and the other was Maritrans, which owned the barge that had caught fire. This became a large and highly visible operation, and there was quite a bit of television and press. My instructions were simply to monitor the operation and the casualty, concentrating on the *Balsa*. The *Balsa* was aground but not otherwise severely damaged. She had some hull damage, but nothing that would cause her to discharge oil, and her salvage operation was concentrated on getting her off her strand and into port, where she could be repaired. I had no oil-spill responsibility to cover for the *Balsa*.

The attorneys for the other vessels, the barges, however, tried to collar me into getting involved in directing the operation of the oil-spill cleanup. I said to one, an Irish attorney from one of the major firms in New York, whom I knew very well, "Gene, you know that OPA 90 requires that the vessel spilling the oil take total responsibility for the cleanup." I told him that I didn't want to intrude on his territory, so he backed off, but he's kidded me about the way I was able to avoid directing that spill ever since.

I took care of the requirements as far as the ship was concerned, helping to get the salvors and monitoring the salvage operation as it proceeded. I was also trying to keep track of the size of the spill, where the oil was going, and what was actually happening to the oil as the casualty progressed. The P&I Club needed to know about the potential liability cost for that. Even though the vessel spilling was responsible for the response, anyone found culpable in a multi-vessel collision was potentially liable for cleanup expenses in the final assessment.

As you will remember, during my very first oil spill, in the Potomac, I had set up a command center in my friend Richard Kingston's boat stationed in Alexandria. It turned out that, in the intervening years, Richard had finally exhausted his welcome in most of the marinas in the Washington, D.C., area, as well as the Potomac and the Chesapeake Bay, and had decided to move to Florida, where he was not as well known. Richard had been in AA for a long time, but during my entire sobriety, he continued to drink, from time to time coming to a meeting to try to get sober again. One of the leading guys in AA in Washington at the time was a fellow by the name of Skip Barclay. He was a B-17 pilot in World War II, was shot down by a German bi-plane, and spent the rest of the war as a prisoner of war in a German prison. Skip had an impressive way of making statements, with his deep, bass growl. Richard had a great ability to imitate people, and he particularly used to enjoy imitating Skip. One day, Richard was at a party imitating Skip, when Skip walked in and overheard. Skip interrupted Richard, saying, "Listen, Kingston, I wish the thing I could get you to imitate was you getting sober."

Richard had some success staying on the program, however, and moved to Clearwater, just above Tampa, bringing his boat with him. I had talked to him a couple of times since he had been there, and when I called and said, "Richard, how would you like to do another spill for me?" he jumped at the chance.

What I needed was to go out and look at the harbor entrance to see where the collision had taken place. By then, the scene was clear, but I wanted to get some idea of what the approach looked like. The collision was around Egmont Key, with the two tows in-bound just as the *Balsa* was coming out of the harbor. It was apparent to me that barges and the *Balsa* couldn't see each other as they approached, because the island, though it wasn't that big itself, it had enough palm trees on it to hamper a visual connection. The ships were in radio contact, but I understood that there was no particular knowledge on the *Balsa* about the configuration of the two tows. So the rest is history, with the *Ocean 255* first colliding with the *Balsa*, and then subsequently with the *Bouchard 155*.

Richard sailed down to Tampa and picked me up, along with an attorney who was also working for the P&I Club on the *Balsa*. I wanted to go out, have a look at the island and survey the beach there. I had cleared our visit with the captain of the port in advance, but when we got out to the island and approached the pilot's dock to land, someone came out and told us we couldn't dock there. It was against the law, he said. I told him what we were doing, and he said, "I don't care. It doesn't matter what you are doing. You're going to need another way to get on the island."

We backed off and went out in the channel. I said to Richard, "Why don't you see if we can get in close enough to swim?" Richard had been a swimmer in college, and if he'd stayed sober, he could probably have made the Olympic team, but he hadn't, though he did continue to swim. He had bathing suits on board, but only the Tarzan trunks that competitive swimmers use. I put a pair on, as did the attorney. They were not very decorous and not the sort of thing that I like to wear. In any event, we swam ashore. We were walking the beach, looking at what oil that was there, when along came a dune buggy with three people on it. One was the federal park ranger. The other two were cameramen from a local television station. The park ranger pulled over and asked us what we were doing. I told him we were representing the ship and were examining the beach, looking for evidence. The ranger asked if we had any authority to be there, and I said that we had cleared it through the Coast Guard, but he started giving us a hard time anyway. Meanwhile, the cameramen had started filming us, and I thought, as we stood there dressed in nothing but these skimpy swimsuits,

"Good God, if our clients see us doing this, they'll really wonder what the hell they're paying us for."

That was just one of the many little things that came up during that operation. The response went at a fairly rapid pace, though it took quite a while for those responsible to get the necessary forces involved. The oil continued to come ashore at St. Petersburg Beach, where I was staying. I remember going down there early one morning and standing on the beach, looking back and forth, and finding black as far as I could see, both north and south. To my surprise, I happened to notice a blue heron not 20 feet from me, standing in the same posture as I was and looking at the oil in the same way I was looking at it, and I realized that the wildfowl had been heavily impacted as well.

The response carried on for some time. The responsibility for the spill response went to the barges, to Marispond, the oil-spill arm of Maritrans, in particular, though Bouchard had a share. Marispond seemed to have the lead in the meetings with the Coast Guard. Coincidentally, many years later, GMS bought Marispond. It is now part of our operation, and one of our leading incident commanders is the man who served as incident commander on the *Ocean* spill, Howard Hile. Howard was a great addition to GMS. He is semi-retired now, living in Western Canada, where he handles a lot of the major and minor operations on that coast. He was the principal responder to the *Selendang Ayu* and the incident commander on the three-year operation that that turned into. Howard, in a way, is an unusual personality in our business, in that he's fairly quiet. As a matter of fact, for some of the spills that we had Howard on, when he was in charge of a noisy command center, we would set up a special routine for when he needed to get people's attention: he would ring a bell to get everybody to quiet down so that he could make an announcement.

The *Balsa* operation continued for two or three months, or at least my input in it did. As far as the ship was concerned, our client came out of the affair responsible for a share of the liability, solely on account of apportionment based on three parties having been involved.

Chapter 26

Gallagher Marine Systems: First Clients

Jeffrey White was a nuclear engineer who had worked for Admiral Hyman George Rickover during the introduction of nuclear submarines into the U.S. Navy and had subsequently established a very successful engineering company. Jeffrey was also an alcoholic, and we met when he joined AA in Washington, D.C., after he had been expelled from his company by his board of directors due to his problems with alcohol. I witnessed his recovery from alcoholism after entering AA and followed his development of an entirely new company that prospered to the extent that it was bought by a much larger company that made him president of that concern. After several years in that position, Jeffrey retired with a golden parachute. Fortuitously, as I was founding Gallagher Marine Systems, Jeffrey willingly agreed to form a board of directors as chairman for my nascent business.

The next thing I knew, I had a board that included the former president of General Dynamics and the former secretary of the Navy. Jeffrey was a tremendous guy, and he helped build GMS into what it became.

One of our first clients was named Peter Cooney. Peter was based in Glasgow and was running a shipping company there. Peter said to me, "I know you're just starting up, so I want to send you all your retainers in advance." That was part of the front money that got us started, and that relationship went very well for a long time, until another company gobbled up Peter's money. At first, I was still running things out of my family's

236

beach cottage at Plum Point, but when I began to hire people, I opened what would be our second office, on the waterfront in Annapolis, Maryland. It was a one-room office with only three chairs. When clients came, one of us would have to get up so our guest would have a place to sit down. Next, we moved to a much larger office, on North Fairfax Street in Alexandria, Virginia. There were a lot more people by that time. We had brought in a retired Navy captain, Charles Maclin, to be our president. He had been the supervisor of salvage for the Navy before he retired. With that experience, he was a great addition to the company and someone very qualified to become the president, while I assumed the position of chief executive officer.

Jack at Gallagher Marine Systems office in Washington, D.C.

Within a year, we moved again to an even larger Alexandria location, about a block away on Slaters Lane. In May 1996, we engaged in our first sizeable spill as GMS: the motor tanker *Anitra*, a French-flagged ship en route for the Big Stone anchorage off the shore of Delaware. Big Stone anchorage is a place where lightering operations are conducted for larger tankers so that they can bring their draft up and discharge the rest of their cargo directly into refineries in the upper parts of the Delaware River. The *Anitra* had anchored at Big Stone preparatory and was awaiting barges that were coming down from the refinery where the cargo was destined. While the crew was exercising the pumping gear, they had an overboard discharge of oil from their engine room into the Delaware Bay. We received a call for assistance.

One of the first problems was that the ship was essentially still at sea. She was sufficiently offshore that there was no way to board her quickly in order to determine what was going on. Our communications with the ship were by radiotelephone, and it seemed to be a relatively minor spill at first. We did not detect any large amount of oil going into the water; it was just an off-and-on leakage through the overboard discharge vent. The problem was finding what was causing the leak and making sure that we had resources lined up to deal with it if it became a greater problem. Most of all, we needed a chance to get a firsthand investigation of the situation.

There was a Delaware Bay Cooperative station located near Big Stone. The co-op covered the whole area of the Delaware Bay for the owners of the surrounding refineries. They had some large skimmers and equipment for dealing with open-water operations, so we had them on standby to respond if that was necessary. As Qualified Individual and spill management team for the *Anitra*, under the terms of OPA 90, it was our responsibility to call the contracted Oil Spill Response Organization, or OSRO, and to direct them, while also coordinating with the Coast Guard and state agencies on any required response. We didn't have any idea how big the spill was at that point, but it seemed to be a relatively minor event that could be handled from aboard the ship. There were no serious reports of oil in the bay, but there was some oil around the ship, and we dispatched the OSRO for that.

Our client had also contracted with an outfit that used the acronym NRC. After this spill, I talked to National Response Corporation about their acronym, telling them that if someone got confused, thinking that contacting them was the same as notifying the Federal Government's National Response Center in Washington, another requirement under OPA 90, we could have a serious problem. National Response Corporation refused to stop using the acronym NRC, suggesting instead, oddly, that GMS change its acronym. So we began referring to National Response Corporation as Narco, and have used that name in all our communication since.

The information we were receiving in bits and pieces was making it increasingly clear that the situation was becoming more serious. The spill was continuing at an unspecified rate. There wasn't a lot of oil flowing, but the discharge was continuous. I then received a report that the ferry between Lewes, Delaware, and Cape May, New Jersey, had spotted oil along its route. Now we really needed to find out what was going on. Our offices were only about two miles from Reagan National Airport, so I went down and chartered a plane to fly up to Delaware to get a first-hand look at the situation. I also asked the charter company to arrange for a helicopter to meet us there so I could take some flights over the shore, over the ship itself, and over the waters in between them to get a better idea of what we were dealing with. When I got up in the helicopter, I was able to see that there was a substantial amount of oil coming out of the *Anitra*. It was entering the water and it was moving along the shoreline inside the bay and out toward the tip of Cape May.

This was in 1996, during the spring, when the terns from the Antarctic migrate to the Northern Arctic, making a single refueling stop—in the Delaware Bay. Similarly, every year at this time, the horseshoe crab, which is really more akin to a turtle than a crab, visits the Delaware Bay and deposits its eggs on the beach. These phenomena attract nature watchers from all over the world. All of this was happening at exactly the same time as the *Anitra* was steadily leaking thousands of gallons of crude oil into the middle of the bay. This immediately increased the spill's visibility. Of course, to us at the time, it was a very large spill because it was our first spill, but now we also had the attention of the media and the surrounding state governments. The governor of New Jersey started holding press conferences on the status of the spill, and our French client decided to send a company representative from France to join the show.

That's when I turned out the firehouse. Oil was continually moving along the Delaware and New Jersey shorelines toward the beaches there. We were coming up on Memorial Day and the opening of beach season. We set up in motel rooms on the Delaware shore and then moved over across to Cape May, New Jersey, moving our communications and organization. It was no small job moving ourselves around, but we had to keep ahead of the spill, anticipating where it was going as it made the turn around Cape May and began to travel up the Jersey Shore on the ocean side. There was a lot of pressure on us. There was one small benefit in the timing along the shoreline, however. The mayors of the towns along the way had so much invested in the summer season that they didn't want too much adverse information to get out. They tried to keep the press down and were also very supportive of our efforts to make sure we got things cleaned up in time. Those were the forces working in our favor on the cleanup operation. The oil eventually made it all the way to near Atlantic City.

Our company president, Chuck Maclin, was schooled in salvage, and we used him to good advantage. He was able to get on board the ship, check the engine room, and identify the problem causing the overboard discharge. Chuck worked on the ship for a couple of days and was instrumental in helping them correct problems on board. Once the oil spilling through the discharge was stopped, the attention shifted to dealing with the spill response. The Delaware Bay resources were at work in the open water. Narco was involved under our direction. There was some skimming going on around the vessel, with some Narco and Cooperative equipment. When the oil hit on the eastern shore of the bay, it was the same beach where a local contractor not affiliated with Narco was doing some drill work. They were in the process of removing their equipment when I learned of them, and I turned them around and had them start picking up the oil that had struck on the beach there. It was lucky they were there, because it would have taken some time for Narco to get their equipment to the scene.

The spill went on for quite a while. The representative from the French shipping company that owned the *Anitra* and I arranged for him to speak with the governor, Christine Todd Whitman. The shipping company representative also participated with Governor Whitman in one of her press conferences. Everything went well. Interestingly, Governor Whitman went on to become secretary of the Environmental Protection Agency.

The Atlantic coast of New Jersey is made up of a series of barrier islands, and between those islands there were generally streams flowing back into the bays behind. One New Jersey environmental group had decided that there was a particular stream that they wanted blocked off with boom, and one man from the New Jersey state government was especially insistent that this be done. We examined the request and realized that the stream was one of the tidal feeds to the bay behind it. Although the flow at slack and ebb tides was not very great, it was extremely strong at flood and outgoing tides. As you might recall from the boom I helped with in Saudi Arabia, oil booms cannot withstand direct flow of over a knot or so without underflow. The current going through there at peak ebb and flow was so great that no boom could stand up to it. We knew that we couldn't keep a boom across it; there was simply no way it would work.

We told the man from the New Jersey government the problem. He said that the Marine Spill Response Corporation (MSRC), a major oil-spill response company owned by oil companies, had done a study of this site and determined that it could be protected with booms. Some time later, I met the salvage engineer who had done the survey for this man while working for MSRC as their salvage advisor. "Well, I didn't tell him that it could be boomed off the way he wanted it," the engineer told me. "I told him we could put booms in the ocean approaches to the stream to deflect oil. But we didn't tell him anything about putting the boom across the stream itself." Of course, I didn't know any of this at the time.

I decided to invite the official to join me in a survey of the stream. We took a boat down to the site, but I made sure that we went during high flood, when the water was flowing through very hard. If you've never seen a flood tide moving through one of these passes, it can really be impressive. I started to turn the boat into the stream itself when he chickened out. "I can see what you are talking about without going any further in there," he told me. I don't think he wanted to risk getting swamped. The official piped down quite a bit after that, though he did continue to grouse about it. When the response was over, he had pretty much come around to our side, as he had realized that we knew what we were doing.

Chapter 27

The Bottom of the World

Some of the more exotic work I ever did came as a result of a request by some students who had been sent to our course at the Massachusetts Maritime Academy from the National Science Foundation base in Antarctica. After completing the course, they asked if David Barry and I could come down and survey their operations at the Pole and assist them in drawing up response plans for their facilities there. Unfortunately, due to the timing and other responsibilities, David was unavailable, so we turned to someone who worked on spills for us from time to time, Erich Gundlach, to accompany me to Antarctica. At first, it seemed like just an adventure, but upon doing some preliminary research, we recognized the seriousness of their needs. The storage, use, and handling of oil at the various installations in the Antarctic is crucial. Oil is the lifeblood of the installations, which can be unreachable from the outside for months at a time.

Erich and I both underwent extensive medical exams before leaving for Antarctica, because it would be difficult to get medical assistance at the more remote places on the continent that we were to visit. This was in January of 1999. After both of us checked out, we were deployed to Christchurch, New Zealand, where there is a station that oversees much of the Antarctic operations of the National Science Foundation. We spent about a week in New Zealand, getting equipped with the gear we would need to survive the conditions we would be experiencing and being trained for the dangers that lurked in Antarctica for every visitor. Once we had completed all our requirements, we put aboard a New York Air National Guard

C–130 and flew down to McMurdo Station for further training. These planes perform similar services for U.S. operations in Greenland and Alaska in the northern winters.

At McMurdo, we were barracked in regular quarters with attached messing facilities much like you would find on a military base. We had a group of Russians come through on their way out to their stations. They were with us for several days, and it was quite a circus with their horsing around. There was nothing untoward, but there was a fair amount of intoxication. Erich and I began to learn the importance of good health and proper training. There were three major aspects to maintaining one's health down there: the first was water—we needed to carry water and hydrate regularly due to the dryness of the air; the second was temperature—we needed the proper clothing against the harsh conditions; and the third was handling the altitude—McMurdo was at sea level, so altitude was not an issue there, but once we got inland, we were going to be crossing extremely mountainous areas.

The mountainous areas of Antarctica are covered, for the most part, by a glacier with a thickness of nearly 10,000 feet. Further, due to the perpetually low barometric pressure there, caused by the rotation of the earth, 10,000 feet can feel at times like nearly 13,000 feet. If you've never felt it, 13,000 feet can be quite something. We were warned in great detail about the dangers associated with altitude sickness as part of our training at McMurdo. Fortunately, I managed not to suffer any serious altitude-related symptoms. When we finally got to the Pole, however, some of my traveling companions were incapacitated for a day or so.

Once we had settled in, Erich and I began to survey the facilities at McMurdo Station, which included oil-storage facilities, machine shops, and multiple airfields for different seasons. To begin, we went through the contingency plans that had been developed initially by the NSF years before. Since then, there had been significant changes in the station. For example, the Seabees, the U.S. Navy Construction Battalion, had built the initial fuel tanks at McMurdo in the 1950s, when the camp was first established. The complex and its oil storage had since grown, and now the station was required to meet OPA 90 standards, just as if it were located in the States. Our job was to survey all the tanks and help the power-plant managers upgrade their contingency plans to ensure that it became a conforming oil-storage facility.

Erich and I were there for a good part of the month and got to see the refueling tanker come in and hook up to load the new tanks for their first use. We went on board the ship as it was pumping oil ashore and examined the procedures both aboard and onshore. A Coast Guard ice breaker created a path in when the tanker came into the pier, stood by for the entire offloading, and broke another path for the tanker when it was time to leave. It became obvious to me that we had been brought down not just to survey the station but also to be on hand for a response should anything have gone wrong. It was pretty clever of them. Once the tanker finished its discharge and left, it was followed by a dry cargo ship carrying supplies for the forthcoming winter as well as the summer that would follow. Members of the New Zealand Army came down with the ship, having been contracted by the NSF to assist with the offloading of the supplies and equipment. Once the ship had its cargo ashore, the army stevedores reversed course, loading back on the freighter all the waste that had been generated in the past winter and summer cycle. The international laws governing the continent require that all such waste be removed by whichever country generates it, and McMurdo Station is the largest installation of its type on the continent.

One of the trips that I took with Erich on the continent was to what the personnel there described as a remote site. When I first heard the term, I thought it was funny—everywhere down there, to my mind, was remote. At this particular site, they were drilling into the glacial cover in a place where the glacier was very deep. The idea was to drill until they hit rock and then to retrieve sections of what they had drilled into. By correlating each section to the historical period in which it had been formed, they would be able to track how the atmospheric contents had changed over time. By coincidence, when I got back from that trip, I learned that they had in fact struck rock on the day I was there. Thus, I had made it just in time, as that was the end of their work at this "remote" site. Of course, they still had to analyze the ice in the laboratory, but as far as the drilling was concerned, they were finished for the season.

The next project in Antarctica for both Erich and me was to go to the South Pole Station and upgrade the contingency plans there. The first interesting thing that I noticed on arrival was that, rather than refueling, our plane proceeded to offload fuel to the station. The refueling went in the opposite direction, as turned out to be the case for all flights out of McMurdo Station. Every time one of the C-130s went out to any of the stations, including the remote one that was doing the drilling, one of their jobs was to top off the fuel tanks. The South Pole Station had recently completed the installation of a whole new fuel-tank system as part of a major renovation. This new tank arrangement was of great interest to us, and we spent a lot of time studying it. Interestingly, there had been at least two previous South Pole observation centers at the site, each of which now lay buried under wind-driven snow. The most recent center was built on stilts above the snow level to protect it from the winter drifts.

While at the South Pole, we also had other missions, such as walking around the world by circling the South Pole marker. As it was summer, it was daylight 24 hours a day, with the sun just circling around at a regular distance from the horizon. It was difficult to tell what time it was or which shift was on. They ran a 24-hour schedule, and there were people working both when we were awake and when we were asleep. Time itself was confusing. We had every time zone in the world there—an anomaly that was interesting to think about.

The accommodations were called "summer camps." However, there was a small contingent of hearty souls who overwintered at the station. In fact, a unique incident happened after we got back to the States and the Antarctic winter had begun. A doctor who was there with the winter team that had come in while we were at the Pole developed symptoms of breast cancer. She was the only physician for the winter maintenance group. She did a biopsy on herself, but it was inconclusive, because the materials at the station were so outdated. The NSF made a risky airdrop of medicine and materials, flying a C-141 out of Christchurch over the Pole. Using the material from that drop, another biopsy was performed. Some of the scuttlebutt among people I knew who were involved was that the doctor picked the team electrician to perform it on her. It showed that the cancer was critical. NSF ended up sending a plane in weeks earlier than usual that spring to get her out. It had never been done before that early at the Pole, and it was a pretty hairy thing to do. The possibility of losing the plane and the crew coming to get the doctor was strong, but they were able to get in, pick her up, and get out without incident. She did recover, as I understand it, though the cancer came back ten years later, tragically.

On a lighter note, one thing I did while I was at the Pole was grow a beard. Everybody down there wore them, so I grew a South Pole beard myself, and wore it until just recently.

PART VII

GALLAGHER MARINE SYSTEMS ARRIVES:

BIG SPILLS AROUND THE GLOBE

Chapter 28

The *New Carissa*

On February 3, 1999, the *New Carissa*, a purpose-built woodchip carrier bound for Coos Bay, Oregon, to load cargo, was prevented from entering port by rough seas on the entrance bar of the bay. She hove to and anchored off the coast to ride out the weather. The next morning, the storm intensified. Winds began gusting to force 8, accompanied by very high breaking waves. The *New Carissa* dragged anchor and was driven aground.

She was carrying an estimated 359,000 gallons of heavy fuel oil and 37,400 gallons of diesel oil on board when she stranded. As one of the worst potential spills ever to hit the Oregon coast, the stranding got immediate and extensive media attention.

The Britannia P&I Club underwriters contacted me early that morning. I had just returned from my trip to Antarctica and was preparing to travel to London for planned meetings with Britannia. I told Britannia I would change my travel direction from east to west to respond to the casualty, and they agreed.

Meanwhile, David Barry was already on his way to the West Coast for a meeting, and upon landing in California, learned about the grounding and took the next flight to Portland and then to Coos Bay. Bill Milwee, our Qualified Individual and salvage master in Portland, Oregon, was also en transit to Coos Bay and arrived around the same time as David. They began coordinating standby resources using the local oil spill coop, and later that afternoon, David drove the SMIT salvage team to the beach where they started to make their initial assessment of the situation. At that time, the vessel appeared stable and SMIT was hopeful that she could be refloated.

Over the next few days, with northwest storm winds unabated and the ship subjected to continuous pounding on the high-energy lee shore, the *New Carissa* was driven further aground. She was upright, partially broached, and hard aground 1,000 feet from the tideline. After three days of such continuous pounding, the first observations of serious structural damage were being reported. We started seeing signs that her oil tanks were penetrated and oil was coming out of her.

On February 8, the salvage tug *Salvage Chief* was unable, in the rough seas and surf, to maneuver close enough to attempt to pull *New Carissa* from her strand. The next day, a transverse crack 10 to 15 feet long was found to have formed in the ship's starboard hull. Further, a rudderpost had displaced, causing flooding in the steering room. Next, the engine room flooded suddenly. What had been our goal up to that point, removing the *New Carissa* from her stand with her nearly 400,000 gallons of fuel still aboard, was effectively scuttled. Getting the *New Carissa* away as an intact structure was now impossible. Duly, the hull underwriters declared the *New Carissa* a constructive total loss, and our salvage operation became a wreck-removal operation.

Under GMS direction, cleanup crews began working on the beach. I expected to see an additional two or three hundred more personnel from West Coast Oil Spill Response Organizations arrive by the end of the day. I also established the Unified Command, as dictated by the terms of the Incident Command System, or ICS. The ICS is a result of OPA 90 and mandates that a "Unified Command" be established by the responding organization in cooperation with the Coast Guard captain of the port for the area, a state oil-spill response official, and a representative of the so-called responsible party, the entity from which the spill emanates. The representative of the responsible party must have sufficient authority to bind its owners to the decisions of the Unified Command, and the state oil-spill response official must have the authority to enact the decisions of the Unified Command.

(Photo U.S. Coast Guard)

New Carissa

One of my innovations at GMS was to create a system for owners who did not have personnel stationed in the United States to serve immediately as their representatives or Qualified Individuals under OPA 90. GMS would provide that service to owners by contract to ensure immediate compliance with the rules. Even though, at the time of the *New Carissa* casualty, OPA 90 rules only applied to tankers, not to dry cargo ships such as the *New Carissa*, Britannia had established a contract with GMS to cover all of their member shipowners as Qualified Individual and salvage master if needed. This would ensure that OPA 90 service their vessels, regardless of the OPA 90 applicability. Other P&I Clubs would eventually follow suit with similar provisions, though not, to our disappointment, all with GMS as their contractor. Eventually, OPA 90 was amended to include non-tankers as well.

Further complicating the casualty was the realization that this was a prime habitat for the western snowy plover, an endangered species. With the ship rapidly showing signs of breaking up, plans were developed through the Unified Command for a controlled burn of the fuel and diesel oil that we knew to be on board. The plan was to blow open the tops of the double-bottom fuel tank with shaped charges. Once exposed, the detonation team would ignite the contents of the bunkers with explosives in jellied gasoline, or Napalm. The Napalm drums were to be deployed by the U.S. Navy Explosive Ordinance Delivery Teams from Washington State.

The first attempt went dismally. However, on February 12, the Navy tried it again, this time with sufficient explosive charges to open those tank tops and expose the bunkers. The result was a spectacular and substantial success. Almost complete combustion was realized in the double bottom tanks that had been breached in the stranding. But, although an estimated 200,000 gallons of bunkers were successfully eliminated in the burn operation, another 100,000 to 150,000 gallons of bunkers were still estimated to remain on board the bow section. Worse, during the burn, the bow section of the vessel had separated from the flooded stern section and drifted some 150 yards away, dragging the bow anchors deployed by the salvage gang before abandoning the ship for the burn. Although separation of the bow and stern sections coincided with the burn, the parting of these two sections was inevitable. The fatal fracture in the hull structure had broken her back, and the stresses imposed on the hull by the scouring sea removed uniform support from beneath the vessel, ensuring complete rupture.

By February 17, SMIT Salvage had developed a removal strategy for the bow section. The Unified Command approved it and preparations began. The plan was to remove the intact bow section from its strand and tow it to sea, where it would be scuttled in deep water. Due to the shallowness of the strand, however, the tug *Sea Victory* could not work in close enough to the wreck. It was decided that we would need a special hawser, one of sufficient length and suitable strength, to make the hook up and the tow. However, the only hawser known to have the required characteristics was a specially designed Dyneema fiber cable, available only in Australia and Europe. We had no choice. SMIT purchased 3,200 feet of ten-inch Dyneema in four 800-foot segments from the European source and had it delivered to Oregon by chartered air cargo.

Meanwhile, heavy storm seas continued to impact the bow section, driving it further aground and closer to the beach. As we awaited the arrival of the towing hawser from Europe, it became possible to work the bow section of the wreck from the beach. Because the threat of continued breakup was imminent, I concurred with a proposal by the Coast Guard Strike Team to attempt a lightering of as much of the remaining bunker fuel from the double-bottom tanks as possible. Since no vessel could conceivably approach the wreck from the seaward, the lightering would need to be done from ashore. We helicopter-lifted eight 21,000-gallon Baker tanks over the dunes and set them up.

(Photo U.S. Coast Guard)

New Carissa

Essentially, we built a temporary oil-storage facility. Our plan was to use Coast Guard submersible hydraulic pumps to move the oil from the double-bottom tanks via a high-line transfer hose shoreside to the Baker tanks. We also called in pumps from Dave Usher's Marine Pollution Control (MPC) to serve as a backup pumping capability. The MPC pumps had boilers and heating coils, which would help in pumping the bunker fuel, which we suspected would be practically solid by this point.

On February 20, we commenced around-the-clock pumping of the double-bottom fuel tanks. It continued for two days, when a pump burnout ended pumping operations. The total volume pumped was reported at approximately 130,000 gallons of oily water. After decanting, this amounted to less than 250 gallons of oil. Given that, by our estimates, there might be as much as 150,000 gallons of oil still aboard the wreck, the pumping effort had been a failure. While we had the MPC pumps available to attempt pumping with heat, the window of opportunity for that had closed—the towing hawser had arrived.

With the towing hawser on site, preparations began for removing the bow section from its strand. The hawser was flaked out behind the sand dunes, and the *Sea Victory* assumed position offshore to receive it. A helicopter lifted one end of the hawser from the shore and carried it to the bow section, where it was attached. The helicopter then delivered the other end to the *Sea Victory*, waiting offshore. It took four days of constant pulling, but finally, the bow section came off its strand. As planned, the *Sea Victory* began the tow toward the agreed upon scuttling site, some 200 miles offshore. However, the drama of this casualty was far from over.

In the early morning of March 2, the *Sea Victory* began to encounter hurricane-force winds. Consequently, she was required to begin steering a best course to ride out the weather. Around noon local time, approximately 50 miles from the Oregon shore, with winds reportedly west-southwest at 50 to 60 knots, the towing arrangement failed. The bow section of the *New Carissa* began to drift in the heavy seas. The *Sea Victory* followed, but in these conditions, there was no question of attempting a capture. With continuing position reports, we deployed response forces northward, toward Newport, Oregon, as we prepared to deal with what was now certain to become a re-stranding. And, to make matters worse, there was an almost 90 percent chance of a stranding on a very rocky shoreline.

(Photo U.S. Coast Guard)

New Carissa

Shortly after dawn on March 3, the bow section of the *New Carissa* fortuitously went aground on a gently sloping beach, about one nautical mile south of the entrance to Alsea Bay and some 60 nautical miles north of Coos Bay, where the towing had begun. With the re-stranding came a spattering of tar balls, concentrated mainly in the area of the stranding. Consequently, we moved our command post from Coos Bay to Waldport to direct the recovery operations in that area. A minimal administrative team remained in Coos Bay to maintain the surveillance over the stern section of the *New Carissa*, which remained hard aground at the site of the original stranding.

After several days of re-rigging the towing arrangement for the stranded bow sections at Waldport, on March 8, the *Sea Victory* once again removed the wreck from her strand, this time with much less effort, due to the gently sloping beach. The *Sea Victory* towed the wreck to the appointed ditching location, where sinking was attempted with explosives. As seemed to be the way with the ghost of the *New Carissa*, the bow section refused to go down. Next, the Navy fusilladed the section with shellfire. It still floated. Finally, and with much fanfare, a Navy submarine fired a torpedo at the bobbing hulk. The mission was a success. It was March 11, some 36 days after the initial strand. To our knowledge, this was the second time that U.S. military warfare assets had been enlisted in the cause of pollution control—the other being the rocketing of the oil manifolds in Kuwait to put an end to Saddam Hussein's release of oil into the Arabian Gulf during Desert Storm in 1991.

With the bow section finally at rest, we thought that the end of our troubles with the *New Carissa* were at last in sight. But, once again, we had underestimated her. Upon returning to Coos Bay to complete what we expected would be the simple job of securing the stranded stern section until salvors arrived to begin wreck removal, we found that oil was continuing to strand on the beaches. To make matters worse, the beaches were where snowy plovers had their habitat.

By April 14, we had pumped nearly 10,000 gallons of lube, diesel, hydraulic, and bunker oils from the wreck. At that point, we determined that the risks of the recovery operation outweighed the benefits. The continued pounding of the stern by the seaway had made the wreck a more and more dangerous workplace. There was still oil in the wreck, but we believed that further pumping efforts would not stop the ongoing discharges, and that tearing the wreck apart was the only way that the remaining oil could be reached. The Coast Guard disagreed and, on April 16, initiated its own pumping effort aboard the stern section. This continued for about a month and resulted in the removal of approximately 2,500 further gallons of oil. With that, the stern section of the *New Carissa* was declared to no longer pose a substantial threat of pollution.

(Photo NOAA's Office of Response and Restoration)

New Carissa incident, Coos Bay, Oregon, February 1999.
New Carissa grounding site after ship broke apart.

The owners of the *New Carissa* hired Donjon Marine and Fred Devine Salvage to dismantle the stern section. They succeeded in removing the house superstructure, the stack, the aft hopper, and the aft cargo crane. They patched the engine-room hull damage, making it sufficiently watertight to re-float. Working against the arrival of winter, they were able, using two large tugs, to move the wreck from the berth it had made in the beach sound. They successfully moved the wreck seaward, but it hung up on the last sand bar. Finally, the tugs had no option but to release the tow. The wreck returned to the berth it had worn into the beach and remained there.

There was hope around Coos Bay, which was severely economically depressed, that the wreck of the *New Carissa* might stay there, adding some much-needed tourism revenue to the area. The Coast Guard had found the wreck remains to no longer be an environmental threat, and there was no impairment of navigable waters involved, which would have required, under federal law, that the wreck be completely broken. However, Oregon state authorities had other ideas. As there were no obvious laws requiring that the owner of the *New Carissa* remove the wreck, the state hit on the novel idea of suing the ship for trespassing. The Oregon courts accordingly found for the government and awarded the state $25 million in damages. The state then hired Titan Maritime, which built a wrecking operation on the shoreline, consisting of two gigantic fixed salvage barges, each with an enormous crane and eight 300-ton hydraulic hoists. Among the ironies of this effort was the fact that, when we first began recovery on the casualty, our prime directive had been to avoid any sort of industrial operations on this sensitive beach, and of course, that is exactly what the Titan operation became. Finally, in September of 2008, nine and a half years after the beaching of the *New Carissa*, the last piece of her was hauled up from her strand.

Chapter 29

Full Circle: Another Potomac Spill

Over the years, GMS staff and I regularly attended the annual meetings of Intertanko, an association of independent owners and operators of oil and chemical tankers. While at the May 2000 meetings in Monte Carlo, David Barry, Robert Carlin, and I got the news that some members of the Marine Spill Response Corporation who were also attending the meetings were packing up and heading back to the United States to respond to a spill. The spill was reported to be at the Potomac Electric Power Company's power plant on the Patuxent River in Maryland. Of course, being based in Alexandria, we knew exactly which Pepco plant they meant. Pepco operated a big one at Chalk Point on the Patuxent, not far from where the river enters the Chesapeake Bay. The spill had occurred at a pipeline feeding fuel oil to the power plant, shutting down the plant's whole operation. As the casualty was tidal in nature, the Coast Guard had gotten involved and summonsed the MSRC group to assist them in overseeing what Pepco was doing in response to the spill. There wasn't any work in it for GMS, as Pepco had already hired another spill management contractor to oversee the casualty.

The accident happened on April 7. We finished our business in Monte Carlo and returned to Washington a few days later to learn that there was major dissatisfaction with the spill management team that Pepco had hired. Actively seeking a replacement, Pepco contacted GMS and asked for a bid, which was accepted. When we sat down to sign the contract, one of the Pepco representatives turned to me and said: "We searched all over the country—to Alaska and beyond—looking for someone to take over this spill. Why don't you guys advertise? It would have made our job a lot easier." I had to laugh, because in fact our GMS offices were next door to another major Pepco facility, in Alexandria. I told him, "We don't normally do power plants; we do ships. But, in the future, we'll consider doing power plants as well."

We took over response for the spill on May 16. To our disappointment, we immediately learned that the Coast Guard was no longer the federal on-scene coordinator for the casualty. The Chalk Point plant and the location of the leak were about a quarter of a mile north of the Benedict Bridge on the Patuxent River. As it turned out, Benedict Bridge was the line that demarcated Coast Guard jurisdiction from that of the Environmental Protection Agency. The EPA had taken over directions of the casualty. As I've written, responses tend to go well when an experienced Coast Guard team is involved. When you get an agency that doesn't have the prior experience, it can be a steep learning situation.

We arrived on the scene of a very large spill—111,000 gallons, by Pepco estimates. It was not a pretty picture. The company leaving was not happy about getting fired and exhibited their discontent. They warned people who had been working for them that anyone staying on to work with us would be blackballed from further employ. We didn't pay much attention to this. As best as we could tell, most of the people who were leaving weren't people we wanted there in the first place.

As part of our response plan, we began an outreach to establish communications with the people who were being affected by the spill. These were primarily customers of the plant, who tended to be very vocal. After all, they had lost their power, and many had suffered damages from the spill itself. We began our physical recovery in the marshy area, cleaning it to the best degree possible with minimal impact on the environment. In the end, it became a massive operation that included reseeding and replanting the land that had been disturbed in the initial response. The project was so large we had to use helicopters to distribute fertilizer over the areas we were remediating.

I had the dubious distinction on this response of sitting across the table from Colby Stanton, the EPA on-scene coordinator. Colby proved to be a difficult person to work with. As I've written, we have strived to create good working relationships with the Coast Guard over the years. With the EPA, in this case, we were starting from step one, and we encountered all the problems associated with dealing with an agency lacking experience and insight in this type of operation.

Among the first of our changes to the earlier response was to move the Unified Command center off the site of the power plant, as our operations were in the way of getting the plant running again. We relocated to the Calvert County fairgrounds, just across the Benedict Bridge and a short drive from the plant. The fairgrounds weren't in use at this particular time of year, so we were able to use two of their large halls for the command post, and supporting offices for media support, community outreach, etc. We were also allowed to use the fairgrounds for the helicopters that we had coming and going on different missions. The Pepco staff also set up communication towers so that we could use marine radios to contact the site operations. Cell phones were not yet in common use.

Our finance department, led by Bob Carlin, set up with the financial people at Pepco. We organized the operation so that all our resources and equipment were ordered through the Pepco ordering system, thereby saving us the manpower and saving Pepco the expense of paying someone to do it.

At the time of the spill, Pepco was undergoing a sale of part of its system to a company called Mirant. The deal actually closed during the response. Fortunately, many of the people involved with the operation from the Pepco side moved over to Mirant, which ensured decent continuity. Also, after some initial bumbling, the Coast Guard was called back in to assist the EPA in conducting the response. The Coasties got right back to doing what they normally do in a spill response in terms of observing and reporting. That expedited the process greatly. We were able, after a lot of work, to remediate the damage done by the spill.

In the end, the Pepco spill turned out to be a big operation that, despite its closeness to the nation's capital, occurred in what is a fairly remote and rural place. We had a lot of people on site during the main part of the response, which lasted the summer months and into the early fall. We billeted our personnel in the motels within reach of the site, two of them in the nearest town, Prince Frederick, and for much of the time, we had most of the other hotels in the area filled up as well. As the response followed the oil downstream, we also more or less took over most of the accommodations as far down as Solomons, at the mouth of the Patuxent River.

To bring things somewhat full-circle, the place where I began the business, my family's beach cottage at Plum Point, Maryland, was within easy reach of the operation, only three or four miles from the site of the spill. This was important to me for a couple of reasons, first of all, because I could go there quite often to get away from the hubbub and catch a night of sleep. The Plum Point cottage was where I had had my first office as a consultant after leaving Lamorte Burns, and it was the place where Gallagher Marine Systems had been founded and had its office during the earliest years. A lot had changed since then. GMS had gone from an idea around the kitchen table to an international company that had pioneered the field of integrated OPA 90 response planning and was responding regularly to major casualties. The Plum Point cottage, on the other hand, had gone from a cramped and busy start-up back to a sleepy cottage by the bay. I was glad for both outcomes.

By the time of the Pepco spill, my daughter, Anne, and her children were living in the cottage. One day, I took one of the helicopters that we had on the response to do a visual inspection of the entire pathway of the pipeline that had ruptured so critically at Chalk Point. From the command center at the Calvert County fairgrounds, we flew first over the Pepco—now Mirant—power plant and then down the shore of the Patuxent River, following the path of the oil up from the discharge terminal at Piney Point at the mouth of the bay. At Piney Point, oil brought up the Chesapeake on tankers and barges was offloaded and stored for discharge through the Mirant-owned pipeline that ran back up to Chalk Point. As we finished the survey at Piney Point and prepared to turn back upriver, I realized that we were fairly close to the cottage. So, by radiotelephone from the helicopter, I called Anne and told her that we'd swing by the beach side and wave to her and the kids. The helicopter pilot brought us down fairly low over the water and then circled back over the beach. I was taking pictures from the helicopter and my grandkids were doing the same thing on the beach outside the cottage. We took another pass, but the downdraft from the helicopter blades started blasting the lawn chairs off the deck of our cottage and off those of the neighbors nearby. We decided that it was time to head out of there. In any event, it was a victory lap for a business that had started with an idea and a shoestring some time before.

Gallagher Marine Systems followed the Pepco project through both the recovery and the restoration. Our participation on the critical restoration probably saved a lot of time and money, in the long run, because normally restoration comes after recovery as a completely separate operation—one that generally runs at an extremely high cost. But, with the support of Pepco and the State of Maryland water-resources people, we were able to work it into our response. Incidentally, some of our success stemmed, in my opinion, from the fact that I already had a good relationship with a number of those state people. They were the same people I had worked with earlier in my career, when I was first on my own after leaving Uncle Paul, running around doing any spill I came across, no matter the size, half the time bringing my boys along to help me. Back then, I'd made contact with the water-quality department in Annapolis and had become a member of their team that routinely met to discuss the problems and the remedies for potential hazards in Maryland waters, particularly for the Chesapeake Bay. It didn't pay me anything, but I got along well with them. We were all committed to keeping the bay safe. And then, when the Pepco spill occurred, that good will went a long way toward helping the success of the response. With the Pepco spill, I knew the proper people in the government and they knew me, and we went to work on those same things we had knocked back and forth years earlier in Annapolis. We trusted each other, and this has always been a central tenet of our business at GMS. With the Coast Guard, with federal and state officials, and with our customers, our relationships are built on trust. On the Pepco spill, as with many others, these relationships paid great dividends.

As we finally closed down the response, Pepco approached us about exploring a longer-term arrangement with them. GMS ended up signing a contract to be their spill management team for any operations they might have with any of the plants that they operated. By this point, their assets included another big station at Morgantown Bridge, on the Potomac River in Charles

County, Maryland, another further up the Potomac, above Great Falls, and one that, as I mentioned, sat right next to our offices in Alexandria. Along with crafting their response plans and serving as their spill management team, they requested that we hold annual classes and safety drills at each of the plants, and this arrangement continues to this day. Incidentally, the Alexandria plant has been closed down due to pressure from the gentrifying residents of Alexandria, who didn't want a power plant in their neighborhood. It just got to the point where the plant couldn't make a profit. It's a shame. Probably the plant will be turned into apartments or something. I suppose that will at least increase the value of the condominium I'm living in now.

Chapter 30

The Baku-Tbilisi-Ceyhan Pipeline

In May of 2002, I traveled to London to begin briefings on a project I had undertaken at the behest of BP: to create a response plan for the BTC Pipeline. BTC was named for the three cities—Baku, Tbilisi, and Ceyhan—the pipeline was to pass through on its way from the oil fields of the Caspian Sea, through Azerbaijan, Georgia, and Turkey, to a port on the Mediterranean. It was a major project. The pipeline was initially slated to carry one million barrels of oil per day, with the possibility that the volume might be increased later without further major construction.

In London, I met with people from BP, which was serving as the lead for several oil companies that were financing the pipeline. I would only be surveying the portion of the pipeline passing through Azerbaijan and Georgia. (Turkey had decided to handle its own spill response planning, independent from BP, and as it turned out, the person they hired was Erich Gundlach, the same man who had gone to the South Pole with me to help set up response plans for the U.S. efforts there in 1990.) From London, I flew to Tbilisi, Georgia, which lay at about the midpoint of my survey, and set up my operations. I connected with the local BP facilities, and they assigned one of their contractors to arrange my logistics along the proposed pipeline paths.

Georgia had been part of the former Soviet Union and had been treated as something of a poor cousin to the USSR. Stalin came from Georgia, which may not have helped their cause.

271

While working along a certain section of the proposed route, we actually traveled near the backwoods village in Georgia where Stalin was born, and I got to see what I suspect is one of the few remaining statues of him anywhere in the world. Tbilisi showed a strong European influence, but the infrastructure in it was sadly decayed. The surrounding countryside was in even worse shape, and most of our travel was over rough roads in a convoy of four-wheel-drive vehicles. Often, one of those would be a security vehicle, as security was a large concern when traveling in the hinterlands.

The first task was to identify the sites where a casualty might have a serious environmental impact. The basic idea was to travel along, or as near as possible to, the route the pipeline was to cover and study the terrain. However, there wasn't a lot of data for some of the more remote locales, and often, when a decent map did exist, it was in Russian. The BTC pipeline was slated to pass through the Borjomi Gorge area, a picturesque part of Georgia that is a popular vacation spot in summer as well as a ski resort in winter. It is also the source of Borjomi water. Famed throughout the region for its supposed healthful qualities, Borjomi water is to Georgia as Perrier is to France and is a major source of export income for the country.

The contingency plans for the Borjomi Gorge were made more difficult by the area's remoteness. Though the region has a long history as a passage between the Caucus Mountains, linking Europe and Asia, in modern years it has been largely bypassed. It is beautiful, but the infrastructure was difficult. There were no high-speed travel routes, and if there were a spill, not only would the most vulnerable sites be the most difficult to reach quickly, but the resources that would be needed were sparse throughout the entire country and it would take some time getting a hold of them.

We were in Georgia for a couple of months in all, collecting information, taking photographs, and painstakingly researching the intended route of the pipeline. While our major headquarters were in an American hotel in Tbilisi, we spent much of our time in the countryside, setting up in small hostels. We looked at every river or stream the intended pathway for the pipeline crossed, visiting some really remote places in the process. Over all, we found the people in Georgia to be friendly. They were effective workers. Most of the communications were in Russian, as several generations under Soviet rule had rendered most of their documents and business dealings into Russian. We encountered no animosity, though there has been a lot of turmoil there since that time.

After completing my research, I returned to the States and, over the course of about six months, came up with a response plan. I turned the plan over to BP for the next stage, which would be the implementation of the plan as they saw fit. BP put the plan out to bid pretty much as I had designed it, and the National Response Corporation won the contract. Some of the people in Georgia who worked with me to develop the plan then went on to work on it with Narco.

Though I was not involved with the Turkish section of the BTC pipeline, on my second trip to the region, BP asked me to go down to the terminal on the Mediterranean at Ceyhan to consult on the emergency response plans they had developed there. In the course of my survey, I noted on one of our charts that there had been some archeological work done on a Roman cemetery near the path of the pipeline. One day, when I had some time, I went over and had a look at it. The dig had been completed, and the archeology team was gone, so I was free to explore. It was interesting to see the manner of burial, in caves with large stones rolled to their openings, not unlike the Holy

Sepulcher of Christ, which was something I knew about, of course, from my days, long before, giving tours of the Franciscan monastery back in Brookland. Now I was in the real Biblical land, however. The town of Ceyhan lay only about 25 miles from Tarsus, the birthplace of St. Paul.

All in all, those trips gave me a good sense of a part of the world that has been important since the beginning of time. They were educational for me. One of my favorite classical pieces has always been "In the Steppes of Central Asia" by Borodin. It's a very important and personal piece for me, and over the years, I'd wondered what the steppes themselves were like, because the tune has such a plaintive melody.

Some years before the BTC pipeline work, I'd been on the Black Sea in Southern Russia, doing training for Russian and Ukraine officers who were going to be sailing one of our Russian clients' ships into the United States. At the behest of our client, we were training them on the laws and protocols involved in bringing oil into the United States. Often while we were on the ships, I would gaze out at the mountains in the distance and know that somewhere beyond those lay the steppes that I had thought so much about but never seen. And then, on my visits to Georgia, I realized that I was at the foot of those same mountains I had gazed at across the Black Sea, the Caucuses, just beyond which lay the country that had inspired Borodin's music. He really did manage to capture the vast loneliness of the place.

The area was so remote and so, in a way, forgotten that you could lose sight at times of how important it had been in history. One night, in Tbilisi, I was out looking for a place to eat when I stumbled on an "Italian" restaurant. I wasn't particularly optimistic, but I had been craving my favorite, spaghetti Bolognese, so our group decided to give it a try. We went into the restaurant and got the menu, and sure enough, they served spaghetti Bolognese. I ordered it, and it turned out to be some of the best spaghetti Bolognese I had ever had. Then it occurred to me that, given the proximity and the history of travel and trade in this region, there wasn't any reason Tbilisi couldn't have an excellent Italian restaurant. It was probably more authentic than anything you could find in the States.

Chapter 31

On the Strand in Cape Town

In the early hours of August 19, 2003, shortly after I had returned to the States from my second trip to Georgia on behalf of BP, the cargo ship M/V *Sealand Express*, at anchor off the Port of Cape Town, South Africa, began straining under gale-force winds and heavy seas. Despite copious evidence to the contrary, the night watch reported "good visibility and occasional showers." By the time the captain came to the bridge around 6:00 that morning, the situation had become dire. The ship had dragged anchor significantly, and the captain ordered the engines readied. At around 6:30, he ordered the anchors retrieved and the engines to dead slow ahead. Eventually, the ship could make no further progress, and the captain ordered the engines reversed. The shallow-water alarm began to sound, but by then it was too late. The sun rose on the Cape Town suburb of Milner to find the *Sealand Express* stranded on Sunset Beach.

Early that same morning, Dave Callahan and Vince Fitzgerald of United States Ship Management (USSMI), called me in Alexandria with news of the casualty. The ship was under their management, laden with over 1,000 containers from Durban and headed for the United States when it had stranded. Immediate attempts to pull her off her strand had been unsuccessful. At that moment, tugs were standing by, awaiting the next high tide to attempt refloating. Their immediate concern, as ours had been with the *New Carissa*, was breaching of the bunker tanks and the possible damage a spill might have on a popular recreation beach at the edge of a large nature reserve. USSMI and *Sealand Express* were both GMS clients, with the ship on lease to Maersk.

(Photo courtesy of Geoff Fairman)

The Sealand Express shortly after having run aground with the heavy seas breaking over her

My first move was to ascertain the current weather conditions and identify what the locally available salvage and spill response resources might be. I called Donjon Marine salvors, who informed me that the local South African salvor, Pentow, had been recently bought by SMIT Salvage, the outfit I had first worked with many years before on the *Akaterini* casualty. I called my contact at SMIT, Richard ("Dick") Frederick, who confirmed that SMIT and Pentow were working together and that they had three tugs in Cape Town. He had not heard of the *Sealand Express* stranding, but told me that he would contact the SMIT headquarters in Rotterdam immediately to learn more. Within the hour, he called back, informing me that in fact it was SMIT tugs that were on the job as we spoke, and that the Cape Town office had already signed a Lloyd's Open Form (LOF) salvage contract with the master of

Sealand Express. The LOF is a common salvage contract dating back to the 19th century. It is distinguished by its simplicity: one page with an accompanying page of explanatory footnotes. It is "open" because it names no budget. It stipulates that the final price of the salvage will be determined by arbitration in London and that, as it famously states at the head of the contract, it is "No Cure – No Pay."

I knew that the National Response Corporation had spill response crew and gear in Iraq, but that was a good distance away. From the International Tanker Owners Pollution Federation, I learned that in South Africa the Department of Environmental Affairs and Tourism (DEAT), was charged with the task of mounting spill response with regard to shipping. As was the case in most countries, the shipowner was ultimately responsible for the bill, but had no role in the spill response itself, which was in the purview of the federal government. I advised Dave Callahan to get in touch with the DEAT people in South Africa and offer to coordinate in any way they saw fit. When Dave Callahan and I next spoke, shortly after lunch, he had been able to reach a DEAT official and had learned that they had personnel on the scene at Sunset Beach; indeed, he was able to contact one of the DEAT people on site and get an eyewitness report of the situation. The *Sealand Express* was still stranded, but there was no sign of pollution. The immediate concerns in the event of a spill were the adjacent wetlands as well as some islands to the north used as a waterfowl sanctuary. For the time being, with the winds from the north and the strand lying south of the wetlands, were a spill to occur, danger to the wetlands would be minimal. The waterfowl sanctuary was sufficiently out of the way that there would be time to intercept any oil that did spill.

On the next high tide, the SMIT tugs again attempted to tow the *Sealand Express* off her strand but were again unsuccessful. The master of the *Sealand Express* suggested deballasting to get the ship unstranded, and using the tugs to keep her from drifting further ashore. In any event, the next high tide was not to occur until 5:30 the next morning.

Early in the evening, Alexandria time, Steve Candito from Narco called with disturbing news regarding the available spill response gear. In his estimation, material from the Persian Gulf was more accessible, but since we needed the equipment without delay, mobilization from the Gulf of Mexico might be more dependable. With the DEAT report in hand, I told him that an immediate response was looking less critical, but that we needed to be prepared. In the morning, I awoke to an e-mail from Steve. His research had indicated that neither option was satisfactory. In both cases, mobilization would be both untimely and extremely expensive. He promised to keep looking, particularly for boom, which would be critical if a spill did occur. When I reached him by phone, Steve sounded more optimistic. Further investigation had revealed that there were some Narco resources available in South Africa, specifically skimmers, boom, some small boats, and some temporary storage tanks. The equipment was spread along the coast as far away as Durban, but a far sight closer than the Persian Gulf or Galveston.

The tugs attempted refloating on the morning high tide, this time using all three of the SMIT tugs, and again failed, with hawsers parting in the process. The DEAT personnel then ordered the *Sealand Express* to commence offloading her bunkers and hazardous material and wanted a plan for doing so delivered by noon local time.

The grim reality was that there existed an immediate danger of a break of the fuel bunkers, which would result in a massive spill. I was still without any significant bathymetry, so I was unable to know whether vessels might get in close enough to effectively lighter the ship or whether, as had been the case with the *New Carissa*, the sea bottom would make a seawise lightering impossible. The good news was, as SMIT had been the salvors on the *New Carissa*, they had the experience that would be needed in either event.

At this point, I recognized that Dave Callahan had not been in direct contact with SMIT, so I arranged a call between him and Dick Frederick. In the process of those communications, both Dave and I learned that SMIT had come up with a plan to offload the bunkers via a hose connected to a lightering vessel positioned outboard of the strand.

Later that afternoon, I joined a conference call from Virginia with Dave and some executives located at the USSMI headquarters in Charlotte, North Carolina. Eventually, the USSMI people inquired about the possibility of a GMS representative being on the ground in Cape Town. Realistically, that meant either David Barry or I would have to go, and since David was still mopping up the *Bouchard Barge 120* spill, that left me. We ended the conference call with the news that the most recent refloating attempt had failed. The sense on site was that the vessel had worked her way into the sand bottom. It was looking as if lightering of cargo, in addition to the lightering of fuel, was going to be necessary to bring her draft up to where she could be pulled out and re-floated. That would take days, if not weeks.

I started making plans for travel to Cape Town. The most logical route passed through Amsterdam, where I thought I might stop at the SMIT headquarters and catch up with them on our plans. While I was considering my options, Steve Candito called with an update on response materials available in country. Unfortunately, the least expensive scenarios would entail a week of transit time, while shorter delivery time would require aircraft charter and considerably greater expense, but it allowed for rapid deployment of the boom that we would need. I asked Steve to work up both scenarios. Soon after that call, Dave Callahan phoned with the news that SMIT intended to commence the first lightering operation at noon that Friday. He wanted me there when it started, if possible, and offered the services of his travel coordinator at USSMI. At 1:30 in the afternoon on Thursday, news came that there was a ticket waiting for me on a flight leaving Dulles at 3:00 P.M. I hung up, threw a few things into a bag, and headed for the airport.

Nearly 24 hours later, I stepped off the plane in Cape Town. I got in touch with my USSMI contacts on the ground, Roger Franz and Vince Fitzgerald, who were at the Cape Town SMIT offices. They recommended that I proceed to the Portswood Hotel on the Cape Town waterfront, where they had established their headquarters. After subsequent delays, we all decided to call it a day and arranged to meet the next morning.

Early on Saturday, I was able to download e-mails from Steve Candito and Dick Frederick. Steve had worked up more specific information on delivery schedules and costs for gear, should it be needed. Dick forwarded me the most recent status report from SMIT, which, of course, was the information from the meeting that Roger and Vince had attended the previous evening in Cape Town. Of most concern was the news that one of the Dyneema towing lines had gotten into the propeller shaft of the *Pacific Worker* as she was performing diving support activities. I knew from the *New Carissa* casualty experience that this kind of line was extremely expensive. The extent of the damage was not reported, but I feared the incident could turn out to be very costly. However, the report also noted that "breaching of the double-bottom plating" of the fuel oil tanks was of prime concern. I had been led to understand that the bunker tanks were saddle tanks, not double bottoms—the double bottoms would better resist damage on the strand.

I also learned from the situation report that an oil-pollution abatement vessel, the SA *Kuswag 4*, was on standby. An oil-pollution surveillance aircraft, the SA *Kuswag 8*, a Partenavia P.68, had carried out two overflights, with little pollution reported. The *Kuswag 8* would continue to overfly the area on a daily basis as required. Further, SMIT had chartered the very small tanker M/V *Oranjemund* to offload bunker fuel from the *Sealand Express*. In fact, I had confirmed with Roger the night before that the lightering had begun, as planned, the previous afternoon.

After an early breakfast with Roger and Vince, we proceeded to the SMIT offices, where I was introduced to Captain C. J. van Essen, known as Kees, the SMIT general manager of operations, and his associate Dave Main. A bit later, I was reunited with Dave Murray, who had been on the South African spill response team that toured the States in the mid-90s. He had heard me lecture on the changes in U.S. spill response since OPA 90 and on the MMA simulator program. Also on hand that morning was Dave Collie, of the South African Maritime Safety Authority (SAMSA), who had also been a member of the South African delegation. As we waited for the first meeting of the morning, we caught up and reminisced.

The meeting commenced with the good news that all fuel had been removed from the double-bottom bunker tanks and that pumping was now underway on the port side, seaward wing tanks. With that, the conversation moved to the importance of a workable plan for the removal of the hazardous cargoes from the vessel as quickly as possible. Dave Collie and his boss at SAMSA, Captain Bill (aka Bull) Dernier, reported that they were under extreme political and media-generated pressure about these cargoes, particularly the uranium ore the *Sealand Express* had aboard. On the SMIT side, Captain Kees van Essen and Captain Nicholas Sloane, who would later gain international fame as the salvage master on the *Costa Concordia* cruise-vessel wreck off the coast of Italy, committed to having a viable plan for offloading of the toxic cargoes ready for presentation the next afternoon.

The fuel offloading was on schedule. We soon got report that, in addition to the double bottoms, port wing tanks numbers two, three, and four were empty, and six and seven were next. The fuel offloaded thus far had been transferred to re-bunker another Maersk container ship in Cape Town, thus answering one of the early USSMI concerns about its disposition. Also, a Russian helicopter capable of lifting a payload of over four metric tons had been identified and negotiations were underway to hire it if the hazardous cargo-offloading project were to commence. One problem was identifying a secure area ashore for depositing and repackaging whatever hazardous materials might be removed from the ship as quickly and safely as possible. There was also the obvious public relations desire to get that material aboard another ship and out of Cape Town as expeditiously as possible. With the next spring tides not due until Thursday and Friday, and a weather report predicting more strong winds for Sunday, it was decided to make getting as much remaining fuel offloaded as possible a priority so that we could disconnect the hoses and get the *Sealand Express* ballasted down to stabilize her against the expected rough seas.

What happened next brought to mind the "Murphy's Law" plaque that Bill Milwee had sent me following the *Aquila* spill off Dos Bocas, Mexico—if something can go wrong, it will. A chemist from the International Marine Organization arrived with the ship manifest and his analysis of it. While the uranium involved in the cargo was a concern, the ship also carried 19 metric tons of chromium trioxide, supposedly held in plastic bags. Chromium trioxide is nasty stuff, volatile and a known-carcinogen: physical contact leads to severe burning of the skin; inhalation, to lung lesions; and ingestion, to death. In the chemist's conclusion, the chromium, not the uranium, was the most dangerous substance aboard. The Russian helicopter, on order at that point, was capable of lifting a load of four metric tons. That meant that, if it became necessary, total offloading would involve five risky flights of containers packed with the toxic chemical over Cape Town bay in severe late-winter weather.

Next came the report from Seshini Pather and Paul Fitzsimmons, representatives of the Nuclear Fuels Corporation, which owned the uranium ore cargo on board the *Sealand Express*. The first plan had been to remove the uranium ore, drum by drum. However, Pather and Fitzsimmons informed us that the drums were not the type we had assumed, that is, the type that could resist high-impact damage of a collision at up to 100 miles per hour. Instead, the ore was being carried in drums that were significantly less impact resistant, rated safe only up to a one-meter drop. Worse still, the ore was in powder form. An exploded drum would likely cause the powder to vaporize, possibly spreading radiation throughout Cape Town. As a consequence, Pather and Fitzsimmons were adamant we leave the uranium cargo undisturbed aboard the ship rather than try to remove the drums individually. They argued that, given the way the individual drums were lashed together within the containers, the real threat was to the salvors who would break those lashings under non-standard procedures. Were a drum to be dropped in transport over water, serious environmental impact would result, but a drop over land would be even worse. A land drop would almost certainly cause breach of one or more of the drums, with attendant broadcast of dust inevitably resulting in inhalation by any nearby individuals.

For the next few days, this would be my routine in Cape Town: Roger and I would meet for an early breakfast to compare notes and review any information that might have arisen overnight. Next, I would travel to the SMIT offices to learn the most recent reports from the strand and attend the morning briefing meeting. The offloading of fuel oil had ceased as planned, and the hoses had been unhooked in anticipation of the weather. A secure container area had been obtained in the port where transshipment of the airlifted cargo could be accomplished. Another, much larger helicopter, of Russian manufacture, with a 20-metric-ton payload, had been found, however, it had a ten-day lead-time and a repositioning fee of $1 million. But the fact was, the salvage was going to need something that big to make a dent in the hazardous cargo. Furthermore, if this ship didn't come off her strand sooner or later, all cargo would need to be removed, and there needed to be a plan for that.

Each day at SMIT headquarters, two meetings would be planned: one to brief the SMIT and support response personnel, the other to report to the media and the concerned public. It was announced at the main meeting of concerned parties that based on analysis of the *Sealand Express* cargo, a "least dangerous cargo off first" strategy would be adopted, based on the theory that we would have worked out the kinks of the transshipment process by the time we reached the uranium ore. This met with

285

general agreement. Captain Sloane explained the specific problems associated with removing individual drums from containers and, for the first time, potential options for removing sandbars blocking movement of the ship.

At the end of the general meeting, Captain Bull Dernier, who was a master mariner and was in charge of that meeting, made an interesting announcement. He stated that his superiors at the South African Maritime Safety Authority (SAMSA) had informed him that they had heard there was a lack of cooperation evident in the proceedings of the assembled response group. It was, he said, the first he had heard of this. "Is there a cooperation problem?" he asked. The room was silent. Again, he asked, "Are there any problems or questions that need answering? Because this is the time and place to air such concerns." And, again, the room was silent. Then he said, "If any such problems come up, you now know where to go with them." There never were any, that I was aware of, but Bull's willingness to meet them head-on was admirable. It was an instance of exemplary conduct by an ideal on-scene coordinator, and we could stand more like him in the United States.

Since I'd been in Cape Town, both Roger and Vince, on the behest of USSMI, had kept suggesting that I might want to go out to the ship for a look. If we hadn't been so busy, I might have considered it right away but there was still much to do to gather necessary information and I didn't see that it could be of much use on board at that point.

Over the next few days, salvors installed a crane and spreader aboard the ship in anticipation of the process of offloading the cargo by helicopter. Some good news finally arrived when we found that the most lethal cargo aboard, the chromium trioxide, had been shipped in 50-kilogram steel drums rather than the plastic bags initially feared. Also, a dredger had been obtained to begin the work of clearing a path for the ship off her strand. Captain Sloane had finalized a plan of action for the aerial offloading, and the routes would be set over water as much as possible. Zodiac inflatables equipped with buoys were to be stationed along the flight paths to provide a means to mark the location of anything that might be dropped into the water as work went on. A repackaging program was established at the container station to process cargo as it arrived. The transports would take place during daylight hours only, and only during favorable weather. The goal was to offload two full containers of hazmat cargo per day.

Another large Russian helicopter had been found in the Democratic Republic of Congo. It had a 20-metric-ton lift capacity and only required a three-day lead. At the same time, however, some people working on the operation were beginning to question the feasibility of such a high-capacity helicopter. No one had ever attempted a lift like this. The massive downdraft the helicopter created might make for even greater problems than were solved with time saved. In the meantime, a smaller helicopter, with a five-metric-ton capacity, was en route to begin work.

By Wednesday, August 27, dredging was underway and most of the bunker fuel had been successfully removed from the ship. Captain Sloane's team had installed stress-measurement equipment aboard the *Sealand Express*, and the readings showed that, despite another few days of serious weather, she was holding together and remained sound.

With the bunkers successfully off-board and the ship not showing any signs of breaking, my active work on the casualty had essentially come to an end. The only fuel the ship had left aboard was the diesel necessary for operating her generators, and it wasn't going anywhere. While real danger still surrounded the casualty with respect to the toxic cargo aboard, that wasn't in Gallagher Marine Systems' brief. I mentioned to Roger and Vince that it might be time for me to head stateside.

At our breakfast meeting, Roger told me that at headquarters in Charlotte, they were still sufficiently nervous about the current situation that they wanted me to stick around for at least another day. They also had another request. Before I left, they wanted me to board the *Sealand Express* and determine if the salvage effort was progressing properly. Roger and Vince had been asking me to go out for some time, but until that point, I hadn't seen the need for it. With the end in sight and my tasks reduced, I acquiesced. At 2:20 that afternoon, Captain Sloane and I boarded a helicopter at the Cape Town Docks for the short flight over to the Sunset Beach area. Once above the ship, the chopper crew lashed both our harnesses to a single knuckle on their wire and lowered us down to the top of one of the containers on the deck of the *Sealand Express*. For the next hour, Nick and I toured the ship, paying particular attention to the crane that was initiating the first offloading of hazardous cargo. All appeared sound. I did note that the ship was lively, even though she was fully ballasted down. At 3:40, we clipped our harnesses back onto the cable dangling from the helicopter that had returned overhead, and they lifted us back ashore. Two hours later, Jennifer, the travel coordinator at USSMI in Charlotte, called to tell me she had tickets for me back to Dulles the next afternoon. Bull had planned a victory party at his home that afternoon, and I was sorry to miss it.

The saga of the *Sealand Express* didn't end with my departure. The tow attempt on that Friday again failed. She would not be floated for another two weeks. On the spring tide of the evening of September 12, she finally made it free of her strand. However, as she was being towed seaward, she collided with yet another sandbar and again stranded. The hawser on one of the three tugs pulling her snapped. High tide would come again at 4:00 P.M. on Friday, September 13. To everyone's surprise, as the two other tugs stood by, waiting for the third tug to return with a repaired hawser, the *Sealand Express* slipped free from her strand unaided, half an hour before the expected flood time. "Like a knife through butter," reported the USSMI spokesperson. In total, the equivalent of a dozen containers of hazmats had been airlifted from her deck during the response. She was towed first to Robin Island for inspection and then to the Cape Town Docks, where the final unloading of her cargo proceeded. Through all of it, not a drop of oil had been spilled.

(Photo courtesy of Geoff Fairman)

Sealand Express stuck on new sandbank with dredger attempting to move some of the sand

Chapter 32

The Casualty to End All Casualties: The *Selendang Ayu*

On November 28, 2004, the bulk carrier *Selendang Ayu* set sail from Tacoma, Washington, bound for China, carrying over 60,000 metric tons of soybeans. The intended course was to follow a great circle route along the Aleutian Chain.

On reaching the Aleutians, the ship began experiencing continuing westerly gales, at times reaching force nine. She transited the Aleutians at Unimak Pass and proceeded on a northwesterly course. About 100 miles beyond Unimak, *Selendang Ayu* began to experience main engine trouble. The problem persisted, prompting her master to shut down power. After completing an assessment of the situation, the master decided to isolate the affected mechanisms, restart the engine, and then reverse course and proceed to the nearest port, Dutch Harbor, for repairs.

Despite the best efforts of the engine-room crew, the engine could not be restarted. The *Selendang Ayu* began drifting southeasterly on the continuing northwesterly winds, which were still blowing at up to gale force. She came to strand on December 8, approximately 2,000 yards off the northwestern shore of Unalaska Island. At the time, David Barry and I were in London meeting with our P&I Club clients. After hearing about the loss of power and the drifting, we knew we had a vessel that was possibly in trouble. We prepared to come back to the States earlier than we had originally planned, but we soon learned that a tug had picked up a tow on the vessel and all seemed to be under control. We relaxed a bit and didn't rush our return, instead resuming our meetings. Upon our arrival back to Alexandria, however, we learned that the towline had parted and the *Selendang Ayu* was again drifting.

When the master of the *Selendang Ayu* felt the ship begin to touch bottom, he ordered engine-room work stopped. He then contacted the Coast Guard and requested helicopter evacuation. The Coast Guard cutter *Alex Haley*, a search-and-rescue detail, was dispatched. As a Coast Guard HH-60 helicopter arrived and moved into position over the ship, crewmembers assembled on the port bow for evacuation. All of the crewmen were boarded by basket lift, except for the master and a Coast Guard rescue swimmer who had dropped from the HH-60 to supervise the evacuation from the deck. As the chopper began its ascent away from the vessel, a giant wave crashed across the ship's bow rising high enough to hit the chopper and douse her engines. She crashed into the heavy seas beside the ship. The *Alex Haley* dispatched a second helicopter, an HH-65, to rescue the crew of the downed helicopter and *Selendang Ayu's* engine crew. The crew of the downed HH-60 wearing exposure suits were all successfully pulled from the seas, along with one teenaged engine-room crewmember of the *Selendang Ayu*. However, the chief engineer, the second engineer, the chief electrician, the chief mate, the third officer, and the bosun of the vessel, all without exposure suits, were lost. None of their bodies was ever recovered.

In the following moments, the *Selendang Ayu* herself broke in half. Still aboard and unharmed were her master and the Coast Guard rescue swimmer. After evacuating the downed helicopter crew and the lone surviving *Selendang Ayu* engine-room crewmember, the HH-65 returned to the foundering ship and successfully evacuated the master and the Coast Guard rescue swimmer. The chopper then made a sweep of the nearby shoreline, searching for any possible survivors of the HH-60 crash. Finding none, the helicopter flew directly back to Dutch Harbor to seek immediate medical care for the master of the ship and the Coast Guardsman swimmer.

(Photo Unified Command)

Selendang Ayu

The hull of the *Selendang Ayu* broke at her cargo hold number 4. The contents of the bunker tank, the intermediate fuel oil tank, and the cargo hold full of soybeans immediately discharged into the raging seas. The sea bottom where the high-energy wave action had driven the ship aground was predominately rock, which crushed her underbelly. Before the crisis ended, the *Selendang Ayu* had released over 280,000 gallons of intermediate fuel oil into the ocean. The northwesterly winds drove most of this oil onto the northwestern shores of Unalaska Island. The spilled oil stranded mostly along the shores of Makushin, Scan, and Pumicestone Bays, also reaching the further finger embayments of Portage, Cannery, and

Anderson. These shorelines, largely cobble beaches and tidal marshes, mostly led to active salmon streams: Unalaska Island was home to one of the largest fisheries in the United States, and the *Selendang Ayu* had just spilled her full contingent of bunker fuel into the heart of it.

(Photo Unified Command)

Selendang Ayu

Command posts were initially established in both Dutch Harbor and Anchorage. At first, I did not believe that much in the way of field response would be possible on the shores of the Bering Sea in the height of winter. I therefore ran and coordinated response communications out of Anchorage, some 800 miles to the northeast. As it turned out, unusually mild winter weather persisted at Unalaska, which allowed me to get into Dutch Harbor and begin field operations on a day-to-day basis. By mid-February, however, the winter weather finally hit, closing down operations in the islands for the rest of the season.

The logistics established during the first phase of the response were essentially ad hoc. The vessels involved were initially chartered by the Alaska Chadux Corporation, known simply as Chadux. Chadux is an Aleut word for whale blubber that came to mean fuel or oil in common usage. As the Alaskan oil-spill cooperative, Chadux was of great help in chartering the vessels used to mount the initial response. However, the principal remit of Chadux was to furnish alternate response compliance for its member companies, which were oil producers and shippers. Obviously, the *Selendang Ayu*, a dry bulk carrier, was not part of the cooperative. As such, Chadux was understandably reluctant to engage in the larger and more vulnerable response operation. Therefore, they told GMS that we had to assume the responsibility for the liabilities coming to the spill management team. Chadux then withdrew from further involvement in the response effort.

Essentially, this left the casualty without a traditional oil-spill removal organization (OSRO), to furnish the cleanup personnel and equipment needed to create the response operation. This required the spill management team, GMS, to take on the unusual responsibility of creating and managing an OSRO itself. Whereas OSROs traditionally have a standing fleet, employees, and equipment, GMS would need to hire cleanup personnel, charter the vessels required, obtain the necessary equipment, and execute the response from scratch. In particular, the chartering of vessels presented a unique difficulty: it required the placement of charterers' insurance, which is generally difficult in Alaska during the winter season, and the inherent perils in winter operations there. Worse, GMS, never having needed to place this kind of insurance before, was unknown in that market. Immediately upon taking on the response, David Barry left the site to work on getting the underwriting.

David's absence in search of suitable insurance coverage led to a memorable event for me. While he was out using all our connections to scour the international maritime insurance market, I took over the Unified Command. The agreed deadline for Chadux to remove their vessels was approaching. By that point, it was uncertain whether we would get our underwriter coverage in time to mount the response. Just a few days before the date that Chadux was due to withdraw, I thought I should inform the Coast Guard executive officer at the command center of the impending situation. I knew that the Coast Guard disliked being surprised by unannounced events, so I gave the officer a heads-up and asked him if there was any possibility that the Coast Guard could help us with vessels if we weren't able to get our insurance in place in time. Upon hearing the request, the executive officer gave me the kind of tongue-lashing that you just don't see outside the military. Fortunately, as I'd had considerable military experience, I had been through this before and knew to wait it out. In the military, you don't make excuses; your commanders just want to know when you are going to do what needs to be done.

Fortunately, David was able to come through with charterers' insurance in time, and we continued the cleanup efforts without interruption. We turned, then, to a series of other, equally difficult logistical problems. We had initially identified 799 segments of coast and stream for analysis, however, via an overflight study, we reduced the number of segments in need of further inspection to 250. In the end, we determined that 123 segments of shoreline throughout the spill area would require mostly manual cleanup. Due to the viscosity of the spilled oil and ambient winter temperatures, most stranded oil set up so quickly that much of it was essentially in solid or quasi-solid form. Recovered oily waste was collected in plastic bags for later consolidation at the waste-staging facility in Unalaska. There was little liquid oil collected along the shorelines. Any remaining fluid oil was generally recovered with whatever substrate to which it had adhered after discharge, such as the ambient sea wrack. That waste was then handled in the same manner as the solidified recovery.

The vast distances involved—770 nautical miles between Dutch Harbor and Anchorage and 1,400 nautical miles between Anchorage and Seattle—created great difficulties in establishing gross logistical streams. Due to post-*Exxon Valdez* regulation, Alaskan law prohibited oil waste from being left in state. As a consequence, the planned destination of the waste stream was a landfill in Oregon, which would be reached via rail from Seattle. Another important element, particularly from the standpoint of the air logistics components, was the prevailing weather on the Bering Sea. This was especially severe and chancy much of the time. The adverse weather conditions, the difficulty in accurately forecasting weather changes, and the rapid arrival of severe weather when it came played havoc with logistics supply and delivery schedules. In fact, it became necessary to retain a full-time National Weather Service meteorologist on the incident command staff in Dutch Harbor. He delivered twice-daily forecasts during the spring and summer operational period of 2005.

Initially, many of the charter flights from Anchorage to Dutch Harbor were via jet aircraft. However, as the operation heated up, the volume of the response traffic began to interfere with international commercial traffic between the United States and Asia. As a result, the charter traffic between Anchorage and

Dutch Harbor was limited to lower-flying turbo props, which substantially increased chartered transit times. And the problems didn't end there: we still had to contend with the weather and the distance. The airstrip at Dutch Harbor, surrounded by water on three sides and threatening mountain walls on the fourth, reminded pilots of the deck of an aircraft carrier. The field allowed only VFR conditions for landings. When bad weather moved in unexpectedly, flights en route to Dutch Harbor often had to overnight at intermediate points, such as Cold Bay, or return to Anchorage altogether. The experience of coming into the tiny single runway at Dutch Harbor, particularly under minimal visual conditions, was not easily forgotten.

The presence at Dutch Harbor of the largest fishing port in the Unites States placed great pressures on the response operation. We needed to ensure that none of the spilled oil showed up in the processing lines at the several plants there. Unfortunately for us, the hydrologic patterns between the western shore of the island, where the spill had occurred, and Dutch Harbor historically proved that floating debris on the western coast could turn up at Dutch Harbor in just a matter of days. Alaska doubled up its fish processing inspectors in Dutch Harbor, and at the end of each day, they delivered reports on the conditions at the fish processing plants to the Unified Command. There was no underestimating the seriousness of the situation. While Dutch Harbor was a rugged little harbor, remote in the middle of the Aleutian Islands, it was the center of the Bering Sea king crab fishery, and the implications were international. For example, in Japan, premium red king crab is an expensive and prestigious traditional holiday gift. Were oil to be discovered in the fishery, it could taint not just Dutch Harbor, but also the entire Alaskan fishery on the world market.

Consequently, the report from the fish processing plants was the highlight of the incident action plan meeting each evening.

We established a helicopter patrol over Unalaska Bay to look out for possible oil slicks. A waterborne response crew sampled the waters in the area continuously. Oil slicks posed a particular danger to returning crab boats, as the crab catches were kept live in the holds by continuous circulation of seawater. Any oil that might be introduced to the holds would ruin the catch. In the end, all of the slicks that were identified in Unalaska Bay were determined to be of local origin and not from the *Selendang Ayu*. Nonetheless, we reported the location and direction of these slicks so that returning fishing boats could avoid them consistently throughout the operation.

The shorelines impacted by the spill were either under the management of the U.S. Fish and Wildlife Service or belonged to various Aleut tribes on Unalaska or the nearby islands. Although these lands were largely uninhabited, the waters off them were sources of subsistence fishing for the local Aleuts. Likewise, archeological sites in the area were of great importance to the Aleuts and needed to be identified and protected. Daily meetings were established for representatives of the various Aleut tribes involved, where we reported our plans and progress involving their lands. We also solicited input from them and respected their suggestions, needs, and concerns. In addition, periodic town hall meetings were held in the town of Unalaska to allow interchange between the residents at large and the Unified Command.

There were no roads outside the towns of Dutch Harbor and Unalaska. Access to the operational areas on the island was limited to air and sea, both of which were subject to weather restrictions. Almost the entire oiled coastline was cleaned by hand. To reach the targeted segments, transportation was generally achieved by helicopter or, at times, by Grumman Goose Amphibians. The weather limitations, a consequence of restricted visibility in the mountain passes at Dutch Harbor and at the scene of operations, often caused cancellation or reduction of local air operations.

Sea transit by chartered vessels working for the response was used for re-supply and crew replacement. All the vessels that we found to work for the response had to undergo special Coast Guard vessel surveys before they would be allowed to sail. This wasn't an idle requirement, as the shortest sea transit was around the weather side of the island. The ships we chartered had to be able to withstand the high winds and heavy seas that were a regular occurrence on that route.

Another unique circumstance in the casualty was that Dutch Harbor was the only place in the United States that had been bombed by the Japanese during World War II. As a consequence, cleanup crews had to be cautioned about unexploded ordinance. Special provisions were developed for dealing with unexploded shells, should they be encountered. Another issue of concern was the possible encounter of the bodies of the six crewmembers that had been lost during their extraction from the *Selendang Ayu*. There was understandably great concern on the part of their family members in India that their bodies should be recovered if possible. Instructions in this respect were given to the survey and cleanup crews, and provisions were made in the event that any human remains were discovered. However, although some lifejackets were found washed ashore, no bodies or other signs of the lost crewmen were discovered.

Another interesting logistical problem came up in the form of communications. A key factor in any activity of this kind is communication between the command center and the field. In this casualty, communications were a continuing headache. The remoteness of the place, the mountainous terrain, the harsh and unpredictable weather, and the distances involved all presented daunting problems. We attempted to boost our communication distances. We set up cellular towers, which were continuously knocked down by storms, and only worked within a narrow corridor that we (GMS Command Post team) affectionately called the "telephone booth." At night, we would often see the vessels (on our VTS screen) aligned within the telephone booth which allowed for calling home and for reports to the Incident Command Post (ICP). Next, we attempted to establish radio and cell phone contact with the field. There was only one provider of cell phone service in the area, Alaska Wireless, and they had as little luck as we did in setting up antennae to enhance the spotty service. A Nextel emergency-response team came to Dutch Harbor to resolve the issue, but after a look around, they determined that their equipment wouldn't work, either. Finally, the U.S. Forest Service brought in their proprietary radio communications system, but that was ineffective as well. The City of Unalaska volunteered its antenna farm as a repeater site. We used this until one of their field repeater antennae froze. After being buried by snow, a fox chewed it up.

In the end, satellite phones were installed on key vessels and other locations where communication was most essential. These worked well when vessels moved offshore, out of the "shadow" that the island cast for the satellites orbiting low on the southern horizon. We learned that, at certain times of day, response vessels could establish communication back to Dutch Harbor and beyond by positioning themselves along the centerlines of the bays in which they worked. By locating themselves as equidistant as possible from the flanking mountains, depending on the weather and time of day, they could usually lock on to a good cell signal. The sight of a number of vessels congregating together in a channel at a certain time of day became common. We called these configurations the "phone booths."

Due to the pristine and fragile nature of the land, none of the property-owning Aleuts wanted to see camps or other sorts of permanent installations established on the shores impacted by the oil spill. This extended to any large mechanical recovery apparatus that might have otherwise been based ashore during cleanup. As a result, the main option available was to establish and maintain a fleet of camp vessels for berthing and sustenance in the bays where the cleaning was taking place. Due to the ruggedness of the local geography and the fact that the impacted bays were on the weather side of the island, shoreline access was limited and often awash at high water. Since weather was such a regular and mitigating factor, having the cleanup crews near to the shore segments was essential. By using the berthing ships, we could keep the crews close to the cleanup sites and provide reliable shelter in times of quickly changing or dangerous weather.

The spill management team in Dutch Harbor established the Grand Aleutian Hotel as its headquarters. This was as good a situation as we might have hoped for anywhere. Although it could get a little tight at times—for example, when fishing crews were coming or going, or when the Discovery Channel was in town filming *Deadliest Catch*, which was in full swing most of the time we were there—the hotel was able to supply the facilities needed to house a substantial command center and breakout rooms. The field workers and field command personnel were berthed on vessels we chartered for that purpose. We also maintained berthing vessels in Dutch Harbor to accommodate personnel to or from field positions. Coast Guard, NOAA, and state oversight personnel were housed aboard our chartered vessels as well.

From the beginning, Dutch Harbor presented significant logistical constraints as the waste-handling center. There was avid competition for the severely limited dock space at the harbor, and the fishing interests had priority over the cleanup interests.

Obviously, another solution was needed if we were going to get the amount of waste we anticipated having to move out of the area and on its way down to Oregon. Due to the expected volume of waste, we decided to put out for competitive bid on a turnkey contract to move the recovered oil directly from the recovery site, bypassing Dutch Harbor entirely. Our plan was to position deck barges in each of the bays where major recovery operations would be conducted to act as waste receivers. When loaded, their cargo would be transshipped to ocean-going barges for delivery to Oregon. This way, we would avoid the problems associated with a crowded Dutch Harbor and with Unalaska Island in general.

After competitive bidding, Waste Management won the contract and towed two deck barges, *Western Venture* and *Chatham Provider*, from Seattle to Juneau. In Juneau, additional equipment was loaded onto *Chatham Provider*, and the two barges were then towed to Unalaska and anchored in Makushin and Scan Bays, respectively. The M/V *American Salvor* operated as a tender for the two barges while they sat at anchor. Both barges were rigged to load, handle, and temporarily store the recovered oily waste. Each barge had a helicopter landing pad in case of emergency rescue. Both had 28-ton forklifts and job shacks to cover and stow gear and supplies for the crew. *Western Venture* came bunkered with drummed gasoline for refueling boats as needed. Most importantly, she carried 108 20-foot open-top waste containers with a 60-ton crane to facilitate their loading and movement.

Chatham Provider carried 150 of the same size containers and had acquired a 90-ton crane in Juneau.

After extensive negotiations with charter-vessel owners and David's placement of charterers' insurance during the winter months, we were able to marshal a substantial fleet to be prepared to deploy cleanup forces to the field and maintain them through the spring and summer. The fleet essentially constituted a floating city of, on average, 250 people and all of their necessary requirements: fresh water, sewage services, medical support, food, and lodging. When the spring recovery began in earnest, the process went smoothly. Each morning, cleanup crews would leave their berthing vessels and proceed to their assigned segment of beach or marsh. A conscious effort had been made to hire as many qualified local people as possible. The general order for hiring workers was Unalaska residents first, Alaska residents next, and then residents of the lower forty-eight. To ensure that interested persons had the qualifications needed to do the cleanup work, GMS offered 40 hours of training in hazardous-waste operations and emergency response to local residents. These response workers would fill individual plastic bags with recovered waste, which would then be consolidated into large polypropylene bulk bags called Super Sacks. The Super Sacks would then be transported to one of the waste barges, where a crane would hoist them by their top-mounted lifting straps and deposit them in containers for loading on barges for further transportation. For the project, we shipped in 36,000 Super Sacks from their manufacturer in Houston.

As detailed in our contract, once the recovered oil was over the barge rail, the responsibility for the handling, storage, and carriage of the load shifted to Waste Management. The containers were filled to a 23-ton road limit, which was measured by a cell on the cranes. When the limit was reached, the containers were closed with canvas covers or fiberglass lids. In approximate twelve-day cycles, Waste Management would send a line-haul tug and barge to pick up the full waste containers staged on each waste barge. Those barges, when fully loaded, were towed to Juneau, where they were transshipped to a subcontractor's semi-weekly barge service to Seattle. Offloaded at the Port of Seattle, the individual containers were then sent by rail to the Columbia Ridge Landfill in north central Oregon, which was owned by Waste Management.

In addition to the Super Sacks and plain plastic bags, huge volumes of other resources were brought on site to ensure the 2005 spring and summer cleanup campaign ran smoothly. We needed to provide rain gear and protective clothing for every cleanup worker in the field. First-aid supplies needed to be kept within easy reach of every working segment on the beach. Of course, portable toilets were provided on or proximate to the beaches where operations were underway. Further, we chartered a fully operational sewage vessel, the M/V *Exito* that served as the sewage tender for the entire response-vessel fleet. The *Exito* routinely traveled between the operating vessels in the fleet to pump their sewage tanks and allow them to stay on station. Sani-Can, whom we chartered out of the North Pole to supply the portable toilets, provided a technician who was berthed on the *Exito* and oversaw the deployment and maintenance of the portable-toilet fleet. Emptied toilets carried by the *Exito* would be exchanged for full ones ashore, and the full ones would be taken aboard *Exito* for cleaning. When full, the *Exito* returned to Dutch Harbor to discharge the collected sewage into the sewage-treatment plant at the port.

On the clean side of the logistics equation, we chartered the M/V *Zolotoi*, normally a fresh-water supply vessel to the fishing fleet, to supply the response with water for drinking and washing. As time passed, we also recognized that we would need to find a remotely operated underwater vehicle, known commonly as an ROV, to check the wreck for oil remaining on board. The engine-room oil had been removed by salvors, but the status of the double-hulled bunker tanks remained unclear. We found an ROV with trained crew in Dutch Harbor aboard a fishing vessel that was heading out in the forthcoming fishery and made a commitment for employment of the ROV upon the vessel's return. Sadly, she capsized during the season and lost most of her crew. We then located another suitable ROV in Santa Barbara and had it brought up. When we finally got the vehicle to the site and running, we found that the double-bottom fuel tanks of the *Selendang Ayu* had been fully compromised. All the oil that was once in them had been discharged into the sea. We conducted surveys of the sea bottom in the area of the wreck for signs of oil waste, but received only inconclusive results.

In addition to chartering the major vessels of the fleet, we needed to provide all the smaller craft that would be needed in the execution of the cleanup. A traditional oil-spill response organization, such as Chadux, would have an inventory of small response boats suitable for deployment under such circumstances. That not being the case with GMS, we needed to scour the local fleets for personal watercraft. Special insurance had to be placed on this watercraft as well: since these boats were not traditional workboats, but considered recreational craft, their owners had very little experience with industrial application. We found ourselves paying compensation for every minor bit of damage done to their vessels in the course of their use.

(PhotoUnified Command)

Selendang Ayu

As for near-indigenous sources, some significant and substantial response resources were available from nearby. For example, a fast-water oil boom, the Current Buster, was obtained from the Alyeska Pipeline Company, which stockpiled that boom for its own spill response operations. A cooperative akin to Chadux, called the Cook Inlet Spill Prevention and Response (CISPRI), furnished us with an aircraft bucket for dispersants. Likewise, Chadux was able to help after it left the response by providing wildlife stabilization trailers: portable structures used as field hospitals for oiled wildlife. Alaska Clean Seas also contributed to the response on this front. As it turned out, the Current Buster boom and the dispersant bucket weren't needed. However, the initial supply of boom from Chadux that we used to protect the threatened salmon streams served additional uses later in the response.

The spill management team was primarily comprised of the GMS Alaskan incident management team: namely the standing GMS team for Alaska as required by OPA 90. We supplemented this central group with other GMS experienced personnel, such as David Barry, myself, and other personnel from our operations around the world. For a project this big, we also called on a broad collection of non-GMS oil-spill professionals covering a gamut of specialties. In a sense, *Selendang Ayu* vindicated a tenet of the GMS operational plan. Even in a remote locale under terrible conditions, a spill response plan and team that had been trained in advance for all eventualities proved to be optimal at responding in a timely fashion and achieving a desirable outcome.

The 2005 cleanup season began on June 14 and stretched to October 18. In that time, 5,400 tons of oily waste were recovered from Makushin and Scan Bays. We oversaw 20,000 paid shoreline days of work and 30,000 skiff-to-shore personnel moves. On average, 250 cleanup workers were on site every day. At the peak of the cleanup, there were 23 vessels and their associated crews at work, eight of them being berthing vessels for field personnel. Ultimately, 123 segments of beach were worked, with less than 20 percent of that accomplished by machine. Over 300,000 plastic bags were filled with oily waste by hand. Over the entire course of the cleanup, there was no reported discharge of oily waste into any waterway or casualties involving personal injury or damage of any kind. After the workable cleanup season ended in October, a reduced spill management team devoted its efforts to planning for the forthcoming 2006 spring and summer operations.

The concerns for 2006 were much the same as they had been for the year before. However, the volume of oil waste to be removed was significantly lessened; the 2005 campaign had been an unmitigated success.

"The cleanup crews have made remarkable progress," wrote Gary Folley, the on-scene coordinator for the Alaska Department of Environmental Conservation, in a report on the response. "These dedicated staff worked long days in some of the harshest weather conditions Alaska has to offer. Everyone involved has done a fantastic job. Local government officials, tribal leaders, businesses, and Unalaska citizens contributed significantly to this ongoing response effort. The level of expertise involved in this response is unparalleled and the results show it."

In spite of the extreme difficulties that weather and the unforgiving terrain imposed on every phase of this casualty, the response to the *Selendang Ayu* disaster was the most satisfying effort in my 35-plus years of spill response. In terms of smooth and effective implementation of plans; the cooperation and collegiality between all elements of the responding organizations; and the support from the citizens of Unalaska, the vessel owners, and P&I Clubs, this was a remarkable achievement that everyone at GMS remains proud of to this day. It is the way all spill responses should work.

PART VIII

CODA

I've always been a storyteller, I guess, at least since that nun at St. Anthony's told my mother she thought I sounded like a Philadelphia lawyer. My stories, like my life, seem to link together like pieces of a chain. I never intended for any of this to happen. I wanted to be in the Navy, but after I went the opposite direction of most of the other students in my year and transferred to engineering at Maryland, the Air Force became the better bet. The University of Maryland was, and still is, one of the best places in the world to study aeronautical engineering: I remember Glenn L. Martin lecturing in my classes. My work at Maryland got me the job at the Allison Gas Turbine division of General Motors, which led to my work on the first generation of jet fighters at the air base in Laon, France.

I might have stayed in aeronautics, but at Laon I learned that I had a knack for problem solving, part of which was bridging the gap between the engineers, who knew what was wrong but had trouble describing it, and the mechanics, who could fix just about any problem if they had clear instructions. I was somewhere in between.

By another bit of fate, I had a friend in the Marines who had graduated a year earlier than me and enrolled in Georgetown Law School. He suggested I give it a try. While I was working on my law degree, I supported my family by returning to an old internship I'd held in college at the Naval Ordnance Laboratory (NOL). Once again, I was in aeronautics, and once again, I was associated with the Navy. Because I had done some original work, and since I was a law student, the guys there encouraged me to try for a patent on one of my inventions. I applied for one and I got it. It was for a device that was specific to an experiment being done at the NOL at the time and had no application otherwise, but still, I had my first patent.

Back at Georgetown, this gave me the idea of pursuing the patent bar, which can only be entered if the lawyer has an undergraduate degree in engineering. I got out of Georgetown, passed the patent bar, and had a couple of good jobs in patent law, which I found pretty boring. I set out on my own, still doing patents, which is how I met Uncle Paul. His inventions, as I wrote, were usually built on other people's ideas, but knowing him did get me onto the deck of a Coast Guard Cutter at the pier in Alexandria on my first spill. It was there that I remembered my first love of the Navy and had the first sense of the career that would shape the rest of my life.

The rest happened pretty quickly. I was lucky enough to begin my career in oil spill practically at the very beginning of what would become a worldwide industry. In the course of that career, I think it's fair to say that I got to know everybody who had a hand in its formation. A lot of those people became good friends.

There were some wrong turns and missteps along the way, but in this linked chain of my life, it seemed like every kink or twist led me in a new and better direction. Meanwhile, the spills kept happening and kept getting bigger and more complex. Each spill had its own twist and unique problems. Much the same as at Laon Air Base, with the Unsatisfactory Reports, there were still engineers with theories about how to remedy the spills and capable spill workers who needed to be instructed on what to do. But now there were more layers. There were the shipowners and the P&I Clubs, whose best interests didn't always intersect. And there was the government, usually in the form of the Coast Guard, sometimes helpful, sometimes not, but always looking over your shoulder. And Mother Nature, unpredictable as ever, played the biggest role of all.

I traveled a lot in those days, across the country and around the world. By the time of the first Desert Storm, I found myself in Saudi Arabia helping in the protection of Saudi oil operations and other factories, and then for several months, helping to protect their potable drinking water supplies. I was also making sure that the King didn't get any oil on his palaces.

One day, shortly after OPA 90 was enacted, my good friend Bob Driscoll, his brother-in-law David Barry, and my family sat together in the dining room of our family cottage on Plum Point, Maryland. We started knocking around ways we might make a plan to work in this new regulatory world. We started small, with just a storefront office in Annapolis. It was so small that when a client came in, someone had to give up his seat so the client could sit down. As with all young companies, things were tough at first. But the spills kept coming steadily and kept getting bigger. It wasn't long before a Gallagher Marine Systems team was on the strand in Coos Bay, Oregon, supervising recovery on one of the worst casualties along the West Coast to this day. We had matured as a company. David and I were running a groundbreaking pioneering program in Marine Safety and Environmental Protection at the Massachusetts Maritime Academy under Admiral Peter Cressy. We were attracting students from around the world and teaching our program from Singapore to Cypress. Many of the standards of teaching oil-spill response today originated from our tenure at MMA.

I had been interested since the advent of the personal computer in something I called Automated Spill Response. By building on the experience we gained teaching at MMA and anticipating the ever-growing requirement stemming from OPA 90, GMS was able to craft a full program of spill readiness and spill response protocols for shipowners. We started the earliest experiments with what would become known as the Qualified Individual. We studied compliance, took the federal requirements and translated them for use by ships' captains, mates, and crews.

Each of these ideas arose from my experiences, going all the way back to serving in the Civil Air Patrol in junior high with my good friend Wally Mitchell. What they grew into was Gallagher Marine Systems, which is today, I'm proud to write, the leader in marine safety around the world. My last big active spill work was on the *Selendeng Ayu*, but I've stayed active with GMS to this day. I am proud to have my name on it.

Stories beget stories: there are many I've left out, some from constraints of space and some from better judgment. All of them remain vivid for me, as do the family, friends, and colleagues who have helped make this a wonderful voyage.

*Jack with Grandchildren on Rehoboth Beach, Delaware 1999
L to R Front row: Morgan Jones (laying on sand); Second row: Sean
& Mary's children—Patrick, Grace & John Gallagher; Third row:
Mike & Susan's twins—Michaela & Liam Gallagher; Top row: Anne's
twin; Bobby Jones*

Gallagher Family Vacation in the Outer Banks 2012
L to R Front row (sitting): Morgan Jones, Michaela Gallagher;
Second row: Patrick Gallagher, Liam Gallagher, Bobby Jones, John
Gallagher; Third row: Susan Gallagher, Mary Gallagher, Sean
Gallagher, Anne Geiger, Jack, Annie Gallagher Jones, Michael
Gallagher, Grace Gallagher

ACKNOWLEDGEMENTS

There are many who have had an impact on my professional life and in shaping the marine oil spill response industry which, by happenstance and serendipity, became my life's work. Some are remembered in the pages of this book; others are not; but all had a hand in influencing my career.

This book was written in part to capture the industry as I knew it from its infancy to the present day and to remember and thank those responsible for its so many successes. Too many of these individuals are gone; all were my friends, including industry founders Dave Stith, Paul Preus, Jim "Pappy" Parker and, most recently, my industry counterpart Jim O'Brien. All are greatly missed.

I also must thank Dave Usher, a great friend and one of the truly iconic founders of this Industry, and Pete Lane and Paul Smith, both known and respected throughout the industry for their numerous contributions and true friendship over the many years. Across the pond, I wish to thank Robert Seward, former Deputy Chairman of Britannia, for his friendship and trust throughout our long association. Also across the pond, my everlasting thanks to Peter Cooney for believing in me and making Acomarit the first GMS client.

The success of Gallagher Marine Systems (GMS) would not have been possible without the steady hand and guidance of its founding board members. I am forever indebted to the late John E. Grey who hand-picked our board and served as Vice Chairman, and those founding members, Robert Blackwell,

Stephen Ritterbush, John F. Walter, and Hillard "Hilly" Paige. That board established the structure upon which GMS has grown. They charted, and corrected when needed, the course of GMS from its founding through 2001. I also must thank Robert F. Carlin, former GMS President, David C. Barry, current GMS President, and the late Carlo Palmieri, former Vice President of GMS, not only for their roles in the success of GMS, but also for their friendship and perpetual good humor.

A special thank you to Mary Gallagher for keeping me alive long enough to complete this book and for her tireless efforts in finding so many of my "lost" photographs that are now captured on these pages.

Lastly, I give thanks to a "Good Faith Payment" (GFP) I received many years ago from a very dear friend (you know who you are). If not for the gift of that GFP, Gallagher Marine, and this book, may not have come into being.

ABOUT THE AUTHOR

Jack Gallagher has worked in oil spill response and marine casualty for over 40 years. After attending McKinley Technology High School in Washington, D.C., he studied aeronautical engineering at the University of Maryland on an ROTC scholarship. At his graduation, he began two years of active duty at Laon-Couvron Air Base in Laon, France. Back in the United States, he worked as an engineer at the Naval Ordinance Lab while putting himself through Georgetown Law.

After nearly ten years of practice at the patent bar, a client called asking him to evaluate a spill resulting from an accidental discharge into the Potomac by his alma mater, Georgetown University. This was late 1970, only a short time after the *Torrey Canyon* and Santa Barbara oil spills. Oil spill technology was in its infancy, but oil spills themselves were about to become an international crisis. Effective response would require visionary thinking, new technology, and powerful organization. The breadth of the work would require communication with everybody involved, from Coast Guard captains, P&I Club board members, EPA officials, and the press, down to the salvors and laborers who would be working the oiled strand. Beginning with nothing more than log booms and bales of straw, Gallagher played an instrumental role in shaping what oil spill remediation and prevention field is today. He participated in many of the most serious casualties in modern marine history, including the *Exxon Valdez*, Desert Storm, and the *Selendang Ayu*. Mr. Gallagher is the founder of Gallagher Marine Systems.

Jack Gallagher

INDEX

Page numbers in *italics* indicate photographs.

Mount St. Helens eruption, 136–137
Mount St. Sepulcher (Franciscan monastery), 37–39
MPC (Marine Pollution Control), 258
MSEP. *See* Center for Marine Safety and Environmental Protection
MSRC. *See* Marine Spill Response Corporation
mules, 87
Mullet Key Channel, Tampa Bay, Florida, 230
Murray, Dave, 282

Naked Island, Alaska, 185
Nantucket Island, Massachusetts, 117
Napalm, 256
Narco. *See* National Response Corporation
Narragansett Bay, 190
NASA (National Aeronautics and Space Administration), 72
National Pollution Fund Center (NPFC), 199–200
National Response Center (NRC), 239
National Response Corporation (NRC; "Narco"), 239
 Anitra spill, 241
 BTC pipeline, 273
 Sealand Express stranding, 278, 279
National Science Foundation (NSF), 244, 246, 248
National Steel & Shipbuilding shipyard (San Diego, California), 188
National Weather Service, 296
natural oil spills, 170–171
Nautilus spill (1990), 192–197
Naval Ordnance Laboratory (White Oak, Maryland), 69–71, 310
Naval Reserve, x, 26
 boot camp orders from, 36–37
 Portsmouth cruise to Jamaica, 30–32
 release papers, *38*
 Robert F. Keller cruise to Portugal, 33–35
 Rochester cruise to Bermuda, 26–27
Navy, U.S., 37, 310
 JG's honorable discharge papers, *39*
 Sea Sentry boom contract, 105–106
Navy Explosive Ordinance Delivery Teams, 256
Navy Yard, Washington, D.C., 26–27
Nepco 140 oil spill (1976), 111
New Carissa spill and wreck removal (1999), 226, 253–263, *255, 258, 260, 262*
New Jersey, 240–243
New Orleans, Louisiana, 122, 123, 128–129
 hot coal problem, 149–150
 JG's ASR work, 167–168

GALLAGHER
MARINE SYSTEMS, LLC

CPSIA information can be obtained at www.ICGtesting.com
Printed in the USA
BVOW08s1906290316

442202BV00001B/4/P